THE SECURITIZATION

OF MEMORIAL SPACE

The Securitization of Memorial Space

RHETORIC AND PUBLIC MEMORY

NICHOLAS S. PALIEWICZ

AND MAROUF HASIAN JR.

UNIVERSITY OF NEBRASKA PRESS | LINCOLN

© 2019 by the Board of Regents of the University of Nebraska

Acknowledgments for the use of copyrighted material appear on page 237, which constitutes an extension of the copyright page.

Library of Congress Cataloging-in-Publication Data
Names: Paliewicz, Nicholas S., author. | Hasian, Marouf Arif, Jr., author.
Title: The securitization of memorial space: rhetoric and public
memory / Nicholas S. Paliewicz and Marouf Hasian Jr.
Description: Lincoln: University of Nebraska Press 2019. | Includes
bibliographical references and index. | Summary: "In The Securitization
of Memorial Space, the authors contend that the National September 11
Memorial Museum is a securitized site of remembrance that evokes feelings
of insecurity that justify post-9/11 policies and war"—Provided by publisher.
Identifiers: LCCN 2019005318
ISBN 9781496215550 (cloth: alk. paper)
ISBN 9781496217325 (pdf)
ISBN 9781496217318 (mobi)
ISBN 9781496217301 (epub)
Subjects: LCSH: September 11 Terrorist Attacks, 2001—Influence. | National
September 11 Memorial & Museum (Organization) | Memorialization—
Political aspects—United States. | Collective memory—Political
aspects—United States. | National security—Social aspects—United States.
Classification: LCC HV6432.7 .P35 2019 | DDC 973.931074/7471—dc23
LC record available at https://lccn.loc.gov/2019005318

Set in Adobe Text by E. Cuddy. Designed by N. Putens.

CONTENTS

ILLUSTRATIONS

ACKNOWLEDGMENTS

Like any assemblage, this book is part of a larger network of institutions, persons, and things that have given it form, and I am happy to acknowledge many, albeit not all, of those relations. First and foremost, I am indebted to Alicia Christensen, Abby Stryker, Elizabeth Zaleski, and Wayne Larsen for all of their assistance and support at the University of Nebraska Press. I must also acknowledge financial, technological, and intellectual support from the University of Louisville's Department of Communication and the College of Arts and Sciences that made this work possible. I recognize both affective support from all of my colleagues in Strickler Hall and the departmental and collegiate financial support that that has allowed me to visit the National September 11 Memorial and Memorial Museum more than once, attend conferences to discuss related content, and, of course, purchase objects such as the camera that produced the high-resolution photographs in this book, office space and writing technologies, and countless books that shaped my thinking about public memory at Ground Zero. That funding came in the form of start-up funds from the college, led by dean Kimberly Kempf-Leonard, and the annual travel and research budget from the department, under the leadership of chair Al Futrell and vice-chair Kandi Walker. The department has also supported this work through the funding of graduate students that assisted with this project in various ways. Special thanks to Jalyn Woodard for her help indexing.

I also acknowledge all of the actors at the National September 11 Memorial and Memorial Museum who facilitated all four of my visits and respected the intellectual freedom that is necessary for any academic piece of work, especially this one. Thanks specifically to the deputy communication manager Margaret Barng, who has permitted the reproduction of photographs of the museum taken by Jin Lee in one of the essays that led to this book. To the NYPD: thank you for tolerating actions that must have seemed strange or suspicious during my visits, such as taking pictures of surveillance cameras, barricades, fences, and signs, not to mention a failed attempt to photograph the metal detectors at the museum's entrance back in 2016.

Last, I have immeasurable appreciation for my family. My parents—Steve Paliewicz and Lisa Fleet—have been there for me whenever I needed a sounding board, life advice, or comic relief. To my brothers Cory and Ryan Paliewicz and John Vincent Fleet: thanks for keeping me emotionally stable and reminding me not to take life too seriously. Thanks, too, for all the therapeutic fly-fishing, camping, and hiking adventures in Duluth, Minnesota, northern Wisconsin, and Michigan's Upper Peninsula. My Kthaw, Ythrung Nongbri, and Kiaw, Grinylda Wahlang, not to mention Lari, Banlam, and Bahep, have strengthened me with love, confidence, and passion. Of all of the people I mentioned here, my wife, Banrida Wahlang, has supported this work in the most important ways. Nga ieid ia phi Rida.

—*Nicholas S. Paliewicz*

The production of a book like this one involves the conceptual and prag-matic labor of many who should be thanked. I begin by thanking editor Alicia Christensen, at the University of Nebraska Press, who helped keep us on track. Abby Stryker, an editorial assistant at the same press, helped move the manuscript through several stages of preparation. I also thank all of the communication scholars in our field who work within the areas of public memory studies. They provide so many of us with intriguing studies of monuments, museums, memorials, and tourist sites that are inspiring. Gratitude also goes to many of the present and former graduate students in the Department of Communication at the University of Utah who have taken my classes and thus tolerated my eccentric ways of critiquing modernist communication theories and methods. Special thanks goes to Professor Kent Ono, whose work on critiques of vernacular rhetorics helped pave the way for studies like ours that focus on securitized spaces in New York. Both the chair of my department, Danielle Endres, and the dean of our College of Humanities, Stuart Culver, helped create the scholarly environment that authors need to work on projects like this one.

—*Marouf Hasian Jr.*

THE SECURITIZATION
OF MEMORIAL SPACE

Introduction

Remembering 9/11 (In)Securities and the Impetus for
National Commemoration at Ground Zero

On September 11, 2001, nineteen al Qaeda terrorists executed the dead-
liest foreign attack on American soil in United States history, claiming
the lives of 2,977 persons from fifty-seven countries. Using four hijacked
jetliners as self-guided projectiles, the terrorists carried out a coor-
dinated plan to crash these airplanes-made-missiles into major U.S.
landmarks to inflict unprecedented amounts of death and destruction.
Terrorists struck the World Trade Center in New York City and the
Pentagon in Washington DC. Another airplane—Flight 93—crashed in
the fields outside Shanksville, Pennsylvania, but, according to some,
the intended target was the White House. What later became known
as "9/11" forcefully and profoundly changed the course of American
foreign and domestic policies in the years that came after.

Archived images and videos of that day, and the weeks that followed,
are constant reminders of the apocalyptic realities that unfolded at
what many consider the epicenter of the American homeland: Lower
Manhattan. Around the tenth anniversary of the attacks the *Atlantic*
reproduced numerous images in several issues to remind readers that
New York, during this time, was nothing short of a war zone. The
Atlantic's visual reminiscences recirculated the now iconic pictures of
the hijacked airplanes, Flight 11 and Flight 175, as they collided with the
Twin Towers. Still frames of the attacks show the North Tower deeply

lacerated with a gash that outlines the shape of an airplane. Snapshots taken while the North Tower was still ablaze and billowing pitch-black smoke into a cloudless sky show Flight 175 heading directly toward the South Tower in a suspended moment before the second deadly encounter between terrorist and target at the World Trade Center. Vicariously witnessing an event through these and other images suspends viewers in a state of helplessness and despair.

And then, of course, images show the exact moment when Flight 175 crashed into the South Tower. The impact that follows is colossal, but it is captured visually in such an evocative way that James Young could describe the pictures as representations that brought to mind the glorified images of Nazi Germany: a "terrible beauty."[1] Angular lines of fire, dust, and debris against the backdrop of a perfect blue-sky day created a sort of tragic, yet aesthetic, masterpiece that takes hold of the viewer. The impact of the collisions formed a cloudlike multicolored conflagration that sent waves of dust into the air and onto the neighborhood. It is an image event that transfixes the viewer in a strange, and terrible, way.

In a frozen moment of time, the South Tower is shattered and instantly transformed into particulate matter. Meanwhile, jet-black smoke rises from the North Tower, creating a vertical line of toxic gas that runs perpendicular to the South Tower's explosion.

Many more pictures from the *Atlantic* photo galleries underscore the magnitude of the tragedy that struck New York. Pictures of the Twin Towers smoldering while local New Yorkers watch in disbelief circulate throughout the world. Entire nations express individual and collective sorrow by shedding tears for the loss of so many lives taken without reason or warning. We see representations of those who cried for friends or family members known to be in the towers during the attacks and never seen or heard from again.

When the South Tower collapsed, video and other media captured people running in terror from massive swells of smoke, dust, and debris that threatened to consume them.

The events of 9/11 were a horror show.

Then, of course, there are the unforgettable pictures of people jumping from the Twin Towers to escape immolation. In one photo, dozens of people hold on to steel tridents while standing on narrow ledges near the top of the tower. Many peer outward, contemplating the jump, while smoke surges from the inside of the building. Because the victims are clearly in a state of perplexity about *how to die*, viewers are put in a similar state of indecision, anxiety, and hopelessness through visual identification. Other images show people who have already committed to the plunge and are in a state of total free fall. Viewers can almost, but not quite, make out their faces. To Barbie Zelizer, these "Falling Man" photos are "about-to-die" moments that spare viewers the initial trauma of gore and tragedy, but their "subjunctive" capacities have also heightened the audience's imaginative capacities for open-ended interpretations in suspended "as if" moments.[2] They too, perhaps, risked suffering from similar fates if attacks persisted.

In the days and weeks that followed September 11, 2001 (9/11/01), nearly ten years before the National September 11 Memorial opened to the public, New York was transformed from a bustling metropolis to a postapocalyptic ghost town covered in piles of dust. Bleak and frozen in time, dust was the substance that symbolized *the absence* of meaning from the attacks. During this time, which became known as the "great dust bowl," more images of persons—especially WTC evacuees—covered in dust from head to toe were circulated. Photos of this strange planet depict people attempting to prevent the inhalation of dust by covering their mouths and noses with T-shirts, handkerchiefs, or their bare hands. Others are running, trying to escape the continual onslaught of dust, while some—as in the picture of a first responder sitting on a bench, dazed from the seemingly endless amounts of work before him—became consubstantial with the dust.

The omnipresence of dust and its transformative potentials illustrate the way 9/11 forcefully created what scholars like Bruno Latour would call a new parliamentarity of disorder. In other words, those who pay attention only to traditional venues for policy formation in discussions of what to do about terrorism miss the more mundane, but just as important, material signifiers found in buildings, ruins, and other objects that have political ramifications.

For our purposes in this book, dust is one example of the material objects that might seem out of place but nevertheless contributed to the ubiquity of insecurity in the aftermath of the 9/11/01 attacks. Here, bin Laden's minions had helped wreak havoc, leading to the material and symbolic "messiness" of a place that some considered to be the economic apex of an ordered society.

The symbolic importance of purity, spaces, and materiality has been discussed by a number of interdisciplinary scholars. Mary Douglas, in her book *Purity and Danger*, sheds light on the materialistic force of dust, as she considers dirt "matter out of place" that "is essentially disorder."[3] Lawrence Wenner goes farther when he views dust as an ideological concept that denotes the inevitable "messiness" of life that travels between cultural sites to render subjects "dirty."[4]

Dust, however, is even more liminal than dirt in its material sense, since it is a sort of absent-present remainder of dirt,[5] which convolutes not only matter but also the orderly relationship it once had with buildings, people, and all of the other objects of Lower Manhattan. It is in transitional moments like these, as Douglas suggests, that objects are most dangerous—culturally and materially—since "danger lies in the transitional states, simply because transition is neither one state nor the next, it is indefinable."[6] In the context of Lower Manhattan, dust became the material manifestation of the terrorist dangers that brought so many insecurities, that forced the hand of those who already worried about al Qaeda before the 9/11 attacks.

In a book titled *Trauma at Home*, Patricia Yaeger convincingly argues that the "transition from rubbish to transcendence describes a first-order response to the phantasmatic piles of debris haunting Ground Zero: namely, the impulse to convert this detritus into something hallowed and new."[7] Ground Zero, in other words, had to be cleaned and purified before it—and America—could be reborn as a securitized, and healthy, state.

We argue in this book that a critical analysis of all of this securitization—symbolized by materials like dust—illustrates the complexity that went into the formation of what Michel Foucault has called the *"dispositif,"* or the state "apparatus" that is put in place when societies must be defended.[8] Until the dust and debris were removed, and the spaces of New York were *resecuritized*, there was little that could be said to heal the traumatic wounds of New Yorkers and American onlookers from coast to coast.

For some, 9/11 exceeded language itself.[9] The familiar and the mundane became unfamiliar and incomprehensible. The iconic Twin Towers—which represented political and economic might—were obliviated in an instant. This total destruction left the living without recourse for traumatic closure. At the core of this trauma was a feeling of irretrievable loss, which was only multiplied by deprivations of everyday ways of making sense of the world. Once the paralysis set in, what came next was a sort of spatial psychosis, wherein publics felt a complete break with the reality that people thought they knew. In essence, what was left behind was a lingering state of physical, affective, and psychological insecurity that would haunt New York and the United States through the condensation of *things* that survived the attacks.

While there are a number of insightful and heuristic ways that scholars, survivors, journalists, and others might approach the study of the 9/11 horrors, this particular book uses an argumentative approach to unpack the *realpolitik* (human deliberative realistic exchanges) and the *dingpolitik* (politics of things) aspects of the 9/11 reconstruction and symbolic rebirth. We contend that the architectural wonders built on these grounds, the National September 11 Memorial and Memorial Museum, reflect the securitized needs of traumatized elites and publics. As some of our colleagues are fond of arguing, place matters.

While other writers might be interested in focusing on the political and financial wrangling that took place behind the scenes, or on the uplifting commemorative messages usually sent during periods of national monumentalization, we are more interested in providing readers with argumentative analyses of the events, images, objects, and other shards of memory and historiography that become a part of antiterrorist security dispositifs[10] at the National September 11

Memorial and Memorial Museum. More specifically, we argue in the chapters of this book that while many commentators mentioned topics like the securitization of these sixteen acres in Lower Manhattan in passing, they rarely provided detailed critiques of all the securitization. For many, there was no need to study any of the realpolitik that might have contributed to the al Qaeda attacks, no need to doubt that the counterterrorist frames were the best way to respond to these threats, and no need to question the idea that the removal of dust, and the building of memorials and monuments, sent clear messages to terrorist foes.

While we understand the traumatizing nature of this situation, we are nevertheless convinced that all of this resecuritization has to be critiqued. We need sustained argumentative analyses—that focus on the political assembly of both agents and things—to see how historical memorials and museums not only represent *but help produce* perceived terrorist and antiterrorist realities. Heightened and sustained states of insecurity are both a cause and an effect of all of this resecuritization as securitized landscapes (and mediascapes) participate in the collective crafting of the "Global War on Terrorism" (GWOT).

The post-9/11 narration of traumatic events circulates through popular culture, public addresses, and, most important for us, *objects*, such as images of the attacks and dust. These things, in addition to the thousands of artifacts stored at the National September 11 Memorial Museum (e.g., an unsent letter, a red bandanna, first-responder vehicles, a rebuilt New York Fire Department [FDNY] motorcycle; figure 1) have functioned as key rhetorical resources for those interested in securitization to bring symbols and material realities together at Ground Zero.

While many might feel that in the wake of 9/11, it is "natural" that these places be securitized in the same ways that airports and military bases are protected, we ask in this book whether prudence has turned into excess, where both presences and absences are used for the formation of a security apparatus that creates more problems than it solves. What if a resecuritized Ground Zero has aided in the production of symbolic systems rooted in neurotic obsessions with security,

Fig. 1. FDNY bike at the National September 11 Memorial Museum.

policing, and military necessities? What if, instead of allowing elites and publics to work through traumas and "master" terrorist pasts, fire trucks and burned columns and old voice records are assembled in ways that contribute to lingering feelings of insecurity and disorientation?[11] Considering the ways that all of the nearly ten thousand artifacts at the National September 11 Memorial Museum have reproduced so much insecurity, grief, and anxiety, what if 9/11/01, and its hypersecuritized, object-oriented politic, should be forgotten rather than remembered? If this happened, would publics suffering from lingering traumatic wounds be more equipped to use mnemonic devices to record and recall injustices that are a part of complex securitized cultures?

We realize that these are complex questions, especially since there are many 9/11 family members, military veterans, police officers, and New York politicians who did not want to see the rebuilding of Ground

Zero send counterterrorist messages to the broader public. At the same time, though, many members of these same factions believed the violent attacks on the Twin Towers meant that these were not just places for a mausoleum, a tomb, or peaceful waterfalls for meditation but rather spaces that needed to be used in instrumental ways to deter any similar attacks on the homeland.

In some portions of the book, we defend the position that the militarization of Ground Zero has impacted more than just the communities living in and around Lower Manhattan. We argue that the feelings of insecurity from 9/11/01 penetrated the American psyche so deeply that nationalistic citizen-subjects are instructed, if not hailed, to remember 9/11 insecurities as they think about everything from potential Saudi government involvement helping al Qaeda to potential governmental lapses in preparedness.

Argumentation and rhetoric scholars might see all of this as a dynamic process that involves both the formation of insecuritization and resecuritization, so critical scholars who want to provide more radical critiques of places like Ground Zero need to be able to provide readers with both diachronic (across time) and synchronic (during the same time period) ways of studying these phenomena. If we are right about the formation of these obsessions, when did it take place, and how did the supporters of securitization stances win the right to chronicle these affairs? Were there ever any dissenters who objected to any of these resecuritization practices, or who wanted to see other usages of these hallowed grounds?

By studying how various social agents used secular and sacred objects to form states of insecurity and resecuritization, we can help readers see how those who were arguing about Ground Zero between 2001 and 2017 did more than rebuild structures that replaced the physical absences of these spaces and places. By inviting visitors to see select displays about terrorism, or by maintaining the presence of security cameras and so many guards, they expected tourists and others to join those who wished to performatively fight al Qaeda or other terrorists.

To get a feel for how the National September 11 Memorial and

Memorial Museum has become a securitized apparatus, the following section considers the political and militaristic context of what has been dubbed "the September 12 Era." We then discuss the heuristic value of materialist approaches to memorialization and other critical, argumentative ways of evaluating the affective powers of the thousands of objects that can be found at the National September 11 Memorial and Memorial Museum. The second section of this introduction also focuses on how participatory critical rhetoric (PCR) approaches help us decode some of the securitizing arguments that were advanced when shoes, fire trucks, holograms, and even "voids" are used to remind us about what might happen if we let down our guard and stop being so vigilant. We conclude with a preview of the overall trajectory of the book and a brief explanation of how each of the following five chapters and conclusion helps us advance our own arguments.

The September 12 Era

The initial impetus for building the National September 11 Memorial and Memorial Museum has everything to do with the early—and lingering—representations of terror, insecurity, vulnerability, and trauma that led to an almost pathological obsession with security. After all, countless other nations had experienced terrorism over the centuries, and even during the GWOT, nations like Afghanistan, Iraq, and Pakistan were feeling the daily ravages of terror attacks with tens of thousands of lives being lost. Yet, for U.S. citizens who believed in American exceptionalist creeds, there was something extraordinary—almost ahistorical—about the al Qaeda attacks on the Twin Towers that necessitated total securitization at home and abroad.

To understand and contextualize the argumentative words, deeds, and objects associated with all of this insecurity, it is imperative we realize that citizens after September 11, 2001, were willing to spend billions on domestic homeland security and even trillions on foreign interventionism. Instead of merely studying New York urban planning or commercialization of Ground Zero, we need to study how this memorial and museum could be symbolically linked to the expenditure of billions of federal dollars on airport security measures, preventive plans for biological attacks, and other counterterrorist and counterinsurgent measures. Those who had watched the collapse of the North and South Towers could also worry about the prospect of terrorists getting their hands on radioactive weapons, such as dirty bombs— which many, including former vice president Joe Biden, have long considered to be one of the nation's greatest threats.[12] Even Richard Clarke—the antiterror chief under President Bush's National Security Council who would be remembered for his worries about another al Qaeda attack—had to admit that some "think the pendulum has swung way too far. . . . Beginning almost the morning after, the consultants and contractors came out of the woodwork."[13]

Unlike other authors who write modernist books that take for granted the existential realities of terrorist threats or homeland security dangers, we argue that Ground Zero's place-based securitization is a rhetorical achievement, a part of an argumentative process that used the ethos of families of survivors, curators, architects, New York police, and other stakeholders to turn this monument and museum into complexes filled with securitized assemblages. In the same way that it is difficult to remember what air travel was like before the arrival of the Transportation Security Administration, any pilgrimage to the National September 11 Memorial and Memorial Museum becomes an opportunity for visitors to perform counterterroristic patriotism through affective displays of vulnerability and insecurity.

In some cases, this argumentation process has involved debates about real or feigned emergencies, but more often disputation between 2001 and 2017 involved talk of how to choose the best policing and military policies that were needed for efficacious counterterrorism. Planners, visitors, curators, and defenders of these spaces began advocating all sorts of ways of making sure that those who traveled to this memorial and museum would "never forget" what happened during an attack that was often linked with Pearl Harbor.

While some of our chapters will put on display the claims advanced by dissenters who objected to the politicization of a place that some believed should be treated as a tomb or a peaceful sanctuary that remembers American innocence, we also analyze how others purveyed more populist rhetorics that reassembled the fragments of 9/11—including, quite literally, the dust and debris—into a securitized apparatus.

Some defenders of harsh responses to al Qaeda attacks averred that security agencies that were not being extravigilant, that were taking only half-way measures, were incapable of reducing the odds of future attacks.

For many, the very building of the National September 11 Memorial and Memorial Museum—and the fact that dozens of attempted attacks had theoretically been foiled—seemed to provide even more evidence that museological, pedagogical lessons were needed to educate visiting publics. In parts of Lower Manhattan, things such as bricks, shoes, and voice records reinforced the beliefs of those who were already predisposed to believe that the nation was at risk. These states of insecurity were so strong that those who argued no one could be blamed for the luck of the nineteen attackers now had to contend with warrants produced by those who were sure all of the dust and the debris provided irrefutable proof of enemy mendacity.

As the ruinous features of Lower Manhattan were getting cleaned up, and impromptu memorials were formed by mourners, people asked whether more could have been done to prevent the attacks. As some members of the 9/11 Commission noted, "the failure of secret services to foresee and prevent the attacks" on September 11, 2001, was a "failure of imagination."[14] To Stephen Brill, a "favorite September 12 mantra in the anti-terror community is: 'The terrorists have to be right only once—but we have to be right 100 percent of the time.'"[15] Such counterterroristic imaginaries created a situation where possibilistic types of argumentation replaced more traditional probabilistic reasoning.

To be right 100 percent of the time, the majority of citizens living in a democratic nation that feels itself to be at war with Osama bin Laden's minions must be constantly persuaded that eternal vigilance—and the support of national security defense policies—also require the building of what we would call post-9/11 "terrorist museums." What kind of consideration does this security logic entail? A robust imagination of terroristic possibilities, to Kevin Fagan of the *San Francisco Chronicle*, goes something like this: "Imagine your most unthinkable nightmare of the next terrorist attack. Now try to imagine something even worse."[16] Publics and decision makers needed to be aware of the need for imagination.

But has this counterterrorist strategy, based on creating and reflecting states of (in)security worked? In an article published in the *Atlantic* on the fifteenth anniversary of 9/11, Brill details a sort of reckoning of America's post-9/11 security obsession. "By my calculation," he states, "over the past 15 years, the American government has spent $100 billion to $150 billion on failed or unworthy homeland-security programs and on acquiring and maintaining equipment that hasn't worked."[17] Considering a host of counterterrorist measures designed to keep America safer and that are endemic to what he calls our "September 12 era," Brill says that we're safer from the kind of attack that shook the world on September 11, 2001, but all of our persistent efforts to securitize the homeland have also opened us up to new homegrown vulnerabilities by those eager to exploit security gaps—such as what happened in the 2016 Orlando nightclub massacre. Such attacks are "less ambitious" than 9/11 but possibly more effective and probabilistic due to their lack of deterrence by the prospect of death and the relative ease of obtaining "military-grade weapons." All of this makes such attacks "harder to detect." In sum, he says, "our defenses are far stronger, but what we have to defend against has outpaced our progress."[18]

Brill would not be the only dissenter wondering about all of these state-securitizing efforts. To Charlotte Heath-Kelly, author of *Death and Security*, the security discourse of resilience is a "disastrous genius" that fails to prevent terrorist attacks but succeeds in creating a narrative wherein civil society embraces "unpreventable insecurity" and hails state actors for facilitating "post–disaster recovery" for an "improved world."[19] Creative destruction thus becomes a rhetorical, argumentative achievement rather than a preexisting ontological reality.

From an effectivity standpoint, more than a few observers have averred that many post-9/11 security strategies do not deter terrorism or eliminate insecurity; rather, they sustain a "neoliberal devolution of responsibility for maintaining security onto the population and local resilience fora"[20] that indexes an important "shift in the articulation of security policy regarding the possibility of providing prophylactic safety."[21] In other words, some security measures do not prevent realpolitik terrorism; they instead function as objects or image events that provide governmentalities with tactics that control populations biopolitically to affirm their own institutional legitimacy.

For a taste of how security has affected memorial space at Ground Zero, consider that when the National September 11 Memorial opened to the public in 2011, it was described as a Vatican-like walled "fortress" as impervious as the "Berlin Wall."[22] Some, of course, found peace and respite, but many others, including one of the authors who visited the memorial during this time, felt that this memorial space was more like an airport, or even a prison yard, than a national memorial commemorating the lives of those who died on September 11, 2001.

Memorial pilgrims were required to show special tickets and endure long lines and metal detectors for admission. Once inside, visitors found themselves surrounded by towering barbed-wire fences and surveilled by closed-circuit security cameras and watchful police guards. The memorial pools themselves evoked feelings of anxiety, doubt, and irretrievable loss.

For Mark Vanhoenacker of *Slate*, the memorial's "iron curtain of security surrounding the site forms its own monument" and creates a sort of "security theater" due to "the measures that are visible or intrusive but also pointless or ineffective."[23] One resident, complaining about the New York Police Department's (NYPD) "fortresslike" security of Ground Zero said, "I live in the City of New York—not 'on campus' or in a gated community. I do not want to prove who I am to come home to my own apartment."[24]

We will have more to say about the formation of these fortresses in later chapters, but suffice it to say here that many ordinary citizens, as well as journalists, decision makers, and laypersons, have paid attention to some of the features of this (in)securitization (see figure 2).

Even though the barricades surrounding this memorial were taken down a number of years ago, the excessive policing and militarizing of this part of Manhattan has produced lingering feelings of precariousness that need to be critiqued. One of the corollary claims we will be defending throughout this book is that consciously or unconsciously, the National September 11 Memorial and Memorial Museum rhetorically function as a policed or militarized memorial space that provides a compelling twenty-first-century example of a security assemblage.[25] Curators and others at the museum may view themselves as apolitical actors who are only bringing together columns, trucks, bandannas, and other shards of memories for commemorative purposes, but all these become parts of contested, as well as complementary, multidimensional counterterrorist memories. We will also be claiming that many mainstream and alternative presses who comment on the building and maintenance of the National September 11 Memorial and Memorial Museum have helped coproduce the security apparatus that reinforces sustained feelings of American exceptionalism and vulnerability.

This particular line of inquiry is important because of all of the obsessions, constant worries, and terroristic phobias that securitization has introduced, produced, and reproduced during the current post–September 12 era. These fears have created what Bruce Janz has called the "terror of place" at Ground Zero.[26] As early as the end of 2001, these feelings would be used as fodder for the securitization of memorial space because they allowed state-sanctioned institutional authorities to use Ground Zero, and the traumas attached to it, as evidence that justified the taking of expensive securitizing measures. Most publics and journalists, in turn, gave their warranted assent to the building of the securitized complexes that would become the National September 11 Memorial and Memorial Museum.

With these concrete, material, and symbolic forces in mind we transition now to a theoretical discussion of what Latour calls *dingpolitik* so that we can use the notion of the "politics of things" to complicate

Fig. 2. The National September 11 Memorial's security apparatus.

the ways that we write about terrorist histories or counterterrorist memories. We feel that scholars of public memory have been moving in directions that parallel Latour's efforts, and what we provide below is a critical engagement with an object-oriented ontology that is capable of understanding the securitized rhetoricity of nonhuman actors (what Latour calls "actants").

Dingpolitik, the Anthropocene, and New Materialisms in Public Memory and Critical Memorial Studies

At least since the time of the publication of Carole Blair, Marsha Jeppeson, and Enrico Pucci Jr.'s "Public Memorializing in Postmodernity" in 1991,[27] scholars within the field of communication have been looking for ways to go beyond the earlier classical or modernist studies of monuments, museums, statues, and architectural designs.

They joined many interdisciplinary researchers who were also bothered by some of the uncritical memorializing that sometimes went on when architects, urban planners, curators, and others built edifices that seemed to hide the symbolic power of epic, monumental, or antiquated structures. Those who were convinced that epic warriors from the past were indeed "great" leaders who served great nations, for instance, not only overlooked the need to interrogate the hegemonic politics that shadowed these revered structures but also culturally reinforced them.

Blair, Jeppeson, and Pucci seemed to gesture in ways that invited some scholars to be dissatisfied with this way of approaching monuments, memorials, and architectural landscapes. Using their own critical reading of Maya Lin's designs and planning for the Vietnam Veterans Memorial as an entrée point for their theoretical and methodological reflections, they argued that we were all witnessing the advent of a new form of what they called "postmodern monumentality."

In this book, we extend the work of Blair, Jeppeson, Pucci, and many other communication and interdisciplinary scholars who are interested in critiquing traditional, modernist, or classical styles of architectural representation. Yet we are also drawn to the work of an eclectic group of poststructural, postmodern, and postcolonial critics who want to study the rhetorical force of these types of structures. Like many twenty-first-century scholars who have profited from the work of Bruno Latour, Gilles Deleuze, Michel Foucault, Judith Butler, and others, we believe that those of us who are theorizing life in the age of the Anthropocene can no longer exclusively focus on what political scientists and others call the realpolitik of contentious affairs.

As Bruno Latour explained in his seminal essay "From Realpolitik to Dingpolitik," the German ideograph "realpolitik" was used to describe a "positive, materialist, no-nonsense, interest only, matter-of-fact way of dealing with naked power relations."[28] Political scientists call this "political realism." In theory, those who espouse these views believe that realpolitik decisions are made by human social agents who make direct appeals to parliaments, congresses, or other assemblies. After periods of deliberation these arguers can agree to carve up territories, distribute scarce resources, or set up rules for civilized warfare.

We can provide readers with examples of these realpolitik concerns when we pay attention to how diplomats traveled to the Berlin Conference of 1884–85, how audiences recognized the persuasive power of the U.S. Supreme Court during the announcement of the decision in *Brown v. Board of Education* (1954), how the victors of World War II cobbled together the military tribunals that served as the venues for trials of the major Nazi criminals, and how the General Assembly of the United Nations met in 2017 to deal with President Donald Trump's decision to recognize Jerusalem as the capital of Israel. Architects, curators, memorialists, sculptors, and others who operated from this realpolitik way of thinking concerned themselves with the valorization—or vilification—of a few select human agents.

Latour was convinced that this primary focus on realpolitik contributed to narrow ways of conceptualizing politics and hindered actual democratic exchanges. As far as he was concerned, all of the architectural and textual focus on realpolitik ideas might have appealed to many political philosophers since the time of Aristotle or Hobbes, but many of the supposed fact-finding efforts that were referenced during traditional parliamentary or other assembly disputations did not necessarily accomplish their tasks. He implied that they hid the artifice involved, and the lack of actual realism that was at work here, in a world that he characterized as being filled with "sophistry." Latour argued that public enchantment with realpolitik efforts led to the use of abusive rhetorics, less civic engagement, poor decision-making, and the acceptance of assertions that were paraded as facts. Even worse, he averred that ironically, all of this primary focus on realpolitik was "deeply unrealistic."[29]

Latour argued that given the ecological damage that came from all of this textual, visual, and architectural focus on realpolitik—which he thought contributed to the coming of the Anthropocene and problems as diverse as fabricated excuses for wars and strange debates about the facticity of climate change[30]—scholars and decision makers needed to focus on more than individual leadership or modernistic parliamentary disputation. He opined that they needed to embrace what he called "object-oriented" democratic ways of thinking that took into account the needs of humans and nonhumans. Latour revised and reappropriated the German neologism "*dingpolitik*" as a term to help put on display the type of change that might take place if global communities were willing to turn "objects" into "things" by paying more attention to what he called "matters of concern." This was the type of perspectival thinking that focused not on the social agency of a few "great" individuals but on the anonymous, overlooked work of assemblages[31] that brought together humans and nonhumans.

To help provide multiple examples of how one might operationalize this dingpolitik way of thinking, Latour would write about these object-oriented assemblages:

> The entry of Turkey into the European Union, the Islamic veil in France, the spread of genetically modified organisms in Brazil, the pollution of the river near your home, the breaking down of Greenland's glaciers, the diminishing return of your pension funds, the closing of your daughter's factory, the repairs to be made in your apartment, the rise and fall of stock options, the latest beheading by fanatics in Falluja, the last American election.[32]

Latour hoped that those who extended his work might see the advantages that came from problematizing the traditional way that we viewed assemblies as we moved toward what many now call the "Parliament of Things."[33]

In *Ambient Rhetoric*, Thomas Rickert speaks about the importance of objects alongside what can be described as his Heideggerian form/thing/theory to help him contemplate the possibilities of what he calls ambient rhetoric. This has to do with *attuning*, or positioning, oneself in an already complex world that is networked, immanent, and object-oriented. This attunement takes place and space seriously, and it invites readers to study the deployment of various symbolic assemblages (memorial, securitization, mnemonic). This, Rickert suggests, is the only way to get a fuller account of the range of objects and senses that shape the multidimensionality of rhetoric's "political ecology" or "ambience."[34]

Rickert appears to be making arguments like those in Jane Bennet's laudable book, *Vibrant Matter*, that remind critics of the need to account for the agency of things. We wholeheartedly agree, and as we hope to show throughout this book, a Latourian take on objects' materiality not only reshapes how we think about the political but also helps in understanding the multidirectionality of public memory. By keeping in tune with this "object-oriented democracy," we can see how spaces and places help with the production of symbolic assemblages.[35] "What Latour finds important about such places," notes Rickert, is that "they help reimagine what politics does: it gathers about things of concern, things about which people disagree."[36] Hence the importance of adopting an argumentative perspective that merges critiques of texts with a "politics" of things at the National September 11 Memorial and Memorial Museum. Chapters in this book will point out that the strategic usages of objects, places, and spaces can sometimes shut down, as well as facilitate, public deliberation.

Studying objects and their "environs" is more important than ever in our current age of the Anthropocene, and Latour's work is representative of some of the most popular academic theorizing that can be found. Readers might imagine that his work can be taken in many directions, but for our purposes here we focus on deterritorializing the spatial and political assemblages that swirled around the planning, building, and maintenance of the National September 11 Memorial and Memorial Museum over a long period. More specifically, we focus on the securitizing and policing functions of objects that turn into "things" as various stakeholders debate over this key edifice that has become a monumental part of America's civil religion.

Throughout this book we extend the work of Latour, but given the spirit of dingpolitik thinking it makes little sense to focus primary attention on the conceptualizations of a single critic when many other influential theorists have mined some of these same intellectual quarries.

As noted above, we have been influenced by those interested in "critical memory studies," studies of posthuman ontologies or investigations of the "new materialist" ways of thinking about the agentic nature of human and nonhuman assemblages.

For example, similarities and parallels exist in the ways that Latour writes about dingpolitik and the way that Gilles Deleuze defines an "assemblage":

> It is a multiplicity that is made up of many heterogeneous terms and which established liaisons, relations between them across ages, sexes and reigns—different natures. Thus, the assemblage's only unit is that of co-functioning: it is a symbiosis, a "sympathy." . . . These are not successions, lines of descent, but contagions, epidemics, the wind.[37]

This refusal to live out the role of objects and relationships in public deliberation also appears in the work of writers like Michel Foucault and Judith Butler. All of this focus on relationality and objects provides local, affective, concrete, and mundane examples of the sites of memory that Pierre Nora once explained allowed memories to crystalize and "secrete" themselves.[38]

The post-9/11 traumas and assemblages that we discuss in this book have everything to do with the ways that we conceptualize both realpolitik and dingpolitik. Unlike Latour, we will not readily dismiss some forms of realpolitik engagement, and one of the contributions that we make in this book has to do with the provision of theoretical and methodological examples of how these notions exist in productive tension.

Later on in this book, we comment in more detail on the importance of studying the realpolitik court battles that are now being waged over whether members of the Saudi royal family, or other influential wealthy Saudis, helped with the financing or planning of the attacks on the Twin Towers. An example of a more dingpolitik analysis appears in the work of Victor Toom, who has written about forensic science, personhood, and ownership of victims' bodies and the remains that are now left in the National September 11 Memorial Museum. As we discuss in greater detail in the following chapter, human and nonhuman elements became parts of assemblages in a "technolegal materialization" during this early periodization of post-9/11, and Toom highlights this point, as do we, by drawing from some of Latour's actor-network theorizing to use networking analysis in explaining the contentious nature of recovery, identification, repatriation, and retention of body parts that are tethered to bureaucracies, bereavement, kinship, DNA, and legal decisionism.[39]

These theories were not circulated in contextual vacuums. Like many before him, Latour could not help noting the way that traumatic events like 9/11 impacted the emotive ways that global audiences discussed topics such as states of exception,[40] and this is why he commented on the necessary recontextualization of the concept of policing. During a 2013 lecture at the Peter Wall Institute in Vancouver, Latour explained that when "you engage in a police operation, you act in the name of a higher authority that has already settled the conflict and you merely play the role of an instrument of punishment."[41] He, like many critical theorists, sensed that securitizing representations were not merely reflecting but (re)producing states of emergency.

One of the questions we seek to answer in this book is whether the assemblages that swirl around the National September 11 Memorial and Museum use objects and relationships to form assemblages that reflect and refract dominant ways of viewing al Qaeda horrors or American governmental responses. Another question has to do with whether publics who visit lower Manhattan are cognizant of these processes.

It is no coincidence that parts of Latour's essay "From Realpolitik to *Dingpolitik*" take up questions having to do with the similar etymologies of "Demos" and "Demons" and the need to critique what he called "teratology," something that he argued had everything to do with branches and assemblages related to politics. The "Demos" and "politics," he explained, had genealogies filled with worries about pandemonium. From "Leviathan to devils, from Discordia to Behemoth," historical communities had to make momentous decisions that dealt with "a whole array of ghosts and phantoms," tricks and "treats all the way down."[42]

Public memory scholars and other researchers who extend Latour's provocations thus need to find critical ways of engaging with all these demons, including the ones that he argued appeared in the guise of "unity, totality, transparency, and immediacy."[43] Using the example of Colin Powell's notorious March 5, 2003, speech before the United Nations, in which he tried to put on display Hussein's weapons of mass destruction to justify interventionism, Latour averred that a dingpolitik approach had much to offer critical observers. They could pay attention to the real matters of concern, keeping an eye on the "provisional assertions" that were made without "imperfect proof," the "opaque layers of translations, transmissions, betrayals," the "machinery of assembly," delegation, and all sorts of "public argumentation" negotiations and conclusions.[44]

In memorial contexts, while purveyors and supporters of classical or antiquarian memorializations might appreciate the representational value of edifices like the Lincoln and the Jefferson Memorials, those interested in more dingpolitik ways of viewing these commemorative architectural spaces may want to study the deterritorializing, or demystifying, aspects of some of this monumentalization. This is what John Law calls the "material semiotics" of these places.[45]

In the case of darker, more teratological spaces, critics might attend to the hybridization of human and nonhuman objects that make up constellations of meaning in these more morbid memoryscapes. Imagine, for example, the dingpolitik roles that skulls play in remembrances of the Cambodian genocide, or how the Treblinka car that appears in the U.S. Holocaust Memorial Museum (USHMM) helps visitors with their affective linkages to traumatic World War II pasts. As one writer for the *Washington Post* noted in an object-oriented critique of the USHMM, there were things that put on display what the Nazi "death Machine could not kill."[46] Perhaps referencing the legibility of some types of artifacts, Ken Ringle, writing in 1993, characterized the USHMM as an "album of agony."[47]

Using objects to evince public memory is indeed an emerging phenomenon locatable at many tragic sites of memory under the title "memorial museums."[48] Holocaust memorials and museums are exemplars of these hybridized places of remembrance because they tend to commemorate mass murder while also offering moral frameworks and visualizations for narrating events.[49] The Jewish Museum, Berlin, for instance, which was designed by the same architect who designed the National September 11 Memorial and Memorial Museum, displays everyday objects, letters, photographs, and interactive media to illustrate the interconnectedness between Jewish life and German history in the wake of the Third Reich's historical attempts to erase Jews as a people. Like the National September 11 Memorial Museum, the Jewish Museum, Berlin, uses objects as dingpolitik testimonials of historical tragedies that support arguments of resilience and survival amid death and destruction.

Object-oriented approaches at museums, statues, memorials, and other topographical places thus allow us to see how demonology and victimage walk hand in hand in so many twenty-first-century neoliberal settings. Is it any wonder that Daniel Libeskind, the architect of the Academy of the Jewish Museum in Berlin and the designer of the Danish Jewish Museum in Copenhagen is also planning to help Kurdish communities with the 2020 unveiling of the Kurdistan Museum? This hauntological site of dark memory will use varied objects to help us remember the gassing of the Kurds by Saddam Hussein's minions at al-Anfal. In place of the traditional "eternal flame"—what might be viewed as a typical example of classical or modernist architecture—visitors to the Kurdistan Museum will be allowed to see inscriptions on tombstones. This type of "physical memory," argued Rachel Shields, Jason Laurendeau, and Carly Adams in 2017, was "manifested in material, spatial objects such as architecture" that placed a key role in "inciting remembrance and encouraging forgetfulness."[50]

We apply this object-oriented consideration to the securitization of space and place at the National September 11 Memorial and Memorial Museum—a place rife with political consideration of things in its own sort of memorial assemblage. Although researchers have analyzed different parts of what James Young has called the "stages of memory" at this place of public memory, many seem to have overlooked the critical purchase of an object-oriented ontology that accounts for the materiality of securitization rhetorics. But as some security studies researchers such as William Walters, Eyal Weizman, and Peter Nyers have noted for some time, material objects are active participants in the shaping of governmental and technological assemblages that affect political disputations and securitized subjectivities.

This book hopes to illustrate the ways securitization is shaped by new materialisms at memorials and museums to open doorways for how objects—and all of their "missing masses"[51]—contribute to assemblages of public memory and (in)security that can mobilize political, performative, and militaristic practices of violence (e.g., the GWOT).

While we applaud, and build on, the work of those who have studied the memorial's irrevocable aesthetics,[52] the power at Ground Zero,[53] and the "kitschification" of New York,[54] we invite readers to review or synthesize analyses that provide diachronic and synchronic studies of these contested grounds. While we share an interest with those who mention the participatory aspect of vernacular memorials and the "public feelings" attached to ephemeral memorials,[55] we also feel that some of this research tends to be generic in its approach to memory, even though memory itself, as Michael Rothberg argues, may be "multidirectional,"[56] or networked, dynamic and coproductive rather than linear, hierarchical, and competitive with other historical memories. We recognize, however, that the need for modernist or structural coherence—as well as perceived needs to respect the dead—may have contributed to oversights that have not focused on the policing and securitization features of Ground Zero.

Unlike many other modernist and linear studies of the National September 11 Memorial and Memorial Museum, our renditions are filled with illustrative examples of contradictory, partial, ambiguous, and sometimes arbitrary arguments as various stakeholders tried to make sense of their insecure world. Over the years, after the fall of the Twin Towers, various individuals and collectives were told at times that all of the policing and vigilance displayed by public and private parties would make them secure (invoking tropes of safety, comfort, freedom), and this in turn added more reasons why many wanted to believe in the necessitous nature of the securitization that might prevent future terrorist attacks.

In fact, such feelings of insecurity at places of public memory have become so widespread that many scholars treat them as features of "dark tourism." Malcolm Foley and John Lennon, in their book *Dark Tourism*, try to account for why visitors are attracted to places and spaces associated with death and disaster.

Thanatopolitics and *necropolitics* are other academic terms used to describe the communicative ways that memories of death and recollections of disasters are mobilized to achieve political purposes in the present. Unlike the life-reaffirming "biopolitics" that Michel Foucault and Giorgio Agamben noted helped ensure the health of populations, thanatopolitics is understood as the appropriation of affective feelings of death and disasters for political objectives.[57]

The following section discusses how the adoption of critical approaches—including participatory critical rhetoric methods—provide guidance for fieldwork types of studies that help get at some of the intersectional dynamics of new materialist approaches. This work is especially important when states of insecurity and resecuritization depend on the establishment of both human relationships and the politics of things.

Public Memory, Argumentation, and Participatory Critical Rhetoric at Ground Zero

While we recognize the importance of studying journalistic, legal, or scholarly accounts of spaces and places like evocative museums and monuments, we are also convinced that something is amiss when these types of critiques do not take into account the affective feelings and other perspectival insights that can be gained from actually visiting these types of places. We need to supplement our traditional rhetorical analyses of press coverage of the National September 11 Memorial and Museum with trips that provide field notes and related epistemic information.

We see memory production as both a product and a process that bring together a range of argumentative perspectives, which in turn give form to complicated, heterogeneous assemblages. These sites of contested memories involve selections and deflections of the past that often shape how we make sense of securitization practices,[58] and some of that shaping comes from interpreting feelings experienced only through actual visits to hallowed grounds.

An argumentation perspective orients us to how commentators write about terroristic imaginaries and how visitors may feel about particular states of insecurity. This orientation is important because, as Charlotte Heath-Kelly argues, the very existence of sovereign security requires a rationalization of "national community (national body)" that "displace[s] the anxiety of mortality" by "effacing" it.[59]

For our purposes here, this burden means that U.S. state actors and institutions have created narratives about the necessity of security to legitimize control of post-9/11 citizen-subjects and to account for the deaths of nearly three thousand individuals on 9/11/01.[60] For those who believe in many resecuritizng narratives, the victims of 9/11 did not die, and should not have died, in vain.

New materialist, dingpolitik approaches to the study of argumentation are both nuanced and valuable because they allow us to pay attention to the role that seemingly apolitical objects play in this welter of claims and warrants about terrorism and counterterrorism. Museum displays of the Vesey Street stairs, which were used by some to survive during the 9/11 attacks, and the Navy SEAL T-shirt worn by one of the men who killed bin Laden, for instance, help ensure that the National September 11 Memorial Museum is more than a tomb. Select usage of objects, such as an interactive lab, brings terrorist dangers alive for tourists.

Oftentimes, as we note elsewhere, these assemblages may appear to be innocuous, quotidian fragments that simply help curators or New York authorities put together some monolithic puzzle of "what happened" on 9/11, but they also can be reassembled in ways that can sustain or challenge nationalistic narratives of counterterrorist security initiatives. Indeed, their evocative power becomes a part of what Eyal Weizman calls "forensic architecture."[61]

We see argumentative practices and the study of diverse persuasive strategies as critical to unpacking the layers of security at Ground Zero because securitization for many audiences can become a type of naturalized rationality that nominalizes certain behaviors, epistemologies, and modalities of remembrance. These must be assessed or critiqued at both the discursive and extradiscursive levels.

Analyzing certain clusters of objects and actors—or what has been referred to elsewhere as *argument assemblages*[62]—enables us to assess how the securitization of Ground Zero was made nominal and common-sensical. Our argument position is similar to the one Gordon Mitchell takes in *Strategic Deception*, wherein he analyzes the complicated argumentative positions and advocacies that led to the consensual attitudes of those who became convinced of the "necessity" for a robust ballistic missile defense during the Cold War.[63] Analyzing the public and technical dimensions of missile defense advocacy allows Mitchell to draw out the enduring effects of American democratic practices, and we see our work functioning in a similar fashion in that we study the multiple variations of security advocacy.

But we make a critical departure from Mitchell and others who might adopt logocentric approaches, since we also view counterterrorist advocacy as a rhetorical achievement that involves studies of both human and nonhuman dingpolitik relationships.

Our argument approach to public memory assumes that space both shapes and is shaped by assemblages of arguments that give form to reticulate sites of engagement. If we assume that argumentation itself is an assemblage of networks, relations, and coalitions—not solely good deliberate reasons—then the way we approach the "politics of things" and material ontologies is altered. [64] Our approach also helps us understand how securitization became almost utopian, common-sensical for audiences who willingly participated in the coproduction of these dispositifs.

The only sure way to securitize the nation, according to those who shared the geographical imaginaries of President Bush, was to rely on the exceptional powers of sovereign authority, which, according to Jenny Edkins, creates a situation where subjects make a deal with the devil: "in exchange for the feelings of security the state gives us we have agreed that our lives are (politically speaking) worth nothing. Life is alienated from itself. Death is not death."[65] September 11 lifted the "veil" that usually covers these political realities.[66] It also warranted state seizure of political rights and liberties so the state could fulfill its exceptional politic. The lingering impact of national (in)securities, as well as the circulation of more materials on the alleged failures of security authorities before the September 11 attacks,[67] created a complicated argumentative situation whereby various security agencies were given authority and the materials to strictly police Ground Zero as a space of surveillance and control.

In the end, to securitize Ground Zero space meant accepting some object-oriented frames while rejecting others. As Foucault argued in his security archives, all assemblages contain ruptures, fissures, and materials that might be used for counterhistories or countermemories.

Heath-Kelly adopted some of this perspectival way of viewing the situation when she noted that sovereigns may assuage the anxieties of those who worry about death, and they may impact ontologies of mortality, but they may also fail when confronted with other competing ontologies of death and destruction at Ground Zero.[68] Certain security strategies, she contends, may conceal the state's "own impotence."[69]

Given the hegemonic power of resecuritization efforts, is this just wishful thinking, or is there evidence that since 9/11, some dissentious communities have used materials within museums and memorials to counter these efforts? Or have their efforts been domesticated and contained?

"Critical" argumentation studies of "terrorist museums" or memorials, then, can be characterized by a set of scholarly tools we use to locate the discursive cracks and fissures that remind us "security" itself is a contested, ideographic term that can be linked to other potent signifiers—iconic materials in museums, water in parks, police devices, and other things. What we hope to show throughout this book, then, is that while many visitors take for granted both the existential threats of terrorists and the need for counterterrorism, these are nevertheless contestable, discursive, and contingent beliefs that may not be necessities.[70] In other words, memorial decision makers who have built structures around Ground Zero did not necessarily have to securitize this part of Manhattan, nor did the curators for the National September 11 Memorial Museum have to use particular exhibits that highlighted counterterrorist efforts.

In some ways, our approach to argumentation and public memorialization is consistent with some of Michael Rothberg's claims regarding the normative need for the multidirectionality of memory, which recognizes that the juxtaposing of several memories need not involve zero-sum games. He notes that some scholars seem to believe that memory work involves the study of scarce resources, where trade-offs have to take place when other genocidal histories are compared with the Holocaust.[71] Rothberg was convinced that if well-intentioned communities used "multidirectional" memories, then they did not need to dwell on the losses that came from losing "competitive" memory struggles. For example, what if a museum could have exhibits that touched on both the Holocaust and terrorist horrors in ways that did not diminish the magnitude of either of these events or the traumas of their victims?

Yet, after spending several years studying the argumentative features of this part of Lower Manhattan, we have become convinced that there were simply times, as a matter of realpolitik, competitive memories did indeed surface to force the hand of those who wished to represent the victims of 9/11 in ways that crowded out what were viewed as unacceptable ways of commemorating those who died on 9/11. Regardless of how one feels about Rothberg's notion of multidirectional memory, there is little doubt that any memory work—especially in terrorist or counterterrorist situations—is an endeavor fraught with controversy.

It is the presentist needs of so many who still feel insecure—even after the passage of so many years—that fuels the rhetorical fires of those who still produce complex, heterogeneous assemblages. As

Kendall Phillips notes, "public memories are those about which we can interact, deliberate, share. And, in turn, these public memories serve as a horizon within which a public finds itself, constitutes itself, and deliberates its own existence."[72]

The constituted public that Professor Phillips describes may not countenance the idea of leaving unpunished those who perpetrated 9/11 crimes. In Foucauldian terms, there are some "effective" histories and others that fail to resonate with generational audiences.

Representing the range of attitudes, beliefs, and feelings in one memorial so that we can trace these effective histories or memories is no easy task, but it becomes even more complicated when we study perceived crises that merge epistemic, ontological, and axiological concerns. In situations where elites and publics have to cope with massive suffering and death, as James Young contends, commemorative practices have to be attuned to even counterintuitive processes of recovery.[73]

It is up to the critical memory scholars, then, to untangle the knots, lines, and ruptures that shape the material and discursive formations of public remembrances made evident at places of public memory. This obligation is especially true when dealing with wartime discourses or counterterrorist spaces and places.

Given what we have said about the need for both textual analysis and field work, we come to the introduction of the concept of participatory critical rhetoric.

Participatory Critical Rhetoric

Our methodological approach to studying the argumentative force of objects at the National September 11 Memorial and Memorial Museum extends the work of those in communication studies who have used a perspectival orientation labeled participatory critical rhetoric (PCR). As conceived and popularized by Michael Middleton, Aaron Hess, Danielle Endres, and Samantha Senda-Cook, this stance attends to the possibilities of investigating the power and flow of evocative rhetorics in situ. This is a rhetorical fieldwork methodology that studies the critical dimensions of rhetoric through participatory *interventions* as a way of examining rhetoric in practice.[74] By the time readers get to the end of this book they will clearly get a sense of how we feel about all of this resecuritization.

Those who defend the value of PCR approaches contend that three key tenets are shared by those who adopt this type of positionality: (1) texts are intimately tied to performances and material contexts; (2) the act of participating in rhetorical events enables a "multiperspectival epistemology" that uses "all senses of the body to discover ranges of meaning,"[75] and (3) studying rhetoric as a material force in places and spaces reveals "complex intersections between words, places, bodies, and context."[76]

We adopt PCR tenets in this book because we believe that doing so is one of the best ways to study both texts and contexts, and thus obtain a textured sense of realpolitik and dingpolitik argumentation. This multiperspective orientation is exactly what is needed to help unpack the dense, securitized features of places like the National September 11 Memorial and Memorial Museum. It acknowledges the importance of studying the rhetoric of architects, the personal anecdotes told by families of the victims, the ideographs and other discursive fragments found in investigative journals, and so forth, but it also highlights the potential contributions that come from multiple visits to the site and the "critical participation" of those who visit and study these hallowed grounds. PCR thus complicates our notions of epistemic knowledge and the production of a rhetorical "text" (e.g., objects, newspaper articles, press releases, academic journals, images, and testimonials).

PCR, we hold, affords rhetorical and argumentative critics with the tools they need to study both cognitive and affect dimensions of memorial and museum visits. Some of the concerns voiced by Middleton and his coauthors find parallels in the claims of some critical memory researchers who attend to the material ontologies produced in memorials and museums that assemble unwieldy collections of objects, bodies, and texts to emotively impact so many. Critics, as well as the observed visitors, get to visit sites where they are asked to relate to the horrors of those who may have been lynched or killed during the Holocaust. PCR orientations take into account how fieldwork allows one to gain an appreciation of the strategic linking of bodies and feelings to particular spaces and places.[77] The feelings associated with public memory formations, after all, are just as important as knowing about these matters, cerebrally. What better way, other than rhetorical field-work, to get a sense of the multidimensional (or competitive) forces of objects found at securitized sites?

While our work specifically focuses on the security assemblages at the National September 11 Memorial and Memorial Museum, we can see many other researchers taking advantage of this newfound theo-retical hybridity, not only at other places of public memory but also in other object-oriented argumentative contexts where researchers can get a feel for the human and nonhuman forces and relations that shape museological controversies.

The analyses in the chapters that follow are thus informed by the insights that come from four visits to the National September 11 Memorial and Memorial Museum by one of the authors and from close readings of purposive samples taken from hundreds of books, essays, and news-paper accounts that discuss these hallowed grounds.

Our chapters attend to the rhetorical force of both the National September 11 Memorial and the National September 11 Memorial Museum.[78] Oftentimes, we trace these arguments by inviting readers to see some of these perspectives through the lens of a "rhetori-cal pilgrim"[79] who visits these grounds. These personal visitations, combined with analyses of textual and contextual materials, allow the authors to account for the memorial's sensory experiences in situ that shape the coproductions of meaning between rhetor and audiences while also aiding the investigation of these sites' rhetori-cal performances that may otherwise be missed through traditional textual analyses.[80]

The next subsection explains how each chapter in the book contrib-utes to the overarching claims that we make about the resecuritization of the National September 11 Memorial and Memorial Museum.

The Securitization of Memorial Space is organized around clusters of actors who had to decide whether they would form alliances with those who assumed the right to "police" or securitize memories of 9/11. Moving chronologically from 2001 to the present, we show each of the different assemblages of arguments that have contributed to the National September 11 Memorial and Memorial Museum's material spatializations of security.

Chapter 1 focuses on the realpolitik and dingpolitik that occurred during the immediate aftermath of terrorist attacks on the World Trade Center on September 11, 2001. This chapter grapples with some of the early tensions that were created when words, deeds, and objects were configured in various ways as audiences sought to make sense of their traumatic experiences. In this portion of the book we show how—even before the dust had settled—all sorts of impromptu, temporary memorials were put in place that hinted at the future GWOT framings of events that would soon dominate so many mediascapes and landscapes.

Chapter 2 analyzes the architectural disputations that went into the designing of a national memorial and museum at Ground Zero. While individuals like Daniel Libeskind may have hoped that their designing efforts would turn this space into an aesthetic, cosmopolitan place of inclusive remembrances, those who were concerned about national insecurities had other plans. For instance, those who wanted to "police" or securitize Ground Zero took advantage of the material features of this landscape as they promoted various surveillance and control schemes. In this way, both the architects and security agencies shaped securitized visions and designs for a reconstructed Ground Zero.

Chapter 3 analyzes how family members of those who died on 9/11/01 attempted to steer the directions of the disagreements that took place over how 9/11 would be remembered at the National September 11 Memorial and Memorial Museum. We argue that although family members sometimes claimed that their personal losses conferred on them a privileged status, this site of memory ended up becoming a polysemic place filled with all sorts of emplotments and emplacements. Additionally, the public and journalistic accommodation of familial perspectives contributed to the securitization of this site because oftentimes their arguments resonated with many communities who also wanted to preserve the "civil religion" of these revered spaces.

Chapter 4 focuses on the policing of 9/11 public memory by the NYPD at the National September 11 Memorial and Memorial Museum. We argue that the NYPD promoted a particular aesthetic of securitization that treated visitors as if they *always already occupied terrorized subject positions* that rendered them vulnerable, insecure, and melancholic. This complicated the efforts of those who were less interested in police security and more interested in finding closure, reverence, or pacifism. Remembrances of securitization—and the role of the NYPD in that policing—clashed with the histories and memories of those who wanted to help with forgetting. Again, this conflict involved both cognitive processes as well as affective states. These concerns manifested themselves during the mediated overage of the New York Supreme Court case *Mary Perillo v. Kelly*. In this case local residents claimed the NYPD's security apparatus at Ground Zero was excessive and interfering with their day-to-day lives. Ultimately, the court found the NYPD's security measures were necessary, and this decision not only legitimized NYPD's current security activities but also paved the way for future securitization of this site of memory.

Chapter 5 argues that some of the securitization features of the National September 11 Memorial and Memorial Museum led to inevitable comparisons with other dark tourist sites. Many could not help linking this antiterrorist memorial with memories of the Nazi Holocaust at the USHMM. Time and again journalists, curators, visitors, and others talked or wrote about how the rebuilding of Ground Zero reminded them of this other thanatopolitical space of exception, which served the somewhat didactic function of teaching tourists to resist terrorists as others before them had avoided appeasing the Nazis. This portion of the book also provides us with an opportunity to critique Rothberg's notion of multidirectional memory, so that we can see whether visitors were learning about both the Holocaust and 9/11 as they traveled to these New York sites of memory. Do rhetorical and field studies provide indications that audiences sensed the thanatopolitical implications of comparing these two horrific events?

The conclusion extends our discussion of resecuritization and national resilience by analyzing how authority figures, such as former CIA director John Brennan, the Navy SEAL Six member who killed bin Laden (Robert O'Neill), and families of 9/11 victims used the National September 11 Memorial and Memorial Museum as a rhetorical platform for justifying diverse securitization practices. By cobbling together stories of heroism and sacrifice, and connecting these tales to objects stored at the museum, the "never again" message of the National September 11 Memorial and Memorial Museum could be linked to broader American domestic and foreign policies. The conclusion also displays how the families of the 9/11 victims could once again raise their persuasive voices as they became activists who helped with the passage of measures like the Justice Against Sponsors of Terrorism Act (JASTA). The families of the 9/11 victims, after years of lobbying, had finally convinced most members of Congress that it was time to go after alleged Saudi aiders and abettors.

Altogether, this book is unconventional. Its authors argue that in varied ways the planning, building, and maintenance of the National September 11 Memorial and Memorial Museum have become entangled in many complex securitizing webs of signification that linked together arguments about everything from the placement of names of the dead to the filing of lawsuits against the "Saudis."

Even today, the millions of visitors who travel to this site of memory are invited to see short video clips on the linking of Islamic fundamentalism and terrorism as they make their way up and down various staircases. Haunting presences and absences have turned this into one of America's most famous "terrorist museums."

We are concerned that all of this resecuritization comes at a high price. These types of commemorative practices, instead of contributing to free speech and open dialogue, make it difficult to confront some of the structural and functional features of terrorism. As Bradford Vivian once noted, some types of remembering foreclose the possibility of forgetting.[81] This belief impacts all types of decisions that have to do with reconciliation, social justice, and mastering of difficult, traumatic pasts.

Granted, there will be those who see nothing wrong with this type of public memorialization, and they will view this resecuritization as the expression of normative liberties, but many of these performances also sustain a topographical manifestation of *alaston penthos*, or mourning without end. And unfortunately, the continual circulation of these unsettled feelings of grief are used to promote constant states of (in) security that oftentimes provide the affective warrants for the "necessity" of accepting aggressive counterterrorism.

1

The Ambiguities and Insecurities
of Ground Zero Space

How Dust and Shrines Threatened the Resecuritization of New York

This chapter analyzes the constellation of events, discourses, spaces, and objects that became a part of the securitization of memorial spaces at Ground Zero during the immediate aftermath of the 9/11/01 attacks (2001–3). Here we extend the arguments that we previously made about material ontologies by highlighting how some acts of outright removals of materials became entangled in local and national debates about the cleanup that was needed before designers and engineers could go to work filling the voids left by the terrorist attacks.

This part of Manhattan was initially characterized as a catastrophe zone that resembled some of the infrastructural damage caused by the dropping of atomic bombs on Hiroshima and Nagasaki, Japan, during World War II, but over time theorists might argue that these hallowed grounds were cleansed and "purified" to help set up spaces for commemoration and public edification. Along the way, a growing number of stakeholders hoped that it would also become a highly advanced security apparatus.

As noted in the introduction, we are extending the work of advocates of critical participatory rhetoric by basing some portions of the book on fieldwork, but we are supplementing this with critical rhetorical and critical studies analyses of the texts that circulated about dust and symbolic cleanup in the first few years after the 9/11 attacks.

With this structure in mind, we invite readers to travel with us back in time, so that they can get a sense of the textured feelings of those who helped coproduce what Michael Rothberg has called the multidirectional and competitive memories that appear in some key rhetorical contexts.[1] As New Yorkers cleared away debris among the ruins, they and other Americans contemplated just how they wanted to set in place the infrastructures that might memorialize the 9/11 tragedies.

While previous researchers often focus on the words and deeds of key architects or mayors or major funders of rebuilding projects, a more "critically" oriented, perspectival approach asks readers to consider how diverse audiences between 2001 and 2003 also play key roles in the production of discursive knowledges as they refracted and reflected nationalistic anxieties about terrorism.

Close textual, visual, and object-oriented analyses—that draw from the work of Latour, Foucault, and others—would ask critics of memorials or related spaces and places to make sure that they do not overlook the role that seemingly mundane objects play in the symbolic formation of key state apparatus. By studying how ordinary citizens, journalists, and others helped with the imbrication of objects such as dust, temporary memorials, and other quotidian objects, critical scholars can illustrate how the "politics of things" (Latour) helps with securitization efforts.

As we explain in more detail below, this was no easy argumentative task, especially between 2001 and 2003, because many were writing as if they were traumatized by the notion that this would not be the last time that terrorists might attack this part of Manhattan, a vibrant economic hub of the nation. What if many other American cities suffered similar fates?

Uncertainty and worries about al Qaeda helped launch everything from the invasion of Afghanistan to the search for bin Laden in Tora Bora. Entirely new organizations, such as Homeland Security, were formed to help prepare the nation for what some critical security scholars called America's "new" way of war. This ushered in an entire generation eager to "take the gloves off" and face the challenges of "hybrid" or unconventional warfare to the point where some pundits were alleged to have characterized the Geneva Convention as some "quaint" paper tigers that should not restrain the hands of aggressive counterterrorist fighters.[2]

Some viewed these worries about terrorism or counterterrorism as "political" or "military" issues that had little to do with the familial commemoration of the dead. Those who argued for discursive or material securitization of the areas around Ground Zero during this early period of memorialization were living at a time that was rife with chaos, confusion, and grief.

All of this collective trauma may help explain why it has taken so long for investigative journalists, academics, and others to focus on the resecuritization facets of post-9/11 planning. For some, the very notion that American publics across the nation might accept the securitization of these hallowed grounds was problematic, in that it could be characterized as an instrumental usage, if not weaponization, of public mourning spaces.[3] For others, the worries about terrorism and New York targeting were palpable and real existential threats that required fewer debates and more counterterrorist actions.

Long before the September 11 Memorial and Memorial Museum finally opened, various stakeholders were trying to influence how we thought about the debris and the material rebuilding after the loss of the Twin Towers. From a Latourian standpoint, this debate involved disputation over the proper reassembly of objects for the reterritorialization of Ground Zero.

The national traumas and anxieties that led to massive changes in airport security and massive growth of other governmental apparatuses have been discussed elsewhere, but less studied are the ways that debates between 2001 and 2003 about Ground Zero were filled with stories about what needed to be included or removed in the name of counterterrorism.

For our purposes, these stories of removal included narratives about public memorialization, makeshift shrines, and altars that were erected by local publics. Eventually the Department of Recreation and Public Works had to intervene and remove some of these structures.

Why were dust and makeshift memorials deemed dangerous by authorities? Is it possible that even before the selection of famous architects, there were ordinary citizens who crafted their own texts and visualities that indicated what needed to be done in the aftermath of 9/11? Is it also possible that between 2001 and 2003 publics were witnessing the Latourian merger of realpolitik and dingpolitik as vernacular rhetorics produced by social agents who reacted to all of these removal efforts?

In some cases, shrines were assembled with nonthreatening objects like ribbons and other mementos. This reaction to the disaster is why Erika Dross, who also found heuristic value in Latourian approaches to objects, explained that in the aftermath of 9/11, written notes, condolence cards, poems, and teddy bears became "things" that were "central to contemporary recollections of loss and social performance of grief." These objects, she explained, may have served the needs of citizens because they were "inexpensive and easily available" in ways that resonated with "literalist beliefs in the symbolic and emotional power of material culture."[4]

In *The Emotional Life of Contemporary Public Memorials*, Professor Doss was focusing most of her attention on theory building that might explain the evocative power of these "temporary memorials," but we extend some of these insights and argue that these material logics and ontologies were being produced long after the cleanup of the temporary memorials.

Moreover, this was also a time when the symbolic and material cleanup of Lower Manhattan became so complicated that it forced the hand of governmental officials, who had to think ahead and plan for what needed to be put in place after the removals. As we explain in more detail below, all of this talk of removal and infrastructural change soon became entangled in conversations about preventing the next potential 9/11 attack.

As is the case with many situations that involve hostile or threatening objects—what W. J. T. Mitchell would call taboo or iconoclast objects[5]—the choice *of how to frame these dangers and how to respond to perceived threats involved both things and human relationships.* In the introduction, we alluded to the material significance of dust in 9/11 commemoration, and it would be during this early period that dust, and the rhetorics about dust, had everything to do with securitization of Ground Zero and surrounding areas.

In many ways Latour was ahead of his time, because all of his theorizing about networks and agentic objects and so forth would soon be echoed by post-9/11 commentaries on chaos theory, "network-centric" terrorism, and algorithmic counterterrorist efforts. Yet, for the local communities who lived in and around Lower Manhattan, it was the symbolic nature of all of this dust and debris that worried those who were familiar with urban ecologies.

Dust, for instance, was materially networked with pulverized body parts, toxic chemicals, and debris from the terrorist attacks. Not only that, but dust was the material manifestation of that which remained after al Qaeda terrorists hijacked two American Airlines aircrafts to topple two of America's most iconic objects. Dust, therefore, was not, nor was it ever, *just* dust; for many New Yorkers and other witnesses to this tragedy, it was always mixed with, and composed of, something else. Dust, in other words, became part of complex material-semiotic assemblages as an early dingpolitik that was associated with these dark times. This importance of dust is especially true considering that it had various elemental, structural, and affective dimensions that could be referenced in complex American security assemblages.

The contents of dust thus triggered widespread debates about to whom, or what organization, the dust belonged, and how it should be treated, especially once an October 21, 2001, forensic analysis revealed that the "dust" removed from Ground Zero and placed in the Fresh Kills Landfill included 4,257 "body parts."[6] What was in the dust, what needed to be done about it, and who was liable for its hazardous health effects postcleanup (or the mishandling of body parts) were just some of the questions that these social agents were asking during these early days.

While many governmental elites worried about public health and counterterrorist dangers, and while others worked at removing dust's "dangerous" materiality, local residents were covering its spaces with makeshift shrines and memorials. These locals were interested in commemorating the dead, and on a more practical level, they wanted to help locate the "missing." Debates about human remains only complicated these matters.

Although these nonofficial acts of spontaneous performativity created a sense of shared solidarity through struggle, loss, and grief, as time passed, the efforts of the locals drew the ire of those who were more interested in removal. The countless individual and communal memorials were deemed disorderly by certain memorial planners and architects because they threatened the futuristic order of Ground Zero and the coherence and stability of more security-oriented stories about 9/11.

Thus, by 2003, the State Department of Parks and Recreation removed these objects of controversy to once again purify New York space and thus regain a sense of spatial control and make way for a securitized national memorial. What was needed, after all, was a functional space, one that was capable of commemorating the lives lost on 9/11/01 but also ensuring the prevention of another attack. Americans, after all, may have wanted to sweep away the horrors of past attacks as they swept up the debris.

At different times, these contested objects served as materialistic reminders of lingering insecurities that had to be removed. Some locals were not impressed when tanks, warbirds, barricades, and the National Guard turned out to militarize Ground Zero.

While some residents complained about the over-the-top presence of these securitized objects, many Americans realized that they were witnessing a necessitous transition from disaster zone to a security complex that could teach others about how to deter future terrorist attacks.

How was this goal achieved between 2001 and 2003? What we provide in this chapter is an analysis of the objects that supposedly threatened the resecuritization of New York, as we also pay attention to the incremental placement of militaristic objects that effectively replaced the debris and some commemorative objects.

To help support the assertions that we are making about removal of makeshift memorials and the symbolic importance of cleanup of dust and debris, we begin with a discussion of the immediate aftermath of 9/11 and the senses of confusion, anger, frustration, and vengeance that swept the nation in the wake of the terrorist attacks. We contend that this groundswell of emotions made for a potent elixir as New Yorkers joined those calling for intervention in Afghanistan and other acts of retribution. We then analyze the material significance of dust as an object that threatened the resecuritization of Lower Manhattan spaces. In that portion of the chapter we comment on the coproduction of many argumentative assemblages that involved responding to familial, institutional, health, or environmental concerns. Next, we write about the dissident efforts of local communities who did their best to preserve the temporary memorials that helped them cope with post-9/11 traumas.

Eventually institutional authorities used their coercive power as they removed the personal shrines, altars, and vigils in 2003 that often had little to do with the waging of war. We would even go so far as to argue that for a time, Ground Zero became a public, institutionally securitized space of nationalist counterinsurgency memory that involved *acts of dispossession*. In other words, the seizure or collection of select objects, memorials, and shrines turned personal grief into public commemoration, and this transition happened in ways that supported the agendas of those who wished to militarize space for the Global War on Terror (GWOT).

If we are right, then by the time architects, politicians, and memorial decision makers began disputing the realpolitik of the National September 11 Memorial and Memorial Museum (chapters 2 and 3), the securitization of memorial space in and around Ground Zero had already begun. Worries about the removal of temporary memorials were replaced by celebration-planning efforts as publics looked forward to the building of the more permanent national 9/11 memorial.

By 2003 it would have been unthinkable not to have these spaces and places configured in ways that did not help with the prevention of the next 9/11.

The September 11 terrorist attacks created not just a perceived military necessity but a *public demand* for the securitization of space due to the inexplicable feelings of insecurity and absence that were left behind after the attacks. The famous 9/11 Commission Report, for example, was a text filled with imaginative arguments about failed security events and ignored warnings.[7] In its wake, various security assemblages—the Office of Public Security, the Office of Homeland Security, and the Division of Homeland Security and Emergency Services—formulated and worked alongside the NYPD to respond to national insecurities. They were supposed to manage high-technology security objects worth tens of millions of dollars and "designed to thwart threats potentially more daunting than another attack on a downtown skyscraper."[8]

Consider just a few of the sundry security initiatives that have been implemented since 9/11: the creation of the Urban Area Security Initiative to increase counterterrorism capabilities with resources to protect high-risk New York neighborhoods; preparations made against possible cyanide attacks on subways; the Lower and Midtown Manhattan Security Initiative, which has allowed for the extreme proliferation of security cameras and license plate readers in "critical areas" of lower and midtown Manhattan; and the Joint Task Force Empire Shield, which is a standing body of military forces from the Army National Guard, the Air National Guard, and the New York Naval Militia at transportation facilities in New York City.[9]

All of this institutionalization of select security concerns did not go unnoticed. In an interview with the *New York Post*, David Cohen—a former CIA official who became the deputy commissioner of intelligence for the NYPD after 9/11—said that striking New York City "is marbled into [terrorists'] thought process. . . . If you want to get into the major leagues in the terrorism business, you come here."[10] Commenting on Ground Zero security specifically, police commissioner Raymond Kelly said that post-9/11 securities have not yet revealed any "immediate threats against Ground Zero, but we are much concerned about that location as projects there go forward."[11]

In the years that followed the 9/11 terrorist attacks, fears of the terrorist "other" were in large part amplified. Part of this increase was due to a sense of spacelessness—where the absence of physical space would be linked to a lack of realpolitik preparation for the eventual GWOT. This new shadow war was considered to be a stark departure from the place-based locations of previous wars where military actors have directly engaged uniformed enemies. In the *Drexel Law Review*, for instance, Nick Sciulo said the "lack of geographical locus" has created a "political paralysis" that "renders people unable to politically engage their world."[12] This deterritorialization of space has allowed security administrators—notably Homeland Security and the Central Intelligence Agency (CIA)—to support arguments of the necessity of war with fantastic stories of the omnipotent other understood as "an enemy who sees but cannot be seen."[13]

This deterritorialization allows for situations where dust, voids, and feelings of unanticipated dread have a disorienting effect on the geopolitical imaginations of New Yorkers and others whose paranoia and fantasies about the unseen other took the place of substantive policies with "definitions, parameters, and certainty."[14] As Sciulo put it, the United States' national security strategy "makes us less secure as it becomes indistinguishable from the very concept it sought to obliterate. We are then the object of our hatred and the very terror we try to prevent."[15]

The September 11, 2001, terrorist attacks thus created a deep-seated topophobia—or fear of place—that penetrated the American psyche on many different levels in the aftermath of the event. Topophobia comes from the merger of two Greek words, *topos*, meaning place, and *phobia*, meaning fear. When you have a morbid dread of certain spaces and places, you suffer from topophobia. Dylan Trigg, in his book, *Topophobia*, explains the relational dimensions and the traumas that contribute to disquieting encounters with select spaces and places.[16]

Many of the post-9/11 traumas contributed to situations where widespread feelings of insecurity were attached to Ground Zero's material spacelessness. This connection in turn necessitated the material resecuritization of Ground Zero that would help provide therapeutic comfort to the afflicted. At the very least, working on security issues allowed for rekindling attachments with Lower Manhattan as an ordered space.

Many decision makers were aware of these anxieties. As Bruce Janz argues, the topophobic effects of 9/11/01 has reduced "place-making imaginations" to a series of manias and terrors rather than the ability to recognize "places as rich, ambiguous and multi-purposed."[17] While Janz speaks of topophobia more broadly in the context of a post-9/11 society, we see topophobia as a recurring pathology that manifested itself in specific ways in, and around, Ground Zero.

Spatial absences, and the presence of debris and voids, contributed to the production of these anxieties, especially during the early days of 9/11 memory-work, when publics were coping with the loss of friends and family members, the Twin Towers, and all the *things* that made Lower Manhattan Lower Manhattan before 8:46 a.m. on 9/11/01.

One can find, between 2001 and 2003, myriad examples of collective feelings of disorientation, fear, and anxiety that support the way topophobia gave way to talk of necessitous retributive justice and the militarization of New York. During President Bush's 2002 State of the Union address, for example, he reminded publics of the necessity of swift and "deliberate" action against the terrorists that were believed to be writ large among terrorist cells. Tapping into the nation's fear of the omnipresent, but invisible, other to justify asymmetrical warfare, Bush said, "America will do what is necessary to ensure our nation's security."[18] While at a service at Ground Zero on January 30, 2002, he pivoted from discussions of unity through grief toward talk of lethal combat. "This conflict," the commander in chief explained, was "begun on the timing and terms of others. It will end in a way, and at an hour, of our choosing."[19]

Although many identified with the president's senses of insecurity and urgency, not everyone was sure how to rhetorically frame these feelings. In a traveling diary about America's post-9/11 moods and sentiments, Ken Wiwa of the *Globe and Mail* commented on the conditions that made Bush's war cry so desirable to millions who thirsted for justice. "If fear is the first condition of war, then America is at war," he noted. "But it is a curious war, undefined, visible but invisible. Paradoxes and ironies are in full bloom. . . . The land of the free is willingly giving up its freedoms. Security breeds insecurity."[20] To Jenny Edkins, this relinquishment of political rights was evidence of the biopolitical reality that was taking hold of the nation. "Security was an illusion," she said. "We were all exceedingly vulnerable," she admitted, but she was also sure that the "horror was that, in being treated instrumentally, as bare life, the victims had been deprived not only of their lives but also of their deaths. They were not the dead: they were the missing."[21]

What then of the terrorized spaces that were used to mobilize this instrumentality of lives during the short but critical time between the attacks and the invasion and occupation of Iraq? Ground Zero was securitized; it was protected by the National Guard and local police forces who stood on watch for suspicious behavior. These guardians stood in front of securitized objects such as chain-link fences, gates, and barricades that separated Ground Zero from the rest of society.[22] Setha Low, who conducted a detailed ethnographic study of Ground Zero and Battery Park during this turbulent time remarked that as "the city cleaned up the rubble from the explosions and the subsequent fires, it also constructed walls, barriers, and temporary memorials."[23]

Due to the utter lack of security, worries regarding the prevention of these attacks, and the feelings of political betrayal, Lower Manhattan became a space that epitomized topophobic fears as so many sought to cope with feelings of insecurity and vulnerability by justifying the militaristic seizure of Ground Zero.

Consequently, critical scholars could argue that many locals were excluded from participating in the search and recovery processes occurring within what Foucauldians might call this heterotopic space of crisis.[24] More than that, families and friends of the missing or dead could not mourn for their loved ones at the place of their disappearance, especially considering many of the human remains were turned to ashes and dust, pulverized. All that many could do was get out of the way and watch the events unfold on their public screens while they were paralyzed by the magnitude of the situation.[25]

Some averred that police forces and first responders left no room for spontaneous public participation, as the dominant roles of actors with moral or ethical agency had already been given to those who prioritized securitization. As Diana Taylor notes, in these select and motivated social dramas, the heroes were the political leaders and first responders. The victims were those who perished. And the spectators were everybody else, who were told to "stay out of the way" and "wait patiently in lines at airports and ballparks, knowing it was for a greater good."[26]

Publics were often told to go on about their days as if nothing happened. In a typical press conference, Mayor Rudy Giuliani affirmed this passive public role when he famously said, "The advice that I would give people today . . . is to stay home from work . . . go about a normal day . . . take the opportunity to go shopping . . . do things. Get out."[27] And on September 27, President Bush seemed to echo this type of message when he urged American publics to "fly and enjoy America's great destination spots" by getting "down to Disney World in Florida" and enjoying life "the way we want it to be enjoyed."[28] Terrorists, after all, and their attacks on Ground Zero and the other sacred sites, were not going to interfere with the American way of life.

This strategic removal of some agency may in part help explain why some, according to Taylor, developed "hero envy" or "trauma envy."[29] Meanwhile, images of terror, death, and disaster were played on an "endless loop" that prevented subjects from escaping the visual onslaught of trauma.[30]

Perhaps because of all of this talk of traveling and consumption, millions of disaster tourists and pilgrims attempted to access Ground Zero in unsanctioned ways. They tried to document the destruction by taking photographs, notwithstanding Ground Zero's highly securitized, war-zone-like status. Tourism, then, along with the fascination with death and disaster (a form of "dark tourism" and thanatopolitics; see chapter 5), adds one more layer of complexity to this securitized space, and it will continue to do so throughout our book.

Consider, for example, the way that some U.S. individuals and communities would travel great distances to take photos through peepholes of "super strong fence three meters high, through which [they would]... push the lenses of their cameras"[31] only to leave feeling more insecure and more uncertain as they boarded planes to take them home. One traveler, for instance, who visited Ground Zero on a tour bus from Baltimore said, "I don't know. I don't know. ... I can't say I feel any better," when asked about her reaction to this space.[32]

Eventually, all of these early feelings of uncertainty, vengeance, and anxiety between 2001 and 2003 would be used as fodder for empowered individuals or collectives who sought the securitization of memorial space. Topophobic feelings allowed state-sanctioned institutional authorities to use Ground Zero, and the trauma attached to it, as they assembled more argumentative justification for hypervigilance during what would later be called a "perpetual war."

In the meantime, New York had to endure a sustained period of spatial and temporal insecurity to warrant the necessity of a carefully controlled, object-oriented security apparatus that could potentially restore feelings of security. Structures of insecurity can take many forms, but during the immediate aftermath of the greatest terrorist attack on American soil in the history of the United States, insecurity was made most prominent, materially, with dust.

The Materiality of Dust (and Its Material Insecurities)

We are convinced that dust became the materialization of dematerialized bodies and objects that refused to disappear. It whirled and lingered with indecipherable, ambiguous, and liminal status. Dust haunted New York for a long period because it simply would not go away. Insecurities over the health ramifications of dust, in particular, wrought by prolific amounts of the toxic stuff, posed important questions about who to remember during the feverish cries for a national memorial.[33] Should the memorial commemorate only those who died from the destruction of the Twin Towers or all of those who survived but continued to suffer from the health consequences of the cleanup stage? What about the undocumented immigrants who gave their health to sanitize New York, or the average New Yorker who developed the "WTC cough?" How can people mourn the dead when distinctions between dust-as-trash and dust-as-human are nonexistent? What should be done with it all? These are some of the questions that were asked by locals, first responders, and politicians during the early aftermath of 9/11—a period that can be characterized as the post-9/11 "dust bowl."

Dust was the material presence of the disorder that lingered and never fully disappeared, even when the National September 11 Memorial and Memorial Museum were fully constructed. During 2001, however, dust became a component of different assemblages, in part, because dust would be the nonpresent remainder of the spatial order that was once attached to New York space. After 9/11 the visual icons of New York—the Twin Towers—were reduced and replaced with nothing more, nothing less, than dust and detritus, which can be read as an erasure of the ordering of time and space that preceded the attacks.

Dust not only signified disorder but performed it, materially, in that its omnipotent presence—and its transformative potentiality—disrupted nearly every facet of normal life. Dust, after all, is a fine and gritty molecular substance capable of blanketing entire landscapes. As an object betwixt and between other objects—which never seem to be quite themselves in a purist metaphysical sense—dust is itself an assemblage that contains numerous different elements with other parts (e.g., it is not quite a solid and not quite a gas). And it is like this all the way down to the molecular level.

The materiality of post-9/11 dust, therefore, teaches us that entities like this are always already something else, what some philosophers call "things" or objects that are tied to other objects with varied sets of relations within different assemblages. Dust is a hybridity, of course, and as such, it is an example of what Bruno Latour calls "quasi-objects" in his *We Have Never Been Modern*. Speaking of how these kinds of objects build relations and formulate what he later calls actor-networks, Latour states that "quasi-objects are much more social, much more fabricated, much more collective than the 'hard' parts of nature, but they are in no way the arbitrary receptacles of a full-fledged society."[34]

As a forceful quasi-object, then, dust was the material manifestation of uncertainty, angst, fear of the unknown, and all of the insecurities that came along with it, not only because dust is the material byproduct of explosion and collapse but because it cannot be reduced to an essence for stable meaning.

Consider how dust includes many different hybridized parts, in trace amounts, that allied with different assemblies. Take the World Trade Center, for example, a space composed of many heterogeneous elements. It was made of steel, concrete, wood, glass, plastic, granite, porcelain, asbestos; and it housed everything one could imagine necessary for the more than 430 corporations to employ over fifty thousand people who worked there.[35] Desks, filing cabinets, computers, printers, telephones. . . . All of it was reduced to dust. In the documentary film *9/11*, one firefighter reflected on this scene:

> You have two 110-story office buildings. You don't find a desk, you don't find a chair, you don't find a computer. The biggest piece of telephone I found was a keypad and it was this big. The building collapsed to dust. How are we supposed to find anybody in this stuff? There's nothing left of the building.[36]

In some places, such as certain department stores, the piles of dust were as much as three feet high.[37]

Everywhere within a three-block radius, dust whirled and lingered as an indecipherable, ambiguous, and liminal matter. One such ambiguity was the fact that in the dust were pulverized body parts, the identification and disposal of which were heavily disputed within technolegal assemblages.[38] This disputation involved organizations such as the Office of the Chief Medical Examiner, NYPD, FBI, and victims' families, who called themselves WTC Families for a Proper Burial and sought legal recourse against the City of New York from mishandling trace amounts of loved ones' remains during the cleanup process. As Victor Toom noted in an essay titled "Whose Body Is

It," dust was the technolegal materialization of the 21,906 reported bodily remains (14,254 remains were associated with 1,637 victims) that involved fraught identification processes about who owned the corpses or to which set of relations they pertained: "Do they belong to the medical professions, relatives, clergy?"[39]

Such insecurities provided fodder for the catalytic turn toward securitization during the early aftermath of 9/11. As Mary Douglas observes, dirt is the materialization of matter out of place that makes things "messy" and prompts processes of "purification" to regain order. When the material force of dirt, specifically dust in our case, is associated with so much carnage, death, destruction, and utter loss of control, and when the material experience of this chaotic assemblage includes visible, tactile, olfactory, and even gustatory forces, one can understand how the ubiquity of post-9/11 dust created an urgency for the eventual ultrasecuritization of memorial space, if at the very least it was to regain a sense of control over one's environment. Years before the memorial opened, when the dust resembled a fresh coat of snow, dust was simply a danger to the order of society and had to be removed as soon as possible.

Extending the work of Mary Douglas, then, in the materialistic sense allows us to study the transitional possibilities of dust, especially during moments of perceived existential terrorist crises. During moments like these, dust and debris were regarded as dangerous—literally in terms of human health, livelihood, and existence.

Consider how to many of those who did not have the luxury of maintaining a safe distance from its fallout, dust was a toxic cocktail that created psychological and physical insecurities for years to come. The deleterious effects of dust were surely on the minds of many health-conscious New Yorkers who were in Lower Manhattan when litanies of this powdery substance scorched the sky and blanketed the ground. However, the exact potency of all of this dust was not known for months and even years after the attack, and this fallout became the object of disputation between New York citizens and agencies such as the Environmental Protection Agency (EPA).

Harold Evans of the *Independent* recalls his difficulty explaining the events to his daughter, Isabel, when she quizzically asked about the "funny smell" that permeated the walls of their Long Island apartment and almost triggered an asthma attack. Evans had an idea that the dust was "the toxic mix of burning flesh, debris and dust," but he did not know how to explain it all to his daughter, in part because he was among millions who did not understand it himself. The dust "lingered for so long," Evans noted, "like the questions of the innocent."[40]

With so many uncertainties swirling around New York, the noxious smell was one of the few empirical certainties that many survivors vividly recall. To Patrick Rhoades, one of the firefighters on the Federal Emergency Management Agency team called in from Denver to assist first responders at Ground Zero, "the smell was like nothing I've ever smelled before, kind of electrical with a little rubber mixed in."[41] Many of the other on-site workers complained about the smell, describing it as a "giant foundry with untold tons of metal burning under the torch." In a sort of explanation to the first responders and locals about what they were smelling, one federally funded worker, who distributed respirators at Ground Zero after September 15, 2001, said, "You do not smell asbestos," he said. "You may smell body parts, you may smell Freon. But it's the things you can't smell that can really hurt you the most."[42]

Ambiguity over the dust's contents contributed to psychological and physiological insecurities derived from the loss of material space at Ground Zero. Awareness of the dust's health risks spread, though, especially after the release of forceful images. Consider the famous "Dust Lady" image, which is a photograph of Marcy Borders—an employee for Bank of America in the World Trade Center—who is covered head to toe in gray dust. This haunting image proffered contemplation about the health effects of exposure to massive amounts of toxic particulates.[43]

Borders's own tragic story speaks to the hidden costs of trauma for survivors, and reminds us of the multidirectional nature of 9/11 memories. She suffered from severe depression, alcoholism, and drug abuse in the years that followed and was, years later, diagnosed with stomach cancer, which she strongly believed was caused by her inhalation of so much dust. She once told reporters, "I'm saying to myself, 'Did this thing ignite cancer cells in me? I definitely believe it because I haven't had any illnesses." She also asked, "How do you go from being healthy to waking up the next day with cancer?"[44] She died from cancer in 2015.

The story of the so-called Dust Lady raised national awareness about the thousands of other survivors who have battled seen and unseen enemies. These survivors silently struggle with obscure and undiagnosed illnesses that were said to have mysteriously appeared after 9/11. It has since been revealed, albeit still contested by some, that 9/11 dust was a deadly chemical concoction of more than twenty-five hundred contaminants.[45] As revealed by a documentary on these health effects, titled *Dust to Dust*,[46] many of these chemicals have been linked to kidney, heart, or liver failure, deterioration of the nervous system, permanent respiratory problems, cancer, and ultimately, long, painful deaths.[47] To name just a few, contaminants included asbestos, gypsum, cadmium, and calcium carbonate,[48] in addition to copious amounts of "caustic, finely pulverized concrete, trillions of microscopic fibers of glass, and particles of lead, mercury and arsenic."[49]

Of course, dust's health-related argument assemblage, and its environmental hybridities, evoked consideration of which institution was liable for articulating the risks of inhalation. The EPA, for example, fell under public scrutiny for telling people that the dust that was scientifically assessed—and ruled not harmful—posed no major health problems. Two days after the attacks, the EPA publicly announced that Ground Zero dust was "unlikely to cause significant health effects."[50] Protective gear such as respirators was not required, and people were told that all air-quality tests revealed the air was safe for inhalation. Six days after 9/11, the administrator of the Occupational Safety and Health Administration, John Henshaw, said, "All of our [air] samples were significantly below our permissible exposure limits. . . . That conveys that the environment is safe."[51]

Today, many of these arguments and environmental worries have been forgotten, but during the weeks and months after the al Qaeda attacks, some of the blanket statements of reassurance circulated by

Henshaw and others stirred up suspicions of misleading information regarding exposure to "wildly toxic" dust.[52] Dingpolitik turned into realpolitik concerns as Democratic Committee chairman Jerrold Nadler blamed government officials for inadequately testing fallen materials, not requiring all workers to wear safety masks, and allowing buildings to be reoccupied, including schools, when they were far from being safe. "Six years later," he said in 2007, "we are just beginning to see the enormous consequences of those actions. . . . Our government knowingly exposed thousands of U.S. citizens unnecessarily."[53]

Altogether, the ambiguities about the dust's substance, and the degree to which it was considered harmful to human health, reinforce the notion that it was a sort of quasi-object that could not be reduced to an essence, and it was this kind of uncertainty that proliferated feelings of insecurity and disputation. Dust was a material force that could not be reduced, yet during times of transition, dust is not only dangerous but also materially forceful, if not outright radical. To Peter Nyers, who argues that the Latourian irreduction of dirt (i.e., its inability to be reduced to something else)[54] in border politics challenges the state's capacity to territorialize dirt for state sovereignty. He asks, "If objects can have a force or direction that is not always controlled, directed or predictable by human beings, can dirt have a force or direction of its own?"[55]

Perhaps it is precisely because dirt is irreducible and uncontrollable that it always seems to fall under the umbrella of security discourses, especially regarding territorial and spatialized disputes.[56] This was at least the case in the aftermath of the greatest attack on American soil since Pearl Harbor. While on one hand, post-9/11 dust is the visible and tactile reflection of society at its existential nadir ("ashes to ashes, dust to dust"), it is also a site of engagement, if not affordance, for purity and rebirth through radical securitization. Dust was both dangerously transitional and politically interventional in the most extreme sense at Ground Zero. So began the transition of Ground Zero's material space from a catastrophic post-fallout area to a highly sophisticated, and sanitized, security assemblage that consisted of its own objects such as NYPD closed-circuit television screens, fences, barricades, and militaristic armory (including high-caliber rifles, tanks, and metal detectors) to replace the dirtied New York space with the materialization of security. What interfered with this state-sanctioned territorialization, however, was a profuse number of makeshift memorials and objects of memory that locals had placed throughout Lower Manhattan in their own attempts to resecuritize space. Like dust, the memorials too had to be removed to purify and reterritorialize the materiality of Ground Zero space.

Ground Zero Dingpolitik and the Vernacular Sacralization of New York

While all of the dust, soot, and ash were still settling, people of many different stripes began to fill New York's vacuumed spaces with secular and sacred objects. Vernacular objects—such as makeshift shrines, altars, candles, images, drawings—performed a different set of ding-politik relations during a time of spatial sacralization when Ground Zero became a political site of struggle regarding the nature and scope of local securitization. Erika Doss explains:

> Things, especially public things, map political cultures and shape political bodies; things, Bruno Latour argues, constitute "atmospheres of democracy" and *dingpolitik* provides clearer and more credible possibilities than realpolitik. Things also, of course, constitute a modern mass culture that valorizes impermanence and disposability.[57]

In other words, some types of deliberative argumentation used by architects, police, judges, or wealthy entrepreneurs may become a part of realpolitik conversations that do not resonate with those who have competing views of commemorative vernacular spaces.

Dingpolitik approaches help academics and laypersons see how microperformances using small objects can put on display how locals attempted to contain the spatial insecurities of post-9/11 New York. By blurring the older realpolitik lines that separated the sacred from the secular, and by allowing critics to focus on the vernacular dimensions of this object-oriented civil religion, analysts gain an appreciation of how publics as well as elites cope with a host of rhetorics of (in)security.

Signs of vernacular dingpolitik were everywhere after the attacks on the Twin Towers. The streets were teeming with them. They were on the walls of Penn Station, the walkways and benches of Union Square, and the security fence that surrounded Ground Zero.[58] Both visual and textual materials were used to display the affection that Americans felt for their lost loved ones, and the mourning included impromptu pilgrimages by individuals to Ground Zero. Journalists and visitors could see pictures of loved ones, signs for local residents, and posters of "I Love New York."[59] Apocalyptic rhetorics were in the air, including pamphlets about World War III, the coming of Christ, and Armageddon.

It would take years before elites and their architects would finalize plans for the National September 11 Memorial, but this delay did not mean that laypersons couldn't work on makeshift memorials dedicated to the dead. In a description of Ground Zero that circulated in December 2001, Stephen Buckley, a reporter for Florida's *St. Petersburg Times*, wrote about the prominence of these eclectic memorials:

> Judging by the array of T-shirts hanging over an iron rail in front of the Trinity Church, everyone loves New York: God loves New York, Oregon loves New York, Holland loves New York. The tributes take all forms: posters with happy birthday wishes to victims, vases of flowers, a Nerf football, an alarm clock stopped at 8:48 a.m., when the attacks began.[60]

According to Johnson, places such as Grand Central Station, St. Paul's Chapel, and random street corners became localized altars of remembrance that were always works in progress. This phenomenon was especially true at Battery Park.

Just blocks from Ground Zero, Battery Park, including the adjacent residential area known as Battery Park City, was physically devastated by the 9/11 attacks. This local community also lost eight members. For many of those who wished to mourn in the absence of an official memorial site, Battery Park became one of the key places for establishing temporary 9/11 memorials. For example, on March 11, 2002, Koenig's Sphere, which once stood in the plaza between the Twin Towers, was rededicated to the victims of 9/11 and placed in Battery Park. On the first anniversary of 9/11 an eternal flame was placed in front of Koenig's Sphere, giving way to an astonishing influx of objects of remembrance. Johnson recorded how there were a number of "material displays[,] . . . candles, a hand-written translation of several paragraphs from the Bhagavad-Gita, balloons . . . ubiquitous teddy bears, and photos of the deceased victims."[61]

In later years, when the Department of Parks ordered the sphere to be removed to make way for a $16 million renovation of Battery Park, the sphere became an object of controversy about where the Port Authority—who owned it—should place it. One emergent defender of the sphere was Michael Burke—brother of Captain William F. Burke Jr., of Engine Company 21, who perished on 9/11. Burke argued the sphere should return to Ground Zero despite the fact that memorial authorities were openly rejecting such a proposition. In response, Burke gathered seventy-two hundred signatures to support his advocacy. "This is a denial of history," he said in his petition. "America has no more vital historical artifact than the WTC Sphere."[62] This would not be the first—nor the last—time that authorized memorial figures clashed with local residents over the nature and scope of 9/11 remembrances.

As readers might imagine, public spaces such as Battery Park became highly securitized by police and military officials who guarded particular private places such as the Sony Building and the Citicorp atriums, and these well-intentioned groups created even more controversies when they asked that all persons show proper identification, allow their bags to be searched, or go through metal detectors for entry.[63]

Many residents were already suspicious when they interacted daily with authority figures, but all of this was exacerbated by the seemingly military occupation of the Ground Zero area. Some residents of Battery Park City talked about "tanks in the street," while others complained about not being able to access their homes due to the security apparatus that took over. In an interview with ethnologist Setha Low—who has done extensive ethnographic work on 9/11 communities and has written about the securitization of suburban communities in other work[64]—one resident talked about her return to Battery Park City months after she and her community were evacuated "in pickup trucks."[65] In this particular interview, she explained that there were "barricades and police all over the place" and that a "policeman with a gun" made her wait before she could return to her apartment to collect her belongings.[66] She also remembers the "little teddy bears" and the way that "people turne[d] against each other," and she recalled seeing "people standing there behind barricades" who seemed "resentful" while they were screaming at us, threatening to report us to the police."[67]

All of this merger of vernacular dingpolitik with security realpolitik from officials created a complicated heterotopic assemblage that severely hampered New Yorkers' ability to cope, mourn, and move on, let alone regain public space. Talking about Battery Park City—which is already home to numerous memorials and museums such as the New York City Holocaust Museum and a memorial to fallen NYPD officers—one resident said, "We're like a dumping ground for memorials. . . . We don't want to live in a graveyard."[68]

These would be the types of dissenting rhetorics, the alternative features of multidirectional memory, that would later be forgotten by those who wrote as if all New Yorkers were enamored by the idea of securitizing Ground Zero and surrounding spaces and places.

Some locals simply wanted to see closure and were not interested in contemplating the economic benefits that might come from the spending by future crowds of tourists who visited these hallowed grounds. No wonder that in November 2001 the *New York Times* reported that most people were looking for closure from the traumatic public memory of 9/11. Whether that came in the form of tattoos, desires for vengeance, or finding the remains of loved ones, New Yorkers were looking for an end to the seemingly endless successions of traumatic memory. To Sandra Owens, a trauma and grief counselor interviewee, the "word closure implies an ending. . . . Those who are looking so desperately for [normalcy], or who think they've found it, are just trying to anesthetize themselves to what's going on."[69] How to communicate, how to act, and how to remember were all new questions that local residents and national subjects had to grapple with on an individual level, and amid so much persistent ambivalence.

The absence of traumatic relief, however, was an emerging trend in American realpolitik affairs. Many members of the nation wanted to feel as though they were doing their part in the GWOT, which oftentimes meant cathartically reliving the visual trauma of the event on a routine basis.

The polysemic and polyvalent nature of multidirectional memory, as well as the absence of any official memorial, allowed this reliving to be experienced in a number of ways. During the months that followed the destruction of the Twin Towers, the attack's meaning was not yet fully articulated, but that did not prevent the journalistic coverage of diverse ways of viewing memorialization practices.[70] The lack of any institutional memorial did not stand in the way of the early "rush to memorialize," which prompted some to ask: "Why wait? . . . I don't think you can do it too soon."[71]

While there were vociferous disagreements about what to build and how to remember 9/11, there was little scholarly disagreement that many publics were in a hurry to commemorate what many regarded as the greatest catastrophic attack since Pearl Harbor. As Rick Hampson observes, memorials are "how we put our stamp on history."[72] To Erika Doss, post-9/11 subjects were swept up as they witnessed the arrival of a national "memorial mania" that incessantly encouraged publics to waste no time constructing any kind of memorial to remember events of the past.[73]

Indeed, many academics argue that memorials have unique capacities to help victims cope with traumatic memories, especially since they have the faculties necessary to organize historical memory[74] and they "define the [spatial] boundaries of memory."[75] Some of the key questions, of course, involve the ideological shapes and contours of those memories, and what do we do when visitors to sites of memory do not seek closure? What if, for example, some securitized spaces contribute to the spread of topophobia?

This situation only complicates the question of who can, or should, speak for the dead when talking about vernacular and official memorialization practices.

While there is no shortage of anecdotal evidence that many locals were patriots who welcomed the prioritization of national security interests and the policing that would become part of so many counterterrorist performances, others wanted to have more say in how the destroyed areas around the Twin Towers would be rebuilt. Between 2001 and 2003, New Yorkers did not mind admitting that they felt excluded from the public, political, and institutional memorial-making processes that millions outside the state were calling for. This exclusion was especially true for those living in Battery Park City, who could not escape the proliferation of memorial space. To Setha Low, "they actually have been left out, even though, along with the victims' families, they will be affected the most by what is built on this site."[76]

While many journalists and those outside local areas wanted Ground Zero to be turned into reverential spaces and places that would allow for tourist visitations by tens of millions of Americans, those living closer to the scene realized that there might be many unintended consequences in the wake of such national memorialization. Many New Yorkers, after all, had more practical immediate needs, such as improved transportation networks, regained commercial space, and local community vibrancies that were lost on 9/11/01.[77] One neighborhood activist said, "There is a sense of anger at the politicians and powers that are ignoring that we are victims too. We lost our supermarket, our buses; it is going to be a construction zone for 5–8 years. No one acknowledges us. They only see the victims, the dead, and their families as victims."[78]

Though these early victimage wars did not capture the attention of most mainstream presses, they provided a potential wedge issue that bothered those who wanted to talk about a united and resilient America where everyone was willing to support counterterrorist efforts and fund what later would become an important part of America's civil religion. For those who believed in the existence of transcendent principles of American exceptionalism, all of this early wrangling and dissension represented chaos, upheaval, and evidence of wounds that had not yet healed. It was thus not uncommon for many journalistic writers to treat some of this dissent and debate as a problematic barrier that obstructed the paths of those who wanted to see the speedy construction of a *national* 9/11 memorial.

Those who searched for monolithic memorial meanings, or univocal support for an institutional and national memorial campaign, had to compete with those who had other motivations and were not afraid to articulate their concerns that official dispositifs regarding victimage and needs need not take center stage. For example, while New Yorkers often agreed that they needed time for bereavement and a place to mourn, there were also countless disagreements about how civil authorities and traditional religious institutions should assist needy publics. In 2002, for instance, a Brooklyn congregation canceled a memorial service for a member of the church who died in the South Tower due to "a dispute over what the remembrance should include."[79] The apparent controversy was between loved ones and church leaders who were arguing about what Josh Gunn calls "voice,"[80] the acoustic registers that filter the sounds that we will hear in ghostly situations. While family members and loved ones of the deceased Brooklyn congregant decided to take their services elsewhere, this minicontroversy can be read as indicative of a larger question facing the New York communities: Who is going to help residents mourn and bring closure to this trauma in situations where the institutional authorities may not want to see that closure?

Although vernacular memorials helped some individuals cope with losses in personal ways, some viewed the surfeit of public displays of veneration and remembrance *as a pathological condition* that was interfering with their normal daily routines. Dystopic rhetorics and talk of maladies circulated at a time when some altars, graffiti, and small memorials were dubbed disruptive and disorderly. For some, too much focus on memorialization could also inhibit processes of grief that were perceived to be necessary for a healthy return to normal life. As one resident of Battery Park City noted, "We are *surrounded* by death memorials. Now we want the opposite: Life and overcoming."[81] Another said, "It's not healthy for me to live in a cemetery."[82]

Some neighborhood residents found their communities flooded with tourists who were "trying to get closer to 'Ground Zero.'"[83] One nearby resident vehemently complained, "We are treated like a freak show. . . . We had people come to our apartment and ask us to view the damage in our apartment. . . . It is disgusting. It is not a tourist attraction—this is a tragedy and a lot of people don't treat it that way."[84]

Is it possible that some state officials reacted to this growing disorder by putting an end to the organic growth of some of these populist signs of performative civil religion? Is it any coincidence that all of this was taking place at the very time that authorities were hiring architects to begin the planning for the mammoth National September 11 Memorial and tanks were rolling through Battery Park? These institutional authorities constructed what Johnson calls "instrumental civil religion, which is a strident us/them discourse [that] had dramatic effects in mobilizing popular support for specific actions, namely, the invasion/liberation/occupation of Iraq."[85]

The famous Powell Doctrine—named after Colin Powell's assessment of the lack of support for the Vietnam conflict—invites military experts, soldiers, diplomats, and laypersons to avoid intervening in foreign affairs or civil wars *if U.S. publics are not firmly behind* the institutional authorities that wish to wage wars overseas. It is possible that Johnson is right, that some types of memorialization and civil religious practices can be used for purposes of mobilizing support for wars. While this type of discourse may appear to be apolitical to some, "it is composed of speeches and ceremonies calculated for political effect, entailing relatively less improvisation."[86] The crowding out of others, and the filling in of "the polysemic space,"[87] preserved status quo hierarchies and helped with the maintenance of sovereign order. Consider how much more potent these pro-war arguments become when the dingpolitik of memorial spaces is used to reinforce institutional realpolitik.

Consider, for instance, how the politicization of things took on new meanings when New York authorities proposed a bill on May 6, 2003, that would ban vendors and peddling tourists within a certain radius of Ground Zero to preserve the sanctity and decorum of the site.[88]

Commenting on this bill, and evoking questions such as those about a possible dress code at Ground Zero and the tackiness of Ground Zero T-shirts, one tourist said, "You can't legislate taste, and you can't legislate sensitivity."[89] Although the bill was not implemented, it deepened levels of distrust between institutional authorities (viz., EPA, Department of Parks and Recreation, NYPD, Port Authorities) and publics that were already on edge ever since the public health disagreements during the dust bowl, in addition to their frustrations over the militarization of their neighborhoods such as Battery Park City.

As noted above, objects of all kinds were made political during this mercurial time of contested multidirectional—and outright competitive—public memories. Makeshift altars, posters, military tanks, guns, fences, barricades, teddy bears, and so forth were all part of this complicated security assemblage that was taking form between 2001 and 2003. In their critique of these temporary memorials, Haskins and DeRose note that "if anything, the noisy democracy of ephemeral street commemorations suggests that the model for a memorial to 9/11 should be an idyllic place that guarantees the rights to express, disagree, assemble, claim, and collectively own."[90]

Indeed, for many dissenters, the right to occupy public space with artifacts of memory is a central component of a reticulate public sphere, one that depends on vernacular discourse to sustain the health of our democratic civil society.[91] At the same time, however, all of the shrines, street memorials, and graffiti were characterized by many citizens as unruly in their natural context and were therefore reckoned more suitable in museum spaces, if not dumpsters. Consequently, the absence of these artifacts, and the processes of mourning that they invited, gave the nation exactly what it wanted with the "memorial fever" that Doss describes: an official history of post-9/11 discourse with a monolithic collective memory about "what happened."[92] The consequence of this, however, was the exclusionary formation of a select national identity that centered on a state-sanctioned securitization of Ground Zero space.

What often gets forgotten is that during this sensitive period (2001–3), relations between grieving New Yorkers and the Department of

Parks and Recreation and Port Authorities were in a constant state of tension. For instance, when the Department of Parks and Recreation started removing shrines and memorial objects as soon as a few weeks after 9/11,[93] many protested for their right to place memorial objects—flowers, pictures, art—on or near Ground Zero.[94] The Department of Parks and Recreation and Port Authorities, however, was more concerned with relocating the material to hangars and warehouses for public safety, and perhaps this was another tactic that could be used to make way for a more official memorial.[95]

By the fall of 2003, on the second anniversary of 9/11, all of the private altars were officially gone. Removed by the Department of Parks and Recreation, the artifacts that became a part of what some might call an "organic" civil religion movement were considered disorderly and thus were hidden from public view.[96] Institutional authorities, publicly charged with establishing a new historical identity, were funneling diverse vernacular religiosities into a singular, convergent nationalistic one that would be recognized as the official "American" public memory of 9/11 victimage. The formation of these assemblages, in turn, allowed for the blurring of the secular and the sacred in ways that allowed stakeholders in the GWOT to use this formation as warrants for even more policing and militarization of these spaces and places.

Many of the personal or vernacular artifacts were moved to museums and historical societies for exhibition, including the Museum of the City of New York, the New York Historical Society, the New York Fire Museum, the New York State Museum, and the New Jersey Historical Society.[97] Haskins and DeRose call this an attempt to create an ideal public sphere, or a political utopia. These are attempts to form a unified, and ordered, public voice that uses artifacts like glass-enclosed exhibitions to legitimate national memory formation by empowered authorities. From a critical vantage point, this is also an example of cooptation, where the securitization of Ground Zero took precedence over competing local motivations and interests.

These securitization performances depended on a host of macro- and micropractices. For example, arguments about aesthetics can be melded with claims regarding counterterrorist decision-making. When the Port Authority of New York and New Jersey built a forty-foot-long, thirteen-foot-high wall to circumscribe Ground Zero, for instance, they did so in the name of memorial art. In reality, the "wall" was an austere fence designed to demarcate Ground Zero space from public space during the rebuilding stages, but the structure was pitched as a space for public expression, as its grammar changed from a "construction fence" to a "perimeter enclosure" to, eventually, a "viewing wall."[98] To Balmori Associates—the company that built the wall—it "looks to those spontaneous, short-lived responses as a way to capture a specific moment of our grief."[99]

We understand this institutional seizure and re-presentation, or even respatialization, of public objects to be one more example of securitized dingpolitik that depoliticizes New Yorkers' matters of concern (the objects used to personally politicize Ground Zero space) and thus present them as trivial matters of fact within state-based nationalistic assemblages.

The seizure, archiving, or recharacterization of these vernacular objects allowed for the formation of governmentalities that provides yet another example of what Eyal Weizman calls "forensic architecture."[100] In this particular case, the outcast artifacts that were removed from public view become curatorial abject objects of antiquity, pre–national memorial objects of curiosity that could be reframed in the security-oriented nationalistic narratives of 9/11 commemoration.

Evidently, the institutional desire to preserve public memories traded off with the actual existence of public spaces in New York. Erasing the memory of makeshift memorials from the streets, then, marked a turning point from chaotic vernacular memorialization to organized and nationalistic securitization of Ground Zero. While this move might be deemed productive by those who search for a consensual "public memory" of this supposed beginning of the GWOT, we need to recall the recursive nature of this memory formation that did more than just "represent" some monolithic 9/11 "history." The selective nature of commemoration and erasure not only helped legitimate the efforts of counterterrorists—it also deprived citizens of their ability to mourn in ways that had little to do with national retaliation against al Qaeda or foreign interventionism.

When former president George W. Bush said, "You're either with us or against us in the fight against terror,"[101] this represented a variant of the Manichean binaries that depended on consensus and the galvanization of American willpower and was said to be needed for the protection of the homeland.

As noted above, those who attempted to localize grief were left out of the picture. One sign of protest, raised in a February 14, 2003, march against war said it all: "OUR GRIEF IS NOT A CRY FOR WAR."[102] This protest would become a voice crying in the wilderness as millions were asked to donate their dollars for the formation of what would become the National September 11 Memorial and Memorial Museum.

Altogether, institutional authorities were able to seize Ground Zero by using their considerable monetary and symbolic resources to clean the streets of New York and pave the way for a more official, nationalistic account of "what happened" on 9/11 and how to remember that catastrophic event. To Johnson, this seizure is evidence of a "symbolic hijacking" that served the interests of political leaders attempting to sell the invasion and occupation of Iraq in addition to the war on terrorism.[103] We would like to add that it was also a materialist hijacking that sought to "purify" New York space to rematerialize it with a national memorial at the epicenter of where the attacks occurred: Ground Zero.

As authorities would soon find out, toggling through the range of opinions about how to remember 9/11 would not be easy, for as soon as Ground Zero was "institutionalized," per se, it also became a battleground where numerous stakeholders would fight over how to "properly" commemorate 9/11 and those who died.

Evaluating the Early Attempts at Securitization of Ground Zero

This chapter has argued that during the immediate aftermath of the 9/11/01 attacks (2001–3), New York was in a material state of transition from disorder, disaster, and confusion to a more purified state that would allow state authorities to construct a national memorial commemorating the lives that were lost on that tragic day. What we have shown is that this was also a temporal periodization of substantial dingpolitik that involved a blend of human and nonhuman actors: local New Yorkers and survivors, dust (and its technolegal relations), vernacular memorials, and state institutional authorities. All of these agents participated in formation of assemblages that eventually gave way to a more "purified" materiality of space through the things that were deemed "dangerous," in their both material and symbolic senses, to a post-9/11 ordered society. Of course, this transition began with the removal of dust—and its complicated mixture of human remains, toxic substances, and other environmental hazards—and then shifted to the confiscation of all the makeshift memorials that locals had put on display to commemorate personal and public losses from 9/11.

While various symbolisms were attached to these New York objects, it was ultimately the materiality of such things that caused argumentative stirs about how to remember. And the circulation of these early arguments, and their cross-pollinations with assemblages in technical, legal, public, and political registers, shaped the contours of the security assemblages that had already taken hold in New York and across the nation.

In other words, the material-semiotic bundle of relations we have described in this chapter has lent itself to the rise of felt necessities of the times, when powerful and highly sophisticated security apparatuses—including, of course, securitized objects such as cameras, barricades, and metal detectors—were already replacing the dematerialization of space at Ground Zero.

The removal of vernacular objects facilitated the transition of this space to one of resecuritization by police and militaristic personnel who replaced public objects of memorialization with securitized objects (tanks, guns, barricades, etc.) to defend the securitized apparatus that was already under construction. In many ways, then, this chapter has also illustrated how dingpolitik can be used to enable realpolitik relations, making the two political orientations complementary to each other rather than mutually exclusive, as Latour mildly suggests.

The following chapter charts the mnemonic contestations that sur-faced over how to nationally commemorate 9/11 at Ground Zero. We begin with a close reading of the architectural disputations over the designs of Michael Arad's winning proposal, "Remembering Absence," between the ad hoc corporation called the Lower Manhattan Develop-ment Corporation (LMDC) and its board members; distraught family members of those who died, who were still grieving and felt they had ownership of how to properly remember; master architect Daniel Libes-kind; and security personnel who were concerned about protecting this space of exception from another terrorist attack. The attempts of all of these stakeholders to fill Ground Zero's material absence with their interpretations of how to best remember the tragedies of 9/11 gave way to a complicated, heterogeneous texture of public memory that would continue to resist a wholly complete, or monoglossic, form of commemoration that could atomistically contain difference, deferral, and mourning. Consequently, efforts to black-box 9/11 public memory only opened up more unsettled questions, beliefs, and interests, which ultimately petrified grief and absence without resolving the traumatic kernels that lie below, subconsciously.[104] More than that, the national memorial (and all the thousands of objects stored at the museum) would become the penultimate dingpolitik object of controversy as architects, politicians, families and other argument assemblages jumped into this mercurial rhetorical situation where everybody thought they knew best about how to remember.

2

Rebuilding Ground Zero

Risky Objects and the Force of Security, 2002–2005

This chapter focuses on the architectural disagreements that were voiced and recorded between 2002 and 2005 about how to rebuild Ground Zero. While many of those who wanted to use militaristic framings for the rebuilding of Ground Zero were adept at turning the site into a material place of securitization, there were other possible ways of remembering 9/11 tragedies. Those who wanted to securitize these key places of memory intervened in the existential removal of threatening objects (e.g., dust and vernacular memorials), but questions still remained about *how* to accomplish these rebuilding tasks while satisfying millions of Americans who wanted to commemorate something else.

What we argue in this chapter is that the nascent securitization assemblage—which included securitized things and the decisions of security organizations such as Homeland Security, the NYPD, and counterterror units—displaced or overpowered other, competing arguments for what we call "symbolistic" relations with Ground Zero. By extending the work of critical rhetorical scholars or critical security studies research, we invite readers to attend to the ways that stakeholders in these debates always seemed to keep one eye on what was happening overseas in places like Iraq and Afghanistan. The "homeland," in other words, could be conceptualized in ways that extended American interest from Lower Manhattan to the mountains at the Afghan and Pakistani borders. This melding of domestic and international concerns meant that the National September 11 Memorial became entangled in intriguing constellations of meaning and securitized ontologies.

The epistemes produced between 2002 and 2005 became a different facet of what Bryan Taylor has called the "media-security relationship," where critical scholarship focuses on "securitization, media framing, media materialism and mediatization."[1]

As we explain in more detail below, the argumentative effect of having architects, New York politicians, or others comment on local involvement in the Global War on Terrorism (GWOT) invited a growing number of social agents to become participants in all of this realpolitik and dingpolitik. By the time Pentagon strategists were planning on invading Iraq, Ground Zero was quickly becoming a space of public memory that would be filled with an increasing number of securitized objects—including the national memorial, the memorial museum, and the thousands of objects that it would exhibit.

A review of some of the conversations that took place during this period reveals that one might go so far as to contend that this space was transformed into some sort of twenty-first-century Fort Alamo capable of withstanding future attacks in the localization of the GWOT. Talks of resilience, survival, coping with risk, and counterterrorist strategizing helped with the coproduction of spaces and places that were supposed to symbolize New York's—and the United States'—survival skills. "Resilience" was an ideograph used between 2002 and 2005 to communicate the idea that bin Laden's minions had failed.

This object-oriented securitized perspective produced a no-nonsense mode of thinking able to cut through the cacophony of bureaucratic and political squabbles that were getting in the way of those who advocated for the symbolic and material fortification of Ground Zero.

Visualities and texts came together to form a dense security assemblage that advanced some of these realpolitik objectives. For example, planners highlighted things such as used steel and concrete to underscore the existential dangers that had confronted the 9/11 victims and first responders.

One could not help noticing the riskiness of objects in Daniel Libeskind's sixteen-acre World Trade Center (WTC) site master plan—which included, among other things, a 1,776-foot "Freedom Tower" and a national memorial depressed into the earth to commemorate loss and absence. As if this object-oriented act was not enough, some members of the LMDC in 2002 wanted to build an International Freedom Center to situate 9/11 alongside other domestic or global histories of suffering.

All sorts of analogies were implicitly and explicitly used to connect 9/11 mourning with other traumatic events. Libeskind's proposed design, for example, was characterized as having been influenced by his personal narrative of immigrating to the United States from Poland. At this time, memorializing symbols infused Ground Zero with deep and abstract meanings that resonated with millions of Americans. Poland, after all, had been invaded by both Nazi and Soviet forces during World War II, and one could only surmise that the lack of adequate fortifications had everything to do with the dismantling of that country. Libeskind, his admirers, and many others who watched what was happening overseas wanted to make sure that Lower Manhattan would be seen by publics as a protected space.

Like many other proposals, Libeskind's plan did not have to be read through an interpretative lens or frameworks that focused exclusively on counterterrorism or continued threats to New Yorkers, but he and many others with competing interests had to cope with stakeholders who surrounded Ground Zero with all sorts of fortifying devices. Some supporters of security—and police forces themselves—began incorporating countless security objects (e.g., bunkers, tanks, snipers) in his design to mitigate terrorist risks. While Libeskind argued that there were myriad reasons why his design was symbolically valuable to those who cared about 9/11 public memories, the security assemblage that would be formed by counterterrorist supporters essentially possessed *argumentative presumptiveness* as decision makers reviewed the WTC site master plan.

How was this fortification, and this sense of argumentative presumptiveness, achieved? As Govert Valkenburg and Irma van der Ploeg explain, Latourian ways of studying security have to take into account how particular translations, trajectories, and "seemingly technical and natural-scientific givens" of securitized spaces involve contestation, competing notions of "democratic governance," and different stages of construction.[2] While many architects, publics, and politicians were calling for a memorial with polysemic symbolicity (multiple meanings)— one that was not just monolithically tied to al Qaeda—others sought more monolithic meanings. From a Foucauldian standpoint, while some wanted to view the new reconstructions as conveying more heterotopic, open-ended meanings, others wanted just the opposite, the narrowing of vision for more utopian, securitized spaces.

In theory, funders or planners might have wanted to build more open-ended structures that allowed for diverse representations of "the meaning" of 9/11, but in reality the power of key decision makers, and communal perceptual views on securitization, limited the force of these other arguments. Although many acknowledged the need for meaningful, inclusive, commemorative practices, they ran against the grain of the realpolitik security concerns of those who believed in the existence of terrorist threats. Human vulnerability was evidenced by the nonhuman rubble of 9/11, and counterterrorist concerns manifested themselves so often that the fight against terrorist evils blurred the lines between the secular and the sacred. Who, after all, wanted to be held responsible for the future vulnerability of the Freedom Tower or other WTC towers, future employees, or those who visited memorials and museums?

Because the building of these security assemblages depended on nationwide alliances, public resources, and convincing New York terrorist attack scenarios, the securitization of objects in and around Ground Zero took on transcendent importance. This focus on securitization also meant that observers who might have hoped for more multidirectional memories now had to fume as winning, competitive securitized arguments won out. Between 2002 and 2005, the growing rhetorical power of securitizing governmentalities contributed to the crowding out of the arguments of those who wanted these spaces and places to symbolize other events or issues.

In fact, the security assemblage grew so large, and became so forceful, during this rebuilding stage that the very concept of security became a part of this dingpolitik of things, as words and objects came together. While we sense that Bruno Latour may not have liked to see the arrival of this particular type of "politics of things," many Americans appreciated the messages conveyed by the objects placed strategically in this part of Lower Manhattan.

To achieve the material securitization of memorial space, decisions had to be made about the placement, or disappearance, of some matter. Some supposedly threatening objects had to be removed, in the name of risk reduction, and these worrisome objects had to be replaced with securitized objects, as noted in the previous chapter. Hence the importance of considering the argumentative force of the militaristic objects that were assembled, both physically and symbolically, in assemblages.

Consider, for example, how NYPD and counterterrorist agencies, including the FBI, were careful to place an abundance of hypersecuritized objects in plain view. They apparently wanted those involved in rebuilding to see everything from concrete bunkers, armored vehicles, and assault rifles to haz-mat (hazardous material) suits, fences, and spycams. These objects would be assembled in ways that helped reterritorialize memorial space. All of this securitization has not only reoccupied and reordered Ground Zero's material space, but it has also, more important for us, produced an incredibly powerful argumentative assemblage that operates by force.[3]

For now, it is simply important to point out that during this particular stage of memorialization, security objects and their "politics of things" forcefully outweighed other symbolic arguments about Ground Zero's spatial politic. This foregrounding of security had important effects on the outcome of not just the national memorial but the former WTC site as a whole: it became a security apparatus that people not only acquiesced to but desired (and eventually performatively commemorated; see chapter 4). And this comes on the heels of the National September 11 Memorial and Memorial Museum's overabundance of symbolism about heroism, resilience, and patriotism, all of which has reinforced the triumph of securitization at this site.

To support these arguments, the rest of this chapter is organized in the following way. We begin with a discussion of the force of memorialization at Ground Zero by noting its conjunctural possibilities. In that subsection we critique Daniel Libeskind's winning design for the Ground Zero master plan, which included a Freedom Tower, two memorial pools, and a Freedom Center. We then discuss the diverse demands of audiences who wanted more inclusive symbolicity at this site, and how those hopes were dashed when their arguments ran against demands for security. Then we analyze the object-oriented conditions of the burgeoning security assemblage to show that the material force of securitization took absolute precedence over all other concerns. All of this rhetoric had even more gravitas when observers noted that this site furnished a securitization space at the front lines of the GWOT, or what might be called the *Local* War on Terrorism. We conclude with a discussion of what all of this meant for the funders and planners who had to carry out these securitizing designs.

The Politicized Formation of the Lower Manhattan Development Corporation

For years, argumentation scholars and other observers have noted that architecture reflects and refracts societal values, beliefs, and ideologies.[4] As Frank Lloyd Wright once famously said, architecture "is the scientific art of making structure express ideas,"[5] and perhaps there is no better example of that expression of ideas than the heated debates that took place over the architectural planning for the rebirth of Ground Zero.

Given GWOT contexts, the architecture that ultimately emerged from the embers of debates about 9/11 public memories and exceptionalist American politics was one tightly bundled up in a security assemblage that privileged, above all else, preparedness for another attack. Stakeholders jostled each other for the right to have the greatest say in the selection of the "master plan," and this power struggle in turn impacted the reactions to the design that was ultimately selected.

All of the additional costs of securitization and potential risk assessments for urban planning also garnered the attention of those who had to come up with the designs that would resonate with anxious taxpayers and their government representatives. As Thomas Fisher put it in *Architecture: The Magazine*:

> The September 11 attacks and the Iraq conflict have demonstrated [that] architecture now stands at the very center of modern warfare, with truck bombs, commandeered planes, and smart missiles able to annihilate buildings with unprecedented precision. This militarization of architecture—especially architecture that has perceived symbolic or strategic value—will change the way in which we design buildings and cities in the future.[6]

The weaponization of memorial spaces thus became a particular example of Latour's dingpolitik.

While some architects would be excited by the prospect that their artistic passions could be used for the therapeutic healing of traumatized wounds and the resecuritization of Ground Zero, others were not so sure. Regardless, more than a few were finding out just how difficult it was going to be to organize the assembly of architects, politicians, and publics to construct a new WTC and a memorial at this site of public memory. This challenge was especially true for the members of the LMDC.

The LMDC was created by New York governor George Pataki in 2001 to help with the selection of a master plan for the future of Ground Zero. This selection process was also expected to rejuvenate New York, as an infusion of federal funds helped ease the burdens of reconstruction. It was through the seemingly apolitical formation of this ad hoc organization that so many initially believed that they would have a voice in the choice of plans. In theory, the LMDC would present the views of the average American person, local persons living in Lower Manhattan, and the families of those who died on 9/11/01 (see chapter 3). Only gradually did some of these stakeholders, who cared so much about their input, learn about the power dynamics that were involved.

The hopes of those who wanted to see a skyline, more open public spaces, and diverse symbolicity were dashed when it became clear that the producers of security assemblages were going to have an inordinate say in the choice of architects, designs, and acceptable building practices. When the LMDC selected Daniel Libeskind to direct the planning for the "World Trade Center Complex," many public communities realized that the rules of the game were in the hands of a few decision makers.

Those of us who take a retrospective view of the arguments that circulated during this period cannot help noticing that a variety of analyzable performative gestures that hinted at what was to come. All sorts of messages were implicitly or explicitly sent out about the narrowing of interests when readers of newspapers, popular magazines, and journal articles learned that Libeskind's proposition for the WTC master plan was going to draw from his experience in building the Jewish Museum, Berlin. Libeskind abstractly displayed a meaningful site of memory that drew from Holocaust tropes of absence and loss as he created what some might view as negative space—what James Young calls a counter-monument.[7]

Many planners and funders hoped that this type of master plan would have wide appeal, but it must be remembered that before Libeskind could carry out his work he had to watch communities debate about how the LMDC was going to reach its decisions.

The LMDC tried to create the impression that many members of the public were going to have a say in matters when it claimed that it would be facilitating "'an open and participatory' process" that Hajer calls a performed "policy process."[8] Yet many felt the LMDC functioned oligarchically to serve the financial needs of those who would privilege capitalistic interests with securitizing interests in this part of Lower Manhattan. This belief was especially strong after the LMDC revealed it was interested in selecting the designs that came from the architectural firm Beyer Blinder and Bell, a firm supposedly composed of what architect Ada Louise Huxtable of the *Wall Street Journal* called "six cookie-cutter losers."[9]

After a blunderbuss decide-announce-defend model of decision making,[10] which was remembered as exclusionary, visionless, and technocratic,[11] the LMDC started again by selecting six teams' designs out of 407 submissions from thirty-four nations and presenting them at the World Financial Center's Winter Garden between December 19, 2002, and February 2, 2003, as a component of what was called the "Innovative Design Study," launched in August 2002.[12] Over one hundred thousand people visited the exhibits and over eight thousand people provided comment cards (there were also four thousand internet comments). In a public dialogue and outreach campaign called "Plan in Progress," almost thirteen thousand comments were provided regarding the planning process and the six proposed designs.[13]

As can be expected, different public opinions were expressed, and not all showed interest in seeing either the commercialization or the securitization of Ground Zero. Some local residents were still wanting a "return to normal neighborhood life as soon as possible,"[14] and traffic concerns took center stage. Kathryn Wyle, president of the Partnership for NYC, complained that "construction and security measures" have been "[tying] up the streets and the pedestrian walkways," making it "difficult to conduct business."[15]

Others sent in comments that put on display the continued calls for the sacralization of Ground Zero in ways that would not necessarily prioritize the allowance for more business space. As we mentioned earlier, security was not on the minds of some of these individuals. In fact, in a poll conducted by the Innovative Design Study, only 2 percent openly expressed concern about security and safety.[16] Rather, publics were more interested in things like regaining the lost skyline (38 percent), focusing more on the memorial (24 percent), and returning to or increasing open, public space.[17]

To us, this lack of interest in securitization indicates that if the process had really been an open one that took into account the views of most citizens living in and around Lower Manhattan, then few would have prioritized the turning of Ground Zero into a defended bunker that was supposed to deter the next terrorist attack. Those in control, however, who tried to argue that terrorist dangers were existential and not socially constructed, ignored the ways that their focus on securitization was creating the very anxieties they claimed came from terrorist planning.

If we apply some of the insights that come from critical rhetorical studies and critical security studies we would find that this incremental, yet powerful move toward securitization involved choices, not necessities. We would go so far as to argue that it was only *after* the National September 11 Memorial was constructed, once the memorial and museum's securitized objects were arranged in such a way that they commemorated security, that so many treated this site's transition to a total security apparatus as a naturalized process.

This incremental process of producing security dispositifs, however, began when the LMDC was pressured into moving in securitizing directions. Additionally, some of this security-oriented decision making was taking place before the 2003 announcement of the invasion of Iraq. Is it possible that before that invasion, there was still a chance that Ground Zero might become a heterotopic space?

A closer look at some of the public commentary that circulated during 2002 reveals that many observers sensed they were about to be bombarded with calls for resecuritization of this part of Lower Manhattan. Some of those surveyed were actually worried about *too much* security at Ground Zero, which, to them, indicated that that self-servicing texts were being produced to instrumentalize 9/11 for militaristic purposes. New York, to them, was becoming a military camp.

Critical analyses of surveys and journalist commentaries reveal that this was a time when dissenting groups were willing to be vocal in their critiques of all of this securitization. For instance, one participant who contributed to the Listening to the City public forum (held before the Innovative Design Study) said, "One cannot turn Manhattan into an armed camp to ensure that security doesn't go too far."[18]

Yet, to be fair, we note that many respondents were proud of the way Ground Zero was being restructured in ways that not only defended Lower Manhattan but also sent a message to terrorist foes. There were plenty of comments such as these: "rebuilding Ground Zero was meant to show America's defiance in the face of the biggest terrorist attacks in history,"[19] and New York should "stick it back to the terrorists."[20] Other commenters remarked that it seemed as though some of those who were working to turn Ground Zero into a "symbol for the ages," were doing "just another schlock job" full of "political pettiness and personal greed."[21]

After getting input from the civic alliance and public commenters, and after showcasing nine possible plans from six architect teams[22]—including Foster and Partners; Studio Daniel Libeskind; Meier Eisenman Gwathmery Holl; Skidmore, Owing, and Merrill; THINK Team; and United Architects—the LMDC made some key moves.

LMDC members whittled the number of their preferred six designers down to *two*: the highly acclaimed architect Daniel Libeskind, who is best known for designing the Jewish Museum, Berlin, and Rafael Viñoly's architectural group called THINK Team, which had designed various urban buildings including a hospital, a university, and housing units.[23]

At this point it seemed as though many members of LMDC shared a strong preference for the THINK Team's design of a vertical memorial shooting from Ground Zero in an interwoven open lattice formation. In theory, this plan removed the burden of replacing Ground Zero with sterile office space and signaled a civic gesture to the world that New York's skyline would be back, in a form that displayed the importance of reverential memories for losses.[24] It was dubbed the "twenty-first-century Eiffel Towers" due to its depiction of two scaffolding steel matrixes resembling the former Twin Towers that were intended to house various cultural and conference centers, a memorial, a museum, and an amphitheater. Here, a host of factors—including the need for open space, aesthetics, proper commemoration, and pedagogy—seemed to motivate those who might support the THINK Team's design.

In fascinating ways, this THINK Team design would have been cosmopolitan, didactic, and very tourist-friendly—but at what symbolic, or political, cost? How would this commemorative construction have helped with spatial securitization?

Despite the LMDC's predilection for accepting the THINK Team design, Governor Pataki intervened, and reporters and others who observed these activities have argued that he more or less instructed the LMDC that Libeskind's Memory Foundations should be the winner—a design that put on display an interconnected plot of land that would feature a memorial, a new WTC complex, and a museum. To Pataki, who was becoming accustomed to using Ground Zero as his own personal "bully pulpit"[25] for reelection, THINK Team's design was "like two skeletons rising exactly where the Twin Towers stood" and "looked like replacing life with death."[26] He was even quoted as saying—"There's no goddamn way I'm going to build those skeletons."[27]

The LMDC now knew what it was like to be part of Governor Pataki's deliberative, and realpolitik, format for reconstructing Ground Zero. The message received was loud and clear: Pataki was using his executive decisional powers to boost his own political standing, and the LMDC should not get in the way. That is why the LMDC conveniently announced that Libeskind was the winner of the design competition in February 2003.[28]

Libeskind's plan featured four WTC towers, a transportation hub, a visitors pavilion, a memorial museum, and a memorial sunk into the earth against the "bathtub" of the former Twin Towers. It was said that he gained last-minute inspiration for this plan while visiting the site with the other architects.[29] In recalling this epiphany, he said, "When I went down to Ground Zero, and when I stood 70 feet below the bedrock and saw those walls, those foundations, continue to support and function, I said, 'You know, that's really what draws together life and the memory and the sacred space of that site.'"[30]

While the specific, object-oriented designs of the eventual National September 11 Memorial and Memorial Museum were to be decided by architects not yet selected (Michael Arad, for instance, wasn't selected the winner of the memorial's design competition until 2004), Libeskind's master plan, for all intents and purposes, was characterized by empowered elites as the official blueprint for how Ground Zero would be built.

Libeskind's design was exactly the sort of plan that Governor Pataki and many publics were looking for, given its evocative nature and

Fig. 3. The Freedom Tower.

idyllic symbolism. It emphasized spacious public spaces while also restoring New York's missing skyline. To Studio Libeskind's "Memory Foundations," the site would "balance the memory of the tragedy with the need to foster a vibrant and working neighborhood."[31]

Libeskind's master plan held out the hope that it was restoring New York's missing skyline with 1 WTC, a 1,776-foot-tall building (figure 3) that Pataki labeled the "Freedom Tower" to "sho[w] the world that we weren't going to be frightened in the face of these attacks."[32] To add to this securitizing rhetoric Libeskind himself remarked that his "Memory Foundations" master plan was simultaneously a "healing of New York," a "site of memory," and also "a space to witness the resilience of America."[33]

The excess of symbolic appeal of Libeskind's design was exactly what many publics were yearning for. Not only was the 1,776-foot height of the tower an intentional reference to the patriotic signing of the Declaration of Independence—it would also be the tallest skyscraper in the Western Hemisphere, with a 408-foot metal spire. No wonder the tower was called "a beacon for the city"[34] that mirrored the Statue of Liberty and poetically displayed the strength of the American spirit. However, the reality was that Libeskind's symbolic overtures not only were just a bit excessive but also overlooked the materiality of all the objects thrown into assembly: security.

The Force of Security: Articulating the Risks of Daniel Libeskind's World Trade Center Master Plan

So far we have discussed the role that business leaders, local communities, and architects played in all of this public disputation over Ground Zero reconstruction, but we need to remember the power of the NYPD and other police officials who called for the elevated securitization of this site. For example, there was talk of the need to ensure that the rebuilding of the tower be done in ways that would have enough structural integrity to withstand "potential truck bombs."[35]

This and other worries forced architects and designers to include more concrete, steel, and buffers to make the rebuilt structures "almost impermeable and impregnable."[36] The effect of the requirements forced the hand of Libeskind and Skidmore, Owings, and Merrill, who now had to turn the base of the tower into what Karrie Jacobs called "a 15-story blast proof bunker trying very hard to pretend that it's not."[37] Nicolai Ourossoff, writing in the *New York Times*, was sure about a "growing apprehension that adhering to new security standards will transform the tower into an armored bunker."[38]

Ourossoff needn't have worried—that is exactly what it did, both materially and symbolically.

All of this merger of dingpolitik and realpolitik ensured that reterritorialized space could not escape the NYPD demands for their objects of securitization. The Freedom Tower actually turned into *two* towers, like the towers that preceded them, says Jacobs: the one that came before security recommendations and the one that came after.[39] In fact, the

Port Authority of New York and New Jersey eventually suggested that the architects drop the names "Freedom Tower," and "Ground Zero" to make the space more appealing for potential tenants who were already leery of leasing what many considered was a "1,776-foot-tall target," as Daniel Benjamin titled his op-ed piece in the *New York Times*.[40] Benjamin, like others, was convinced that the Freedom Tower would "become a top target for Islamic terrorists as soon as it is occupied."[41] Others, such as Ron Rosenbaum of the *New York Observer*, said things like "the building will be Terrorist Target No. 1 as long as it exists. To deny that reality is not to let the terrorists win, but to give them a chance to win big."[42]

All of this obsessive commentary on security concerns raised the ire of Libeskind and Pataki in the spring of 2004, but their feelings did not stop Raymond W. Kelly—the NYPD commissioner—from telling WTC leaseholder Larry Silverstein that he was "deeply concerned about the Freedom Tower location and design from a terrorist standpoint."[43] Kelly asked for documentation showing that planners were taking into account the need for assessments of threat risks.

Even though the proposed tower met New York standards for security standards, and in spite of the fact that it was deemed acceptable by a judge working in a federal courthouse, police officials thought otherwise, claiming that security had to be substantially increased. In this particular dispute, the Port Authority of New York and New Jersey's executive director, Joseph Seymour, blatantly expressed the view that "doing it at the courthouse standards was going far enough."[44] When police officials did not provide any specific alternatives, Mr. Seymour was left thinking that "the NYPD was really not receptive, in my opinion," he said, "to the idea of building a Freedom Tower at all."[45]

And indeed, some anecdotal evidence supports that viewpoint. In later years, for example, former FBI specialist agent Don Borelli asked rhetorically, "You look at all of the people that want to visit this beautiful site, and visit New York City and Times Square and everything else. And how do you protect all of those people without just being in some kind of lockdown state?" "You really can't," he concluded.[46] It should be no surprise, then, that it "irked the police" when Pataki laid the cornerstone for the WTC tower on July 4, 2004.[47] For some, this was too much political grandstanding and idealism, and not enough attention being paid to realpolitik matters of counterterrorist security.

Almost two months later, the police deputy commissioner for counterterrorism, Michael Sheehan, wrote Mr. Seymour that the proposed Freedom Tower was at an "insufficient standoff distance" from West Street and that the glass floors on the lower level of the tower were a security threat. These concerns, he was sure to mention, had been noted, and then ignored, in previous letters. After receiving no reply from Seymour, Sheehan wrote in another, more deliberate, letter, "Due to the history of al Qaeda strikes at this location and the symbolic nature of the Freedom Tower itself, it seems clear that this building will become the prime terrorist target in New York City as soon as it is occupied."[48]

In spite of these anxieties, construction continued. Reflecting on these tensions, Daniel Doctoroff, the deputy mayor for economic development and rebuilding, said the Port Authority and Silverstein did not merely have "their heads in the sand" but rather "didn't want to slow things down."[49]

And there was good reason for the motivations to "soldie[r] on" with the construction of the Tower,[50] considering that by this time there had already been numerous setbacks due to political wrangling, disagreements over security risks, and spiraling financial costs. All sorts of wedge issues brought bitterness and resentment as financial stakeholders, political figureheads, the Port Authority of New York and New Jersey, the architects, and, of course, the NYPD all participated in heated exchanges.

Perhaps the biggest trigger for ensuing security debates—and bureaucratic entanglements of propriety, liability, and responsibility—would be the NYPD's 2005 demand for increased fortification of the structural integrity of the WTC site so that it could withstand "potential truck bombs."[51] This was due to the increased distance between the tower and West street, which made it more vulnerable to such an attack.

The more that publics and elites mentioned the importance of Libeskind's master plan and the need to visit Ground Zero, the more that the NYPD expressed concerns over the securitization of these key spaces and places. Recursive arguments circulated regarding cause and effect, securitization and attraction at Ground Zero. To Healy and Rashbaum, "many . . . fear that the mere public discussion of security worries could damage what they regard as a hard-won optimism about the site's future."[52] At the same time, however, actors such as the LMDC, Larry Silverstein, and Governor Pataki were dismayed by the perceptual belief that the NYPD had interceded in these affairs so late in the design debates. John C. Whitehead, who was a chairman of the LMDC, provided typical commentary when he stated, "I don't want to say the police have been irresponsible, but where were they until this month? . . . I wish they had called attention to the seriousness of the problems earlier, rather than at this late stage."[53]

These were arguments not against the securitization of Ground Zero but against the nature and scope of that type of rebuilding. This dispute was all about power politics, the ones with final say, the pace of construction, and the ultimate look of the project after paying attention to so many factors.

More than a few wrote and talked about the need for greater preparedness against car and truck bombs. In an interview with Jill Gardiner of the *New York Sun*, Jeff Kern of John Jay College said, "I don't think there is anything mystical to it.[54] . . . If you have more distance it means that any intruder has further to travel from public streets.[55] . . . The most inexpensive way to topple something is to drive a truck loaded with explosives."[56] In his polemical article "Ground Zero Hype: Is Giant Skyscraper a Freedom Folly?," Ron Rosenbaum suggested that the

"security concerns" being addressed mainly involve protection against a truck bomb—including features that will certainly have al Qaeda tearing up its plans, such as smaller windows below 150 feet. As if a truck bomb was the only threat; as if anyone can guarantee that any World Trade Center replacement is going to be able to be made safe from aerial attack.[57]

These types of framing of affairs treated Ground Zero as if it was going to continue to garner the attention of a host of terrorist foes.

For some of these commenters, the best security measures were the ones designed to prevent another 1993 WTC bombing, but this time the preparations had to take into account twenty-first-century counterterrorist requirements. This type of argument became a part of the ideological security assemblages that invited readers or listeners to think more imaginatively about omnipresent and omnipotent threats. One redevelopment security official arranged to bring together security specialists from Britain's MI5 with a group of Ground Zero government officials. When the officials got together it was said of the British security service that "these guys were laughing at us," and they ridiculed the "idea that Jersey barriers and bollards would protect the tower when terrorists have become more sophisticated."[58] Those who read these rhetorical fragments might ask, Why not get ahead of the curve and plan for hybrid wars, fourth-generation warfare, irregular battles, and other kinds of nontraditional, asymmetrical campaigns?

It was one thing to hear all of this security talk coming from police officers, field agents, and those with a vested interest in selling heightened security, but it was quite another to hear some of these concerns being voiced by laypersons using vernacular arguments. To Karl Joseph, a forty-seven-year-old carpenter from Newark, "It's all for the better. As far as all that big-number stuff, moving it, if it's safety, it's for the better. If it gets built six months or a year from now, either way, we're going to build it."[59]

There were also times when journalists and laypersons recognized the resonant power of this securitized rhetoric, but instead of embracing it, they worried about it. Did this talk of military necessities and the securitization of Ground Zero threaten taken-for-granted civilian freedoms? Adam Brodsky of the *New York Post* expressed a dissenting view when he asked:

Must every American alive today sacrifice and live in fear—forever? Sure, concessions for security are part of the price of terror. When thugs leveled the World Trade Center, they scared folks away from buildings that tall. So, offices in the Freedom Tower are to rise only 70 stories, not the 110 of the Twin Towers. And even that isn't enough: Now truck bombs are the issue. . . . Sure, security measures are needed for a while. But the priorities here seem topsy-turvy. . . . If our leaders are talking about building low-rise fortresses and keeping them out of harm's way for 100 years, it's time to rethink not the Freedom Tower plan—but the war plan.[60]

Few, however, were willing to go in this direction and interrogate present and future war planning.

In some cases, it would be the specificity of the suggested changes that gave their purveyors some credibility. At this point, for example, the NYPD had three major security recommendations that were delaying the tower's progression: more distance, or "setbacks from surrounding streets"; a sophisticated security screening of incoming cars and trucks that entered the underground garage (what eventually became the Vehicular Security Center); and mitigation of the glass on lower floors.[61] One anonymous government official involved in these security conversations became convinced that in terms of security, "basically nothing can satisfy" the police.[62] This same commentator understood the views of those who cared about the sanctity of this site, but he plainly laid out the predicament as he saw it: "Here's the dilemma. . . . If you put too much security into the building, it's going to look like Fort Knox and no one will rent it. If you don't put enough, it could end up with catastrophic results, not only catastrophic for the tower but for the surrounding buildings as well" (figure 4).[63]

From a critical security perspective what we are witnessing is a complex recursive process that allowed the NYPD to provide suggestions that did more than hint at their own power and indispensability. The objects that went into the building of the Vehicular Security Center, the use of preferred glass, and other measures in turn conveyed a "politics

Fig. 4. Vehicular security complex at the National
September 11 Memorial and Memorial Museum.

of objects" that reiterated the message that police and security messages
were needed, long after 9/11.

These policing messages did not resonate with those who sought
some balance in the life of New Yorkers. Alexander Garven, a professor of urban planning at Yale University, explained that either "we
live normal lives with normal streets and normal sidewalks, or we go
back to living in fortresses as they did in the Middle Ages."[64] Kenneth
J. Ringler told the executive director of the Port Authority that there
"is no question that it is a more secure building."[65]

After Pataki announced that the Freedom Tower would be redesigned
with the oversight of his chief of staff, John Cahill (dubbed the "security czar"), journalists noted that this change seemed to be a response
to NYPD demands for stronger security measures. Silverstein went

"apoplectic" when he recalled some of the delays that had taken place because of these types of security concerns, and they were labeled "an unmitigated disaster." He elaborated by noting that they "had wasted two years, and, as I pointed out to the governor, inflation was starting to take hold in the construction trades and everything was going to be more costly."[66]

All of these delays became a seemingly never-ending source of disputation between 2002 and 2006. The second president of the LMDC, Kevin Rampe, became so frustrated that he resigned from his duties, explaining that the "minute the governor made the decision to redesign the Freedom Tower, people said, 'Hey, if you can redesign that, why not rethink everything else?'"[67] Suffice it to say, noted Rampe, "that there is not going to be any other building in the world built to these safety standards."[68]

Were these necessary or unnecessary delays, and was this hyper-vigilance or just the right amount of prudential precautionary counterterrorist activity? To Pataki—who was at the time contemplating running for another term—"rebuilding Ground Zero was . . . his political magnum opus," explained David Usborne of the *Independent*.[69] It is no wonder that Pataki said valiantly, "Failure to rebuild is not an option," and we will "not tolerate unnecessary delays."[70]

That said, the vociferous demands for more securitization could not be ignored, even in situations where meeting those demands brought delays and greater costs. Pataki and Bloomberg's redesigned plan increased the distance between the tower and the curb and included an "almost impermeable"[71] bombproof concrete and steel base two hundred feet high. In a documentary titled *Ground Zero Supertower* David Childs, who was hired by Larry Silverstein to help redesign the Freedom Tower, said, "One of the things I've learned about safety is *the appearance of safety*."[72] Commenting on the final design, he said, "This building is a strong, visible image of our resilience, coming back after this terrible tragedy."[73] Paula Grant Berry, whose husband died on 9/11, and who served as a memorial board member, reiterated this point in saying, "This, to me, is resilience. . . . This is resilience."[74]

Additional waves of security arguments arose when one of New York's largest commercial actors—Goldman Sachs—used its financial and political networks to move the planned construction of a tunnel on West Street that, it was feared, would increase traffic concerns and create a "security nightmare."[75] After the giant company threatened to cancel its plans to build its $2.9 billion headquarters across the street from the WTC site, political authorities enticed Goldman Sachs to keep its plans by eliminating the proposed tunnel from WTC plans and offering another $1.6 billion in Liberty bonds.[76] Even after these concessions, this multibillion-dollar company wanted the NYPD to send it a detailed security plan of Lower Manhattan for review before finalizing the deal and releasing a $161 million rent payment from an escrow account.[77]

The problem, however, was that the tunnel was considered a necessary component of the site's structural security due to its ability to contain damage from potential car or truck bombs. The tunnel would also eliminate the need to extend the distance between West Street and the Freedom Tower, something that was creating "bunker-like reinforcements."[78]

Indeed, it is atypical for a corporation to have so much say in the securitization of a particular site, but exceptions for Goldman Sachs were made not only because of the employment that they provide the city but also because their proposed headquarters would make them both property owners and tenants, since they would be the only ones in the building.

At times visual argumentation supplemented more logocentric types of disputation. At one point, when advancing their claims for more security, company representatives showed the NYPD a film depicting a vehicle with over ten thousand pounds of explosives blowing up, "leaving a huge crater" to demonstrate the necessity of "hardening" infrastructure from such impacts.[79] Not long after that, the NYPD, according to Deborah Sontag of the *New York Times*, outlined plans for building the Freedom Tower that were akin to "the security standards of an American embassy."[80] This would be just one of many examples of rhetorical fragments that linked domestic architectural planning to foreign interventionism.

New York was left with an assemblage of actors (human and non-human) who were all trying to securitize space in different, and decentralized, ways that seemed to traverse time and space as New Yorkers were thinking about everything from embassy bombs to bunkers. A type of siege mentality set in that looked much like some of the discourse that appeared in Giorgio Agamben's descriptions of historical states of emergency and exception.[81]

Yet it would be a mistake to think that CEOs were the only ones helping coproduce these securitized dispositifs. For instance, while Goldman Sachs was giving orders to the NYPD to increase the overall security of the site so they could feel more comfortable relocating across the street, the NYPD was also debating with the fire department about who should have "haz-mat" first-responder status, and if and when civilians should call in after an attack of this nature. In the meanwhile, Battery Park City Authority was turning "bus shelters, bike racks, boulders and trees into vehicle-proof obstacles"[82] to minimize possible explosive impacts at the same time that the LMDC and its own security advisers charged the replacement of "metal barriers with a wrought-iron fence" outside the New York Stock Exchange to satisfy Pataki's demand to halt "obnoxious security measures."[83] And while the NYPD was both responding to demands from Goldman Sachs and imposing its own on the LMDC—the company in charge of the architects—the Port Authority of New York and New Jersey was in charge of securing areas within the WTC site fence and walkways on Church Street, per a previous agreement with the NYPD.[84]

The Port Authority owned the site, after all, but it were also working with Silverstein to ensure he was satisfied with the plans, since he would be renting it for ninety-nine years. All the while, architects like Libeskind, David Brody Bond, and Michael Arad were supposed to take all of these variant, and sometimes competing, interests and turn them into not just operable designs but ones that also preserved their style—if not their original intents—in ways that gratified politicians, pleased locals, and uplifted the American public. This complex security assemblage, therefore, comprised an array of emplacements, meanings, and strange juxtapositions that were caught up in bundles of dingpolitik and realpolitik relationships. They provided yet another example of why so many involved in security studies have taken what Valkenburg and der Ploeg call the "material turn," where researchers study the police and other social agents who control the "translation" of security problems, "concrete policy," "technological requirements," and so on in ways that ensure that "many sociopolitical and technological factors influence the trajectory and co-produce specific security devices."[85]

For some, this proliferating interest in securitizing Ground Zero reduced anxieties and put on display American exceptionalism and resilience, but for others, these preparedness activities raised many questions. According to one security official involved in these space-based security entanglements, "The police would say, 'Based on our knowledge and our intelligence, we think you can do more to make the building safer.' We would say, 'Tell us what.' The cops would say, 'We're not engineers.' We would say, 'O.K., tell us what we need to tell our engineers to protect against. And it became this long, drawn-out back and forth."[86] "This is a remarkably complex security question, and every time you turn one dial, you end up turning many other dials on the security issue," said Deputy Mayor Doctoroff.[87]

Yet, to others, especially some of those who felt there was no such thing as too much security, all of this equivocation signed the presence of some corrupt governmentalities that cared more about themselves than cooperatively working to ensure the absolute securitization of this space. Monica Gabrielle and Sally Regenhard, coleaders of an organization called the Advocacy Safety Campaign, had lost loved ones during 9/11, and they were skeptical of some of the claims they heard regarding impregnability and counterterrorist prioritization. "The claims of being 'the safest building in the world,'" they averred, "pale at the realization that these buildings are nevertheless exempt and immune from all New York City building codes and fire codes, because of the Port Authority's exemptions."[88]

Libeskind, meanwhile, was close to feeling defeated. All he wanted, after all, was to use his creative, postmodern architectural talent for remembering tragic events—which had been proven with his involvement in building the Jewish Museum in Berlin. Libeskind once responded to security complaints in the *New York Times* by saying, "We are responding to the need for security, but we are also responding to life. We cannot make the Freedom Tower a tower of fear."[89]

This rhetoric did not sit well with some who viewed it as delusional and idealistic. There were always people like Ron Rosenbaum, who called such comments "hubristic bloviation"[90] and personally attacked Libeskind as one of several "egotists, idiots, political opportunists and incompetents"[91] who were downplaying the true security risk of the site. Reiterating a point made by radio host Kurt Anderson, he asked, "Will the inspirational jolt we enjoy in 2009 by having demonstrated our architectural gumption outweigh the horror we will feel if that [edifice] is bombed in 2010?"[92] Not to be outdone, the nation's future commander in chief, Donald Trump, too, attacked Libeskind's final design by saying, "It looks like a junk yard, a series of broken down angles that don't match each other . . . and we have to live with this for 100 years? It is the worst pile of crap architecture I have seen in my life."[93]

Libeskind charged on, though, commenting once that "security is clearly the paramount concern." "While the shape and details of buildings may change," he explained, "the intent, spirit and direction of the master plan remains intact."[94] He also had help, even if he did not appreciate it, from David Childs, who Silverstein hired to complete the tower, since Silverstein saw it as his "absolute right"[95] to select his own designer. Despite Silverstein once saying that "[Libeskind has] never designed a high-rise in his life,"[96] and Childs himself being what Elizabeth Greenspan labels "anti-Libeskind,"[97] the two architects worked together in "meaningful collaboration"[98] to fulfill all of the demands from so many different stakeholders. Libeskind once admitted that he "never intended to build this whole project."[99]

Having Childs on board actually allowed decision makers to assure local and national publics that Ground Zero would be properly securitized, despite Libeskind's disgruntlements and even pressing a lawsuit against Silverstein for unpaid architectural fees.[100] Pataki once commented on Child's unique ability to securitize the "Freedom Tower" by saying, "I have no doubt that David Childs will come up with yet another magnificent design that will once again inspire the nation and serve as a fitting tribute to freedom."[101]

Pataki continued to reassure people of the safety of this site against growing anxieties about spaces and places of terror:[102] "I think it will be very safe."[103] If one of his children worked at the Freedom Tower, he said, he would be "confident in their safety."[104] Childs himself commented on the state-of-the-art security by saying, "Remember, we're going to have 5 million people a year come in and go up to the observation deck. . . . So it will have a lot of public use, but it will be extraordinarily secure. I don't know of any other building in the world, apart from the Norad defense facility, that will have anything near this kind of security. Yet we've done everything in our power to not have it appear as such."[105]

All in all, this incremental type of securitization, which gained momentum over the years, allowed many journalists, decision makers, and laypersons to comment on either these secure spaces or the *appearance* of securitized places and the mitigation of objects' risk. Material realities merged with potent symbols in a foundational assemblage that allowed Ground Zero to be conceptualized as a military fortress that could be visited, safely, by those who might be oblivious to all of the preparation and delays during these architectural debates.

Granted, local communities, commercial ventures, and leading New York politicians may have occasionally complained about the Port Authority or NYPD's planning, but they could not escape the snare of hegemonic, discursive formations that were coproduced by those who understood that rebuilding Ground Zero had to appear to be primarily a securitizing venture.

Fig. 5. Port Authority Command Center.

Although there was a point of arbitrariness and ambiguity about how to securitize this space of memory, once the NYPD made suggestions to prevent car and truck bombs and increase the distance between the tower and the curbside, the security bug went around and everybody, it seemed, rallied behind those who argued for the "necessity" of securitizing Ground Zero (figure 5).

While Governor Pataki was saying that the Freedom Tower "is going to be a symbol of our freedom and independence," folks such as Steve Rose of the *Guardian* claimed that "the new tower, braced for disaster and infused with paranoia, will hardly ring out as a victory. Rather, it is an acknowledgment of how dominant security has become as a design factor."[106]

When Michael Arad was passed the baton from Libeskind, he too soon learned what it was like for architects and designers to have to negotiate this treacherous post-9/11 terrain.

While debates about securitizing the Freedom Tower were swirling around Lower Manhattan and the rest of the country, another set of arguments was taking form regarding what Pataki's chief of staff and downtown development official John P. Cahill called "the soul of our rebuilding efforts": the national memorial.[107] These concerns had everything to do with the microdecisions and the more specific architectural planning that had to be made in the wake of the acceptance of Libeskind's master plan.

This is where disputation centered on the acceptability of Michael Arad's winning design for the National September 11 Memorial, titled "Reflecting Absence." Since January 6, 2004—the date that the LMDC selected Arad's specific designs—arguments about securitization of space once again took hold as various actors engaged in protracted debates about freedoms, necessities, and the actual shape and contours of some sixteen acres of hallowed ground (figure 6).

One disagreement, for instance, revolved around what to do with the two one-acre memorial pools, or "footprints," where the Twin Towers once stood. What would visitors make of the cascades of water plummeting in their descent thirty feet below ground? While Arad was caught up in debates with family members about issues such as the placement of the names on the memorial, security officials worried that Arad's design posed yet another security threat for the museum's vent shafts that, apparently, were not high enough to prevent a possible terrorist from "lob[bing] a device in" and compromising securities against "chemical, biological and radiological attacks."[108] Saddam Hussein's minions were apparently not the only potential enemies who might be carrying weapons of mass destruction with them.

Additionally, officials wanted to make sure that the vents were not interrupted by memorial objects—such as the hundreds of swamp white oak trees that landscape architect Peter Walker wanted to surround the memorial pools—because they may interrupt security guards' line of sight in properly surveilling the premises for potential lurking

Fig. 6. Aerial view of the National September 11 Memorial and Memorial Museum at Ground Zero.

terrorists.[109] To Cahill, the security concerns about the vents were of utmost importance for public safety. Commenting on the issue, he said, "When you think about the thousands of people who could be below grade at any particular moment, . . . the ability to provide for their public safety is of utmost importance."[110]

Another security issue arose when the LMDC asked David Brody Bond to assist Arad with the design of the memorial. Bond's concerns were voiced when he was chosen to design the underground museum, even though Bond had already submitted his bid for the $160 million underground museum while working with Arad. Some of these disagreements arose when observers commented on the specific location of four L-shaped ramps that descended to underground galleries beneath the memorial. In his counsel to Arad, Bond claimed that the memorials' "voids" should be centered above the actual footprints, thus, eliminating the necessity of four ramps since only two would be needed. This claim was warranted by the fact that it had "meaning to families"[111] because, as Pataki said, families could "bend over and touch" the bedrock[112]—to which Arad replied, "They didn't even know the pools weren't centered on footprints."[113]

Bond wanted to make room for the underground museum that he had in mind, but he had not shared all of this plan with Arad. Both propositions—the one for the four-ramp and the one for the two-ramp scheme—evoked security concerns that included concerns such as safety exits and possible security checkpoints.

Defending Arad's original design against critics, Stefan Pryor—the president of the LMDC who replaced Kevin Rampe—claimed the design of four memorial ramps included exit stairs that could support four times the number of people at any point in time.[114] Jake Pauls, however, a consultant for building codes and public safety who was working as a technical adviser for a coalition group organized by families of victims called the Skyscraper Safety Campaign said that all of this was "playing games" with numbers and also challenged the design of six emergency exits at the main memorial level, which were "behind corner doors in the galleries" that led to "fire-protected, blast-hardened, pressurized stairwells and corridors."[115] Pauls said, "'If the exit is not used normally, you can just kiss it off in an emergency.... People won't know about it. The authorities won't know how to deal with it. And how do you redirect people from a normally used path which they want to use to a distant, well-hidden but relatively safe, narrower, longer, more arduous route by stairs?"[116]

Others had qualms when they heard about the single-ramp idea advocated by Bond. To Monica Iken, founder of a group called September's Mission and who lost her husband on September 11 said, "We're glad the governor and the mayor have addressed the safety and security issues of the Freedom Tower, but we hope that now they will address the issues of the memorial itself. Its single-ramp design is not safe, and beyond that, the memorial needs to be more prominent, and the Freedom Center needs to be off the site."[117]

In the meantime, security officials were debating where to put possible security-screening magnetometers and whether to impose "some other" security methods to securitize the memorial.[118] Bond, for instance, in suggesting placing them on the descending ramps, said, "You don't want this to be like an airport."[119]

Going to the National September 11 Memorial, however, did indeed feel like going to the airport when one of the authors visited these sacred grounds in 2012, just one year after it officially opened (September 11, 2011; see chapter 5). Before any of these security plans were finalized, however, security assemblages had to be assembled and defended.

Conclusion: Evaluating Concerns over Securitized and Risky Objects

Whereas the previous chapter discussed not only the threat of certain objects to the rebuilding of Ground Zero but also the planning of the security assemblage, this chapter has discussed how calculations of risk, and perceived terrorist threats, impacted the debates about the WTC master site. While some selection processes for design plans were framed as though they took into account local concerns about traffic, the aesthetic desires of architects, or the views of those who worried about hypersecurity, the final decisions were primarily made on the basis of security concerns. This emphasis on security took precedence over all other design considerations in spite of the fact that polls showed New Yorkers and others wanted a 9/11 memorial that would not look like a bunker or a space for counterterrorist deterrent practices.

In many ways these resecuritization efforts depended on the persuasiveness of rhetors who were armed with everything from risk assessments to videos that showed the police what might happen in the event of a terrorist attack on key infrastructures in and around Ground Zero. Between 2002 and 2006, those who wanted to prioritize securitization gained hegemony by circulating texts and visualities that effectually crowded out the competition from more cosmopolitan, multidirectional memories.

We have argued that some of these security assemblages were constructed by those who refused to believe that any of this was hypervigilance. Terrorist threats were created at the very time that they were described, and vernacular discussions of issues like traffic control looked pedestrian in comparison with the risks that were said to be associated with inadequate architectural planning or poor reconstruction efforts. So did all of the elite discussions of the need to factor in commercial and capitalist concerns.

These types of hegemonic concerns about vulnerability influenced the rejection or acceptance of many parts of Daniel Libeskind's master plan. The only sure way to eliminate risk, after all, is to anticipate every single possible terrorist plot and then prevent it—an integral component of what Richard Grusin calls premediation.[120] When the NYPD seemed to be using these types of premediation strategies—which found flaws in almost all architectural schemes—those who sensed that vested interests were behind all of these delaying tactics were infuriated.

But, of course, the security assemblage could not possess absolute control over the architectural process of rebuilding Ground Zero, given the national desires that were expressed by some for symbolistic meaning and structures of representation that might help them cope or recover from the traumas of 9/11. Ultimately, as we have shown, securitization rhetorics garnered the attention of many, but Ground Zero might have looked even more like a replica of Fort Knox if other social agents, including some families of 9/11 victims, had not intervened in these situations.

Those interested in promoting "bunker" ways of viewing rebuilding efforts at Ground Zero were able to form a strong, if unwieldy group of American decision makers and laypersons who grudgingly accepted the "necessity" of weaponizing Lower Manhattan architectural designs. By taking advantage of both the dingpolitik and realpolitik of these spaces and places, those interested in underscoring the riskiness of objects in Libeskind's master plan could point out the reasonableness of their meticulous calculations as they went over nearly every conceivable terroristic scenario. Even though such considerations went against the spirit of symbolic overtures that Libeskind and Arad initially wanted, eventually even they were forced to compromise and alter their design plans so that they would at least appear to be a part of complex security assemblages.

By the end of 2006 New Yorkers and other Americans were left with a complicated hybrid assemblage that would be configured as an essential geopolitical space in the battles that had to be fought during the GWOT.

The suggestions for improving the security of both the Freedom Tower and the National September 11 Memorial were not made in some political vacuum. They were advanced during periods of continued feelings of vulnerability, several years after 9/11, when the debris had been removed. This was a time of lingering feelings of loss and absences. Those who wanted to securitize Ground Zero perhaps sensed these structures of feelings, as they demanded that architectural designs and reconstruction planning signal resilience and counterterrorist preparedness.

3

Policing Memory with Moral Authority

The Idealistic Visions of Family Members of the Deceased, 2004–2014

The securitization of Ground Zero, and the public circulation of proliferating representations of these hallowed grounds, took place during a time when this site's symbolic appeal and its overall mystery were growing in intensity throughout the nation. While New Yorkers continued to be some of the major stakeholders in debates about these spaces and places, the perpetual nature of the Global War on Terrorism (GWOT) meant that counterterrorist threats were here to stay. The confluence of realpolitik and dingpolitik factors meant that Ground Zero was incrementally, but quickly, becoming a memorial for the ages.

The gravitas of the situation was not lost on members of the memorial jury, who formed their own type of Latourian deliberative "parliament" as they announced the design competition for the National September 11 Memorial contest in 2003. The committee received 5,201 design propositions from architects in sixty-three different countries, and all of this publicity increased the fervor of those who wanted to use the memorial to converse about the imaginative potentials of recovery, remembrance, and rebirth.[1]

But, as we noted in previous chapters, these were not just debates about winning designs or conversations about abstract goals but were also rhetorical situations that involved disputes about the inclusion and exclusion of specific material objects. While many wanted a design that heroically and openly displayed American resilience and its ability to survive another possible attack, many of the families of the 9/11 dead wanted a more private, mausoleum-type setting. Still others took the more controversial stance of calling for a rebuilt site like Maya Lin's Vietnam Veterans Memorial, a dark and somber place that allowed for silent, critical reflection about global affairs.

While questions about who would become the winning memorial architect and how that choice would influence the overall "story" of the place loomed over the nation circulated, cultural debates about the memorial persisted until Michael Arad's design, "Reflecting Absence," was selected in 2004 (two years after Libeskind's master plan for the entire Ground Zero site was chosen).

To get a feel for some of the broader sociocultural implications of selecting the design of the memorial, consider Amy Waldman's novel *The Submission*, which speaks to the politics of mourning that many were dealing with during this time (2004–14).[2] The book offers a narrative of a Muslim American, Mohammad Khan, who wins a design contest with his anonymously submitted draft of a memorial featuring a walled, rectangular garden that creates a contemplative space for victims' families and publics. Unfortunately, but also unexpectedly, the announcement of Khan's winning design triggers nationwide uproars from vocal pockets of American society, mirroring fragmented American political communities divided over race, culture, and religious identifications in the wake of an event that many thought had brought the nation together. Writers for the *Guardian* opined that the book "reveals much about the frenzied, divisive political climate produced by that catastrophe, which is still very much in evidence today."[3]

Yet many parts of Waldman's book also hint at the dominant rhetorical responses to the polarization that took place after 9/11. Often during these turbulent years, the views and stances of Muslim Americans took a back seat and were marginalized as fissures created between "good" Muslim Americans who denounced Jihads and bad "Islamic fundamentalists" whose silence could be configured as problematic.[4] To us, *The Submission* could be accurately described as a melodramatic illustration of the moral polarities of post-9/11 political discourse that might have provided more peaceful and less terror-centric ways of conceptualizing Ground Zero spaces. The book implies that we all need to critique the artificial us/them dichotomy of major 9/11 counterterrorist narratives and, of course, some of the more problematic racial, cultural, ethnocentric implications of not listening to the views of individuals like Mohammad Khan.

The Submission invites consideration of the negative cultural auras produced in ages of massive insecurity and vilification of morphing terrorist enemies. This culture of fear was part and parcel of an era that witnessed post-9/11 hypersecuritization in a post-9/11 world. Waldman's analysis allows readers to sow the multidimensional nature of collective traumas, where feelings of vulnerability contributed to situations in which those who suffered from posttraumatic stress disorder were also victims of horrible attacks. This trauma, in turn, bred political and ideological extremism. In terms of the materiality of the memorial itself, the book, of course, also evokes questions that many were asking during the memorial design competition: Whose designs, and views, should be included in all of this memorialization?

While some of those who look back tend to lump together the concerns raised by different stakeholders, decisions made during this crucial period—between Michael Arad winning the memorial design competition and the museum opening to the public—impacted what would be left out of some design planning. The numerous conjunctural possibilities for this memorial space should remind readers that ultimately, the memorial did not have to turn into the security apparatus it is today. But as we have shown, the "felt necessity of the time" (Oliver Holmes Jr.)[5] meant that securitizing objects and spaces became a transcendent goal that impacted the trajectory of argumentative presumptions in these debates.

This chapter focuses on one of the key factions that influenced the securitized directionality of the politic of mourning at the National September 11 Memorial: the families of those who died on September 11, 2001. Although they often disagreed about the perceived "politicization"

Fig. 7. Objects of memorialization at the National September 11 Memorial.

of Ground Zero, many influential family members joined the ranks of those who wanted to territorialize this place in ways that commemorated the sacrifices of lost loved ones. A narrower position taken by some families was that the proper commemoration of the dead had to also involve efficacious counterterrorism.

As readers may be aware, many 9/11 survivor families became part of the planning teams for the selection of architects, the choice of designs, and the planning that went into the building of the National September 11 Memorial and Memorial Museum, but readers may not know that these interventions were not the only times these particular social agents became vocal, and often respected, commentators on a host of national security issues. The ethos they gained as members of the victims' families helped them garner the attention of journalists, politicians, urban planners, and others who realized that these stakeholders could not be ignored. Many representatives of these families used their elevated rhetorical status to interject their own beliefs regarding the propriety of local, regional, or national policing or counterterrorist measures.

The families of the victims, as well as representatives of organizations that claimed to speak for these families, used their ascribed or achieved moral authority to join others who would critique the counterterrorist and counterinsurgency policies of both the George W. Bush and Barack Obama administrations, even in situations where the topics of conversation looked as though they were only tangentially related to the urban planning for this part of the sixteen acres in Lower Manhattan. For example, in May 2011, when then-president Obama announced that bin Laden had been killed in Abbottabad by U.S. forces, word of bin Laden's "death triggered spontaneous demonstrations at Ground Zero and the White House."[6] One of those who lost a loved one on 9/11, a "prominent critic of the Obama administration's anti-terrorist policies," explained that while she thought this was the "beginning of the end" she nevertheless hoped that Americans would be able to see bin Laden's body to help end conspiratorial talk of his escaping.[7] The perceptual moral authority of the 9/11 families would become an important part of many U.S. geopolitical imaginations, especially in terrorist-related contexts, and even the framing of some critics' arguments could be reframed for strategic purposes.

Although some of the survivor families supported peace efforts or resented the instrumental use of the histories and memories of their loved one by those interested in resecuritization, there would be no shortage of those who not only condoned but applauded the idealistic efforts of some, like Debra Burlingame, the sister of Charles "Chic" Burlingame, one of the pilots who died on 9/11. Burlingame apparently wanted to have an inordinate say in how to convey "the truth" about what happened on September 11, 2001, and even today she is regarded by many members of mainstream media outlets as a "voice" for the survivor families (see conclusion).

Debra Burlingame did not hesitate to speak her mind on a plethora of subjects. On a popular website that she helped establish, called "9/11

Families for a Safe and Strong America," Burlingame would speculate about whether leaders were actually sincere or whether they provided "swift and certain justice" to the nineteen September 11 hijackers.[8]

During that same year, when National Public Radio audiences were hearing experts converse about what led up to the recent bombing of an Iraqi base by a former Guantanamo Bay detainee, Debra Burlingame was asked to explain her take on how individuals like Abdallah al-Ajmi, who was imprisoned in Cuba for five years, became radical Islamists. Burlingame, adopting a typical conservative line, had this to say about Ajmi, who allegedly drove a truck full of explosives into an Iraqi army base, killing both himself and thirteen Iraqi soldiers:

> I'm speculating just like anyone else would be speculating, because his profile before he arrived in Guantanamo wasn't as bad as the profile of some of the other Kuwaitis, and some of those are pretty bad. But I take issue with the idea that if someone isn't a terrorist mastermind or a senior operator that they're not dangerous. Some of the 9/11 people who boarded those planes, none of them, with the exception of, say, Mohamed Atta, would be considered a mastermind. Some of them, called the muscle hijackers, the ones who probably killed my brother and the other pilots, they were not high up at all. They would have been called the lowly foot soldiers that were found at (unintelligible) training camps. . . . He was already radicalized to go and fight Jihad, to fight holy war. So, it wasn't that there was a major conversion experience that happened at Guantanamo.[9]

Like many other Americans, Burlingame wanted to argue that Islamic fundamentalist terrorism was a foreign threat involving both high- and low-level detainees, and she was sure that the acts of individuals like Atta or Al-Ajmi had little to do with U.S. social agency. Many of her narratives were explicitly or implicitly supporting the positions of those who wanted the National September 11 Memorial to be a place where reflection about absences would aid the cause of patriot counterterrorists.

The vignette about Abdallah al-Ajmi and Debra Burlingame illustrates the potential reach of what might be called the populist nature of the survivor family rhetorics that helped form the realpolitik and dingpolitik of this period. These positions were coming from those who wanted to represent the views of the dead and others who might have cared about "swift and certain" justice. Regardless of whether decision makers and their constituents were talking about the discernible truths revealed by the 9/11 Commission or the role the Saudis played in helping the 9/11 hijackers, it was often taken for granted by journalists that at least one of the family members had to be interviewed for their take on these subjects.

Oftentimes this involvement meant trying to control the polyvocal nature of the discourse surrounding these hallowed grounds so that it would appear as though most, if not all, of the 9/11 victims' families were unified in demanding that the American government continue to hunt down those who brought down the Twin Towers. This hunt soon evolved into a search for both "high-value" detainees and any other terrorists who threatened American embassies or the lives of allies.

For more than a decade—especially during the immediate aftermath of the attack on the Pentagon and the Twin Towers—talk of the designing plans or the rebuilding of towers in Lower Manhattan would be tethered to conversation about dominant survivor family needs and desires.

For example, some representatives of the victims' families tried to shame those who were not doing enough to track down Osama's bin Laden's minions, destroy Taliban strongholds, or dismantle al Qaeda networked cells. More than a few appeared before Congress or in front of teams of journalists as they talked about Guantanamo detention policies, the use of "enhanced interrogation techniques" on terrorists, the policing of memorial sites, and even the extraterritorial use of drones by the CIA or the Department of Defense. Along the way, they oftentimes conversed about the preferred patriotic monovocal tale that should be told about the rebuilding of this part of Lower Manhattan.

Not surprisingly, the epistemes and rhetorical fragments in the argumentative clusters used by some family members were often filled with commentary on the victims, the undeniable evil of their attackers, and the need for reverential memorials or respectful museum displays.

While these family members often tried to comment on others' politicization of 9/11, what they often hid was the rhetoricity of their own select narratives.

What many scholars—even those who commented on the rhetorical status of these families—have underestimated is the impact this argumentation had on the final decisions made about the reconstruction of this part of Lower Manhattan. Citing the views of 9/11 family members served as a persuasive vehicle for critiquing many liberal or moderate ways of carrying out America's securitization policies.

Some of the survivor families were so successful at extending the reach of their commentary that they infuriated the minority of families who were peace activists. After all, if idealists are supposed to focus their energies on some single, identifiable reverential goals—like the sacralizing of the spaces at the National 9/11 Memorial and Memorial Museum—then why were some of the more conservative members of survivor family committees becoming entangled in more divisive debates about U.S. foreign policy or military strategies and tactics? But, as Michael Middleton, Aaron Hess, Danielle Endres, and Samantha Senda-Cook have pointed out, sometimes rhetoric can be happening "with place as opposed to happening in place,"[10] and it would be difficult to think about the National September 11 Memorial Museum without seeing the victims and their families as a part of those (in)securitization grounds. Over time, it became inevitable to think of the planning and building of this space as counterterrorist in nature.

Even as we focus on the way 9/11 families and others used their individual social agency and political authority between 2004 and 2014, our poststructural sensibilities remind us that these rhetorics may have reflected the structured views of many other public actors, especially those who believed in the need for aggressive warfare or the dangers of Islamic fundamentalism.

The 9/11 family members' realpolitik views of the national memorial provided examples of fairly typical conservative, populist, or Judeo-Christian ways of writing and talking about America's civil religion and military obligations. Those who were shocked by Donald Trump's election to the presidency in 2016 might have profited from studies of some of this populism, especially in security contexts.

Others before us have noted the symbolic capital, and the authoritative ethos, of these particular stakeholders. Jay Aronson has argued that even after the passage of some fifteen years, the "political power of the 9/11 victims endures."[11] We would go even farther and claim that the longer it took to identify the remains of the dead, the more time their families had to speak for them as they intervened in myriad policing and securitizing controversies.

Make no mistake; others besides these family members could take advantage of the aura that surrounded the suffering and mourning. Aronson would go on to note the dynamic, recursive nature of some of this casuistry when he averred in 2016,

> The political power of 9/11 victims was marshaled by politicians, especially then-President George W. Bush, Vice President Richard B. Cheney, Defense Secretary Donald H. Rumsfeld and their backers to justify both a widely supported war against the Taliban and al-Qaeda in Afghanistan and a more contentious one against Saddam Hussein in Iraq. . . . The victims also underwrite the metastasizing war on terror across the globe. . . . These wars and lethal actions undertaken, at least partially, in the name of victims have pockmarked parts of the Middle East and Africa with mass graves and unidentified remains.[12]

The family members, in turn, wanted a hand in persuading Americans and foreign powers that they too had an obligation to stop the metastasizing Islamic terrorism that might produce the next 9/11.

Aronson's academic linking of human remains of the victims of 9/11 to other sites of destruction during the GWOT would not have resonated with most of the families or most Americans, but it did illustrate how interdisciplinary scholars were noting the rhetorical usage of all of this framing. This rhetorical situation did not prevent Aronson from pointing out that while "most [victims around the globe] were not directly killed by American military personnel or drones, hundreds of thousands have died as a result of the chaos and instability that has enveloped the region since the invasion of Iraq in 2003."[13] This we view as an intriguing, but dissident, way of configuring American memory-work during the GWOT.

We have contrasted Burlingame's with Aronson's readings to point out that the families' apparently unified tale of "what happened" during 9/11 is just one of many plausible ways of configuring historical causes and effects, terrorist phenomena, or the efficacy of particular counterterrorist strategies and tactics. The textual and intertextual readings in this chapter help with the discovery of some of the antecedent genres that would influence the framing of the narrative argumentative arc that would later appear during the opening of the National September 11 Memorial and Memorial Museum.

The polysemic and polyvalent nature of this hallowed ground itself, as well as the mediated representation of these spaces and places, has created rhetorical situations where elites and publics will continue to evaluate, and modify, the ways they talk and write about the role of the families who wanted to protect the image of these sacred places. Like all spaces and places of reverence, many would agree, this is a special site of remembrance, but this belief does not resolve the personal, organizational, or nationalistic controversies regarding *how to operationalize* that remembrance. As Joanna Slater explains, decisions had to be made about how "to tell the tale of the worst terrorist attack on American soil in the very place where the violence occurred," while at the same time navigating "between the needs of victims' families, the sensitivities of survivors, the wishes of local residents, and the obligation to educate future generations."[14]

While many journalists, politicians, architects, academicians, New York residents, and other participants in the formation of securitized texts or image events have been sympathetic when they assessed the major role that these families of the dead played in salient museological and memorial disputation, there are some who expressed reservations about the monolithic nature of what might be regarded as an "idealistic" way of conceptualizing these key spaces and places.

As we noted in the introduction, we are not interested in providing readers with some single prescriptive, modernistic commentary on how some groups may have lost their moral compass and deviated from proper memorial practices as they fought over the design, planning, building, or maintenance of the National September 11 Memorial Museum. Granted, we need to pay attention to some of the dominant positions of empowered rhetors and communities who represented majoritarian views regarding how to remember those who died on September 11, 2001, but following Bruno Latour, we are also interested in tracing the argumentative forces of objects that have become securitized at Ground Zero.

We also join those critical scholars who invite us to listen to some of the marginal voices of those who speak out and contribute to the polyphonic nature of these grounds. As Ross Wilson has argued in his study of popular museums in the United Kingdom, those who follow in the footsteps of Michel Foucault or Michael Bennet, and care about "governmentality," need to make sure that they do not forget to study how audience-centered places involved negotiations between hegemonic communities who want these places to be "repositories" of national values and the "demands" of minority groups who want critiques of dominant cultures.[15]

Yet one of our key theoretical contributions is displaying how notions of perceived domination and marginality *are themselves part of all of this memorializing contestation.* For example, Debra Burlingame sometimes claims that she is one of those marginalized voices.

This is why, instead of treating the families' views as morally privileged or presumptively on point regarding what "happened on 9/11," we view them as empowered stakeholders who have participated, since 2001, in heated elite and public security and policing debates.

Although representatives of the families sometimes disagree among themselves about whether their views have been forgotten and marginalized, many representatives of survivor family organizations act as if they had little power in the face of larger structural or material forces in these commemorative debates.

It will be our position that these families were much more influential than they let on, and that the circulation of their patriotic ideas often resonated with those who shared their views regarding the proper way to remember the dead or protect the living during the twenty-first century. In spite of their protestations, representatives of the families were constantly being interviewed by members of mainstream and alternative presses, they were putting up blog posts about their work, they were treated as honored guests as various commemorative functions, and some were even viewed as expert authorities on counterterrorism.

To provide just one example of this inordinate argumentative power, we note that there was no shortage of stakeholders who were adamant that pedagogical functions or security interests should take a back seat to the reverential remembrance of the more than twenty-nine hundred who died on September 11, 2001. Individuals who had competing interests—like Larry Silverstein and the architects who sent in building designs—sometimes tried to advance their own competing viewpoints that might potentially marginalize the heroic tale that the families wanted to tell.

At other times, alliances were created when material needs, social interests, and personal motivations converged. For example, in 2008 when a developer was suing to win $12.3 billion in damages that also involved families of some victims,[16] those who wanted to highlight the importance of transcendent reverential needs could have configured these lawsuits as materialist efforts that undercut other messaging. Most of the time, though, the public persona crafted by representatives of empowered victims' families highlighted the complementary nature of the reverential narratives that resonated with many journalists, politicians, lawmakers, architects, and other stakeholders.

To help trace some of the evolutionary nature of the persuasive influence of these familial discourses about the National September 11 Memorial and Memorial Museum, we begin with an overview of the mass-mediated coverage of the families' demands that followed in the wake of 9/11.

The Rush to Memorialize and the Idealistic Demands of 9/11 Survivors
Following the events of 9/11, Ground Zero almost immediately became an example of what Pierre Nora called *les lieux de mémoire*, or sites of

memory, where "memory has been torn" for communities that long for a "sense of historical continuity."[17] Early purveyors of post-9/11 rhetorics about Ground Zero focused on a "rush to build memorials"[18] that was spreading throughout the nation,[19] and a host of private and public memorials were dedicated to the dead long before the official opening of the National September 11 Memorial and Memorial Museum. For instance, famous pizza parlors became places where families tried to get information about loved ones, and for weeks and months New Yorkers looked for their own ways of memorializing the dead.

Impromptu or temporary memorials helped many of the living with their bereavement, as we discussed in chapter 1, but there were also those families of the dead who wanted to see the nation display more permanent, and more reverential, representations of those who died on September 11, 2001. This tragedy needed to be viewed as a national, as well as personal, one.

Family members of those who died on 9/11 quickly emerged as important stakeholders in the controversies that arose over the potential rebuilding of the World Trade Center, and they were not always pleased with the architectural designs and organizational plans that were advanced by those who sought to commercialize or politicize this site of memory. Family members often worried that the renovated Ground Zero areas were going to be used as cosmopolitan spaces for general tourism, pedagogical sites for cultural education, or spaces for private entrepreneurship that would help with the rejuvenation of Lower Manhattan.

The polyvocal nature of the site, and the cacophony that swirled around the early debates about what to do with Ground Zero, troubled many families who lost loved ones on 9/11, because, they often argued, all of these vocalized disagreements were detracting attention away from what they believed should be the dominant usage of this space: reverence for the dead and acknowledgement of their sacrifices.

By 2005 various fragments of context were used by families in the production of this monolithic tale about 9/11, and many family members who shared this antiterrorist vision established an organization for social change called Take Back the Memorial (TBTM). There were several organizational reasons why the TBTM was able to contest the heteroglossia of early design planning for Ground Zero. First of all, they were viewed as other traumatized victims of the 9/11 attack, and early on few doubted that they should have a major say in the commemoration of those losses. As can be expected, for the next several years after 9/11, negotiation processes between the TBTM and other stakeholder organizations such as the LMDC were sensitive.

We also believe that there is a second reason why the 9/11 survivors were viewed as primary stakeholders in the early debates about the trajectory of Ground Zero plans—the 9/11 surviving families were positioned as social agents who represented the views of typical Americans across the country, who also wanted to see aggressive counterterrorism at the same time that they commented on respect for the dead. In other words, we take the contentious position that the views of the 9/11 surviving families represented the idealistic dreams of many patriotic Americans who cared about national preparedness, and the actions of the TBTM were characterized as deeds that represented traditional American ways of treating the war dead.

This representation of idealism involved the production of constitutive rhetorics that had to hide their artifice to be successful. Theresa Donofrio has noted that when other stakeholders were advancing competing agendas about commemoration, Ground Zero became a "stolen" object to families who rhetorically positioned themselves as "'owners' of this possession"[20] that was "bestowed upon them . . . as a condition of their status as bereaved."[21]

Professor Donofrio and others have been able to see how select rhetorical fragments were used to cobble together this monolithic, yet persuasive metanarrative. To TBTM members, Ground Zero is "a place akin to a cemetery, shrine, battleground, or crime scene,"[22] and we are convinced that sizeable communities of Americans felt the same way.[23] After all, if the Twin Towers could be attacked by foreigners, then what was to prevent similar terrorist attacks from occurring in places like Chicago, Atlanta, St. Louis, and Denver? No wonder that so many in the weeks and months after 9/11 talked about "hunts" for Osama bin Laden or the need to intervene in the affairs of those nations that might have been harboring or aiding terrorists.

The TBTM became entangled in a host of organization disputes about how best to turn this part of Lower Manhattan into that shrine for those who died on 9/11. During these early years, the TBTM began its campaign by opposing the LMDC's plan to build an International Freedom Center (IFC) adjacent to where the Twin Towers once stood. As initially conceived, the IFC would have put on public display various U.S. histories of oppression and freedom to paint a *multicultural* type of multidirectional narrative that expanded the range of potential factors leading to traumatic events like 9/11. TBTM members sensed that perhaps some of these factors might involve critiques of "state terrorism." This stance was not going to be tolerated by those who viewed multiculturalism as a more "competitive" (Michael Rothberg) strategy that could take away from the proper commemoration of the dead.[24]

This way of contextualizing the attack on the Twin Towers also tapped into America's civil religion, but now decision makers were having to choose between a more inclusive type of civil religion that would recognize America's history of racial inequality, or a more exclusive type of civil religion that focused only on the 9/11 victims and terrorist horrors. The potential addition of the IFC was treated by the TBTM as a "politics of things" that swerved away from the more classical memorialization of the sacrifices of 9/11 victims. Just as potentially problematic was the idea that the addition of the IFC might trigger victimage wars, where the specific details of Islamic fundamentalism and the attacks on the Twin Towers might get lost in all of this multicultural memory-work.

The LMDC plan would resonate with those who cared about multiple generations of people that may have suffered from diverse historical causes. This plan still underscored the importance of American ideals, but these ideas now included possible referencing of global histories of prejudice, enslavement, and oppression. For example, the LMDC's plans would have symbolically linked the events of 9/11 with the Holocaust perpetrated by Nazi Germany (see chapter 5), the struggles of Chinese dissidents, the trials and tribulations of Chilean refugees, the historicizing of Jim Crow politics, and the Native American genocide. Frustrated TBTM members might well ask: What does any of this have to do with the evil that caused the loss of three thousand precious souls? Was this a savvy, politicized way of critiquing America's counterterrorist efforts and overseas interventionism?

What some might call the "liberal" or transgenerational broadening of these scopic visions invited viewers and listeners to think about more than the deaths of pilots, first responders, and other individuals who died on 9/11. For puzzled families of the victims, this welter of topics spoke volumes about the values of the LMDC, but these same acts seemed to be sacrilegious acts of memory-work that deflected attention away from both the dead and their families.

Many family members starkly opposed the LMDC's plans for the IFC on the grounds that all of this historical contextualization would be done in a way that would prevent future visitors to the memorial from seeing the unique sacrifices of those who died on 9/11. In their minds those who died on that day were heroes who acted in extraordinary ways, and they did not deserve to be treated as mere mortals whose deeds would be mixed in with the acts of ordinary humans suffering from myriad problems that had little apparent links to the nineteen attackers, al Qaeda, or the values that were held by TBTM members.

Families and their supporters conjured up myriad arguments about why the LMDC plans were problematic. For example, one family member argued that LMDC plans would be a "magnet for protestors."[25] Representatives of the families, or members of the TBTM, could join those who argued that these fancy didactic plans for multicultural learning, or these suggested atrocity lessons, were interfering with the telling of a preferred, monolithic reverential story that needed to be told about 9/11. By blending "the" 9/11 story with other memories of historical American suffering and terror that surviving families found unrelated, organizations like the LMDC risked expanding the "scope [of] the place-making imagination"[26] in problematic ways.

Some critics such as Theresa Donofrio and Robert Kolker[27] have configured the TBTM as an interloping group that interfered unnecessarily with the progressive building of both the 9/11 Memorial and the Museum, but we would argue that their idealistic visions were contagious and some of their geographical imaginations were shared by other Americans who also wanted reverence to be the primary commemorative function of this space. The positions of the TBTM could be thought of as a form of populism that demanded that this reverence for the dead be linked to concrete social or political action on the part of the National September 11 Memorial and Memorial Museum as well as those who had the power to aggressively go after al Qaeda. The rhetoricity of this securitized object-oriented politic may have bothered those who wanted to see more heterogeneous, heterotopic usages of these spaces and places, but these more utopian positions could not be easily ignored, as the previous chapter argued.

To give readers a sense of what this rhetoric looked like during these early years, note the response to the arguments that were presented by Debra Burlingame—who also became a member of the board of directors of the World Trade Center Memorial Foundation. In a widely discussed 2005 letter to the *Wall Street Journal*, she commented on the difficulties that came from having spatial designs that tried to do too much. While Burlingame recognized that there were some "histories" we "all should know and learn," she believed the National September 11 Memorial site was not the place to be teaching those lessons because "dispensing it over the ashes of Ground Zero is like creating a Museum of Tolerance over the sunken graves of the USS Arizona."[28] Would this mixing of genres produce an injustice to those who believed in the uniqueness of both the Holocaust and the terrorism of 9/11?

Allegedly, some of the LMDC planning was creating a situation where commemorative representations of different battles and various temporal periods were becoming entangled in unproductive, competitive ways that did little to help with proper commemoration or bereavement.

This dispute over LMDC planning should be viewed not as some minor squabble over memorial planning but as an illustrative example of the emotive and symbolic importance of the National September 11 Memorial and Memorial Museum that TBTM members and others wanted to see ensconced as a major heroic part of the nation's unique civil religion. This desire in turn implied that it had been American exceptionalist values that contributed to the heroism of those who tried to fight the terrorists on the planes or who risked their lives responding to the attacks. Producing a more reverential and securitized space only etched in stone the fundamental values that TBTM members believed existed apart from all of this squabbling.

The particularity of the terrorist injustices is what took center stage in the idealistic narratives crafted by TBTM members and their supporters. These memories of American courage had to be fought for and preserved—especially when potential critics of American domestic or foreign policy wanted to use the space to debate alleged historical injustices. What family member wanted to see 9/11 horrors linked to postcolonial critiques that mentioned American genocidal treatment of indigenous populations in places like the Dakotas, California, and Florida?

TBTM members wanted to celebrate America's inherent values and the heroes who embodied those virtues, and the last thing they wanted to see was their loved ones being used for anti-American diatribes or harsh critiques of overseas military interventionism. In another article, Debra Burlingame was quoted as saying, "If you want to debate, go to Columbia or NYU. Don't do it on the ashes of all these people."[29] Note the implied claim that academics who wanted to broaden the scope of the National September 11 Memorial were not in tune with lay perceptions of those who didn't want to turn these hallowed grounds into some ivory tower.

Burlingame's arguments resonated with supporters of the TBTM and put on display the politicized nature of all this early planning. As Gregory Hoskins has explained, the TBTM movement, which was partly inspired by the editorial work of Burlingame, should be linked to threats of congressional investigations and a campaign to block some fund-raising efforts. This stance, we argue, led to the IFC being officially removed from the World Trade Center Memorial site by New York's governor.[30]

Although the IFC proposal was eventually dropped from the 9/11 memorial plans, idealistic narratives of sacredness, reverence, and spatial exceptionalism continued to be deployed as normative ideals for commemoration, and groups like the TBTM continued to complain about other heterotopic usages of this sacred site of memory. As we note in later chapters, these types of idealistic arguments would be recirculated for many years.

The clash between utopian and heterotopic ways of conceptualizing commemorative space and place even impacted the ways that architects and their supporters debated the placement of names or the remains of the dead. For example, surviving families of the 9/11 dead also opposed Michael Arad's original architectural plan to place the names of victims in underground galleries beneath the memorial pools. Arguing that such a proposal was not commemorative enough, families fought for the right to have the names inscribed above ground, at the plaza level. The families got their way, better preserving the visible memories of those who died and allowing generations to see the names of the victims more easily. Arad's plans could be considered objectionable dark spaces that were too, too underground and too dreary, and a threat to those who worried that their loved ones would be forgotten. Michael Palladino, the president of the Detectives' Endowment Association averred that "if you want to put people underground, go build a cemetery."[31] Political undertones of these debates were sometimes inextricably linked to aesthetic debates about classical, modernist, or postmodernist architectural planning.

Some of the mass-mediated representations of this idealistic visioning included commentary on how to arrange the names to be inscribed above ground. Surviving families pressured designers to replace the random arrangement of the names that Arad had in mind with one focused on topographical, communal loss of love. Some of the surviving families wanted the names to be arranged so that visitors could see where the victims worked and who died beside them.[32] The TBTM—and its supporters across the country—were thus able to flex their rhetorical muscles to police memory by altering the architectural designs proffered by Michael Arad and the LMDC. At the same time, the TBTM legitimated more conservative ways of contextualizing this hallowed ground while helping with the securitization of 9/11 histories and memories.

The materiality and symbolicity of memorials are often intertwined and shaped over time as generations of publics contemplate them and give them form. Although some of the idealistic strands of commemoration that families advocated for influenced the trajectory of planning at the National September 11 Memorial and Memorial Museum, it must also be remembered that 9/11 was also a national tragedy that affected millions through what Marc Redfield has called "virtual trauma."[33]

Even though numerous other factions had competing ideations about how to remember 9/11 at the National September 11 Memorial, it was primarily the families of the 9/11 victims who had an inordinate say when it came time to actually implementing some of this planning. Kolker, writing in 2005, noted that no one said the 9/11 families weren't entitled to expressing their pain, but he wondered why a "small handful of them should have the power to shape Ground Zero."[34] As we noted above, some family members would deny they had this type of political power, but we are convinced that plenty of evidence illustrates the substantial rhetorical influence of TBTM supporters.

The Continuing Resonance of the September
11 Victims' Families Arguments

The power of the victims' families did not end in 2005. For example, a study of the evolutionary nature of the memorialization and securitization rhetorics that circulated between 2006 and the opening of the National September 11 Memorial Museum in May 2014 shows that many surviving family members became involved in a host of other securitizing issues. Families doubled down their focus on securitization in spite of knowing that other stakeholders were continuing to write about the didactic or cosmopolitan functions of the national memorial that threatened to interrupt the prioritization of the reverential qualities of this space. As Donofrio has argued, "9/11 must be understood as more than the aggregate of nearly three thousand individual deaths," and focusing only on the TBTM metanarrative promotes the "rhetoric of American innocence" and truncates "our ways of understanding trauma."[35] One wonders, of course, whether Donofrio's views represent those of academic dissidents or *most Americans* who may sympathize with members of the TBTM.

All of the many arguments produced by the victims' family members between 2004 and 2014 provided the argumentative fragments, the warrants, and the epistemic templates that would ideologically drift through time. For example, during the first half of May 2014, interest in the views of the victims' families once again spiked as major mainstream outlets covered their response to the opening of the National September 11 Memorial Museum. For years there had been behind-the-scenes debates about what to do with some eight thousand unidentified remains "from the terrorist attacks,"[36] and now journalists noted how the commercialization of the gift shop and the high price of admission could be juxtaposed with the families' interest in having solemn commemoration. Jim Riches, for example, lost his firefighting son, Jimmy, during 9/11, and the elder Richeses thought it was a disgrace that his son's friends had to pay $24 in order to pay their respects. Diane and Kurt Horning told *ABC News* that they were appalled by the "greed and commercialization" that seemed to be part of the ambiance of the museum. Jim Riches similarly complained that this place appeared to be the "only cemetery in the world where you pay a fee to get in."[37] These materialist critiques seemed to echo the lamentations of those who commented on the efforts of billionaires like Larry Silverstein.

During the spring of 2014 some surviving families critiqued the decisions that were made about the treatment of the remains of the dead. Vocal relatives of missing World Trade Center victims wanted the remains to be moved out of the 9/11 Museum and placed above ground like the dead at the Tombs of the Unknowns at Arlington National Cemetery,[38] but this was not to be. This denial of their request would contribute to their feelings of being ignored, marginalized, or betrayed as tourists and tourism seemed to become the focal point of so many crass entrepreneurs.

In the days leading up to the grand opening of this museum, a handful of stories were circulated about the appropriation of grief and disaster to represent a larger-than-life panorama of dramatic scenes. Several organizations and groups of stakeholders were involved in the creation of an underground repository in the museum that would house some fourteen thousand unidentified remains.

Families of the 9/11 victims performatively expressed their displeasure with the placement of the remains. On Sunday, May 10, 2014, the *New York Times* featured an image event of families wearing black cloths over their faces as they protested their lack of voice in the repository decision-making process. Stephen Farrell, who covered these demonstrations, commented:

> Alexander Santora, 77, a retired deputy chief in the Fire Department, was among those who wore gags. "We had no say in what was going on here," said Mr. Santora, whose son Christopher, 23, a probationary firefighter, was killed in the attacks. "You can't tell me that tour guides aren't going to be going inside that building and saying, 'Behind that wall are the victims of 9/11.' That's a dog and pony show."[39]

In theory, some of the survivors were not interested in large, public displays of affection or commemoration that might attract tourists—at the cost of deviating from solemn reverence. Travel to these hallowed grounds ought to be viewed as pilgrimages and not as just one of many secular or ordinary places to see while visiting New York City. Tourists, and their supporters, were turning the heroic into the mundane, the sacred into the profane.

As we will explain in more detail in chapter 5, by the fall of 2014 some journalists who covered visits by mourning families characterized the National September 11 Memorial and Memorial Museum as a "shrine" that would now be open to members of the public.[40] During this period some of the surviving family members implicitly or explicitly argued that they had the authority to police Ground Zero as a place of reverence and repose, and they sought to convince other Americans that this needed to be an "uncontaminated" place of sacral decorum.

We would argue that this attempt at monopolizing the planning resonated with all American audiences, in part because most Americans living during the "perpetual" war against terrorism see the 9/11 dead as just some of the potential victims of al Qaeda attacks. Why, for example, could this memorial and museum not be a place that memorialized the suffering of all terrorist victims?

This is not to say that the surviving family members did not realize that they were only some of the stakeholders in these heated debates. The rhetorical nature of this secular and sacred site meant that no one organization—no matter how powerful—could totally stop the flow of the competing forces that worked to turn Ground Zero into a material space that involved many different layers of spatial meaning. As Michel Foucault and others have noted, even the most hegemonic of power relationships, and the most well-respected monumentalized national archives, still contain fissures, ruptures, and cracks that can provide spaces and places for the disempowered who need what Foucault called "subjugated knowledges." As Richard Jackson explained in a 2012 essay in *Critical Studies on Terrorism*, Foucault's concept of subjugated knowledges got at the notion of suppressed or silenced narratives being masked by more dominant, hegemonic forms of knowledge.[41]

The families of the 9/11 victims dominated some of the mediascapes and landscapes of these Lower Manhattan sites of memory, but that did not mean this was no longer uncontested ground. For example, various stakeholders wanted this place to be an aesthetic architectural wonder, a commercialized tourist attraction that would help recoup the $700 million spent developing the site, a counterterrorist "bunker" that demonstrated New York resilience, or an area that would help rejuvenate the local community. As we noted in earlier chapters, the resecuritization of these spaces depended on the abilities of the empowered to hold off the other stakeholders.

Some members of the TBTM movement aptly described Ground Zero as a "battleground,"[42] but over time they may have underestimated their own influence in shaping the development of these sacred grounds. When we take into account the concessions that had to be made by both Daniel Libeskind and Michael Arad, we can acknowledge that some cosmopolitan heterotopic visions had to make room for the haunting rhetorical power of at least some idealistic, nationalist remembrances of the Americans who died on September 11, 2001. After all, the rhetorical making of places of public memory involve a rich and complex "bundle of relations"[43] that can transform places like the World Trade Center site into a material space of many "utterly different emplacements."[44] This, however, does not mean that idealistic visions always lose their rhetorical power.

Indeed, it could be argued that by the time of the May 2014 opening of the September 11 Memorial and Memorial Museum, the patriotic themes that became a part of the story of the attacks was capacious enough to contain both heterotopic and utopian elements. Holland Cotter, who wrote an essay on the opening that went viral, explained that the museum "is simultaneously a historical document, a monument to the dead [and] a theme-park-style tourist attraction."[45] He also said that the museum tells "the 9/11 story" "at bedrock," and delivers an emotion as "powerful as a punch to the gut."[46] Featuring superfluous objects such as a wrecked ambulance car, devastated fire trucks, and left-behind everyday items such as unopened letters, piles of shoes, and firefighter helmets, visitors are bombarded with fragments of trauma in a visceral way. The use of these abject and moving objects of memory by the museum complements the messages sent by the massive voids one sees at the national memorial. We would argue that perhaps Cotter overlooked the ways these same objects were entangled in a "politics of things" that invited visitors to feel that if they paid enough attention, they could become a part of securitized assemblages. This ambiance, we speculate, pleased many families of the 9/11 victims who did not have to witness the building of more multicultural ways of framing these tragedies.

We will have more to say about the museum in later chapters, but for now, suffice it to say that 9/11 families had myriad ways of intervening in debates both inside and outside museum walls.

A Space for Private Mourning: The Formation of the "Family Room"

Disputation about the nature and scope of the National September 11 Memorial planning was just one facet of these complex memorialization contests. When the administrators who cared about views of surviving families wanted to find a place of commemoration, they could turn to a place, known as the "Family Room," that allowed for mourning and meditation. For about a dozen years the Family Room served as a "most private sanctuary from a most public horror," and its very existence and whereabouts were known only to those "who needed it."[47] Before some of the objects in the Family Room were moved to the National September 11 Memorial Museum, a small office space at 1 Liberty Plaza was reserved for surviving families so that they could be by themselves in a "temporary haven where they could find respite from bad weather and the curious stares of passers-by." Characterized as an impromptu site of memory that did not involve elite planning, this vernacular place of memory was "transformed into an elaborate shrine" known only to the families.[48]

During the memorialization and museological contests that took place over the years, there is little question that the Family Room had a great deal of symbolic importance for survivors' families. For Nikki Stern, whose husband, James Potorti, died on September 11, 2001, the "Family Room was the beginning of the storytelling that was controlled by the families."[49]

Some of the rhetorical fragments that would become a part of the morphing Family Room were collected when well-wishers began gathering tributes, messages, and photographs that had been left on an outdoor viewing platform overlooking the World Trade Center. With the approach of winter, family members needed a more private, indoor space for commemoration and quiet reflection, and over time, representatives from Brookfield Properties on the twentieth floor of

One Liberty Plaza donated space that was closed to the public. For approximately a dozen years, families from around the globe who had lost loved ones on 9/11 could visit the Family Room, and they could leave their own tokens of remembrance. As Tara Snow Hanson explains on a website devoted to providing information about the Family Room, this special location "served as a place for mourning, especially for those who never received the remains of their loved ones."[50]

Over the years, what began as a wooden platform on a surviving building was transformed into part of a familial movement, as the administrators of the National September 11 Memorial and Memorial Museum decided, in April 2014, to open up a new Family Room. This one would build on the symbolism of the One Liberty Plaza room by establishing a committee that would attempt to document, interpret, and preserve the materials and panels that had been a part of the Liberty Plaza Family Room. This transfer, according to Tara Hanson, illustrated how the new Family Room might provide a tangible connection to the room's historical legacy," and the New York State Museum would later be given the task of preserving what could now be viewed by members of the public.[51] After September 2014, for the first time in more than thirteen years, the photographs, private messages, and other memorabilia that had belonged to the victims' families were put on display at the New York Museum in Albany.[52]

Conclusion

We have argued that the National September 11 Memorial and Memorial Museum is a securitized space of remembrance that has juxtaposed many different emplacements into one setting, and this mixture clearly bothered family members who were interested in more idealistic, utopian usages of these spaces and places. Marita Sturken once asked, "To whom does the site of Ground Zero belong—to the city, the Port Authority, the developers, the families of the dead, the architects who re-envision it, the tourists, the media, or the nation?"[53] Some of the families obviously could answer this question in their own ways by reminding us of ever-present Jihadist foes. They would also answer that question in dingpolitik ways, by asking us what some objects, like the "white rose," could tell us about some victims' birthdays.[54]

From a post-structuralist vantage point, it is impossible to essentialize and only focus attention on the reverential functions of this place, even though some victims' families have attempted to do just that. After all, what has occurred at Ground Zero has been nothing shy of what Judith Butler calls the politics of mourning.[55]

The echoes of myriad cosmopolitan, universalizing, or multicultural architectural ideas that were circulated during the first decade of the twenty-first century remain with us, and they need to be juxtaposed with the more monolithic, idealistic visions of American exceptionalists who wanted to underscore the heroism of first responders or the resilience of family members who left messages for their loved ones just minutes before they died.

This fetishization of "stuff" is in many ways resonant with the work done by Clare Pettitt[56] and Bill Brown[57] regarding the symbolic attachment and commemorative value of things from the past, but we want to highlight the populist nature of some of the persuasive arguments that had patriotic, reverential, or nationalistic overtones.

As we will explain in more detail in later chapters, the realpolitik and dingpolitik arrangements in the museum—from the textual biographies of the dead to the displays that beckoned viewers to think about the nineteen terrorists who caused so much havoc—blurred with material realities to commemorate U.S. losses and traumas in particular and strategic ways.

In some cases, the need to remember the losses of the victims' families become *our* potential losses as we are invited by Burlingame and others to feel that in spite of the passage of years, our insecure world may bring another attack on the homeland if we do not learn the lessons that can be taught by the dead.

As mentioned earlier in this chapter, many are not happy that the remains of their loved ones might be turning into a "dog and pony show."[58] One survivor said the museum "was made for people who don't really know what 9/11 is about."[59] Another blithely stated he "won't visit it anytime soon" because "it promises to be filled with gawking, ghoulish out-of-towners who will overwhelm the New Yorkers, who lived through the sorrow of those days and will have a hard time getting in."[60] Sadly, this reminds us just how many Americans lived through those horrific times.

And recall that the museum is almost entirely underground, absent of natural light. The recordings of people screaming during the attacks, the ghostly objects left behind, and the chilling narratives of those who were never found put visitors themselves in a victimized subject position that must always be on the lookout for terrorist activities.

In sum, we believe that heuristic critical frames that take in all of this trauma open up a gateway for understanding how commemoration works as a material, unfolding force that brings together a clash of dominant and subjugated knowledges. The Take Back the Memorial Movement may have derailed the efforts of those who wanted to build the International Freedom Center, but it did not have total control over these heterotopic spaces of remembrance. The movement's power did mean, however, that it could form alliances with those who wanted to rush to naturalize counterterrorist activities and their varied representations.

4

Melancholic Commemoration and "Policing" at the National September 11 Memorial, 2011–2014

On the tenth anniversary of the September 11 terrorist attacks, the National September 11 Memorial opened to special guests, including family members, first responders, and invited politicians. It was a somber day full of reflection and contemplation. New York firefighters Joe Conzo and Miguel Flores were among those who walked these sacred grounds on this special day of commemoration. Reflecting on some of the delays in constructing the memorial would become a part of all of this memory-making; Conzo told journalists that the memorial "should have been built years ago." He was nevertheless "pleased to see the memorial open to the public and to see the Freedom Tower rising from the ashes." Flores said that the city was "healing." "It's closure," Conzo added. "We lost so many."[1]

Although some, like Conzo and Flores, talked about how the memorial provided them with spaces for healing from the wounds of September 11, there was also the sense that national anxieties about the GWOT and the local worries about the "policing" of this part of Lower Manhattan helped with the securitization of these memorial spaces between 2011 and 2014. This time frame is unique because it was a momentary pause for all the stakeholders who had contributed to the architectural formation of this site. They could now stand back and reflect on what they had created, making decisions about the future securitization and reterritorialization of the site.

Indeed, between the opening of the memorial on September 11, 2011, and that of the museum on May 15, 2014, numerous fissures opened up and allowed for potential critiques of the "idealistic," utopian stances of the families we mentioned in previous chapters. There were also legal disagreements, for instance, between a coalition of local residents who called themselves the WTC Neighborhood Alliance and the New York City Police Department (NYPD) about whether the securitization of space had gone *too* far. Even though deputy police commissioner Paul Browne said that the NYPD and port authorities were working "to provide for a safe, inviting and commercially viable World Trade Center site," and not a "fortress-like environment,"[2] leaders of a local community board were not so sure. They felt that their neighborhood was fast becoming a sort of militarized space that was utterly different from the rest of Lower Manhattan.

This chapter continues our chronicling of all of this realpolitik by focusing on what could be called the "policing" of the National September 11 Memorial and Memorial Museum. By this we mean that the local NYPD worked in performative ways to illustrate how they, like the military warriors fighting in places like Afghanistan and Iraq, were also involved with homeland security. They were still being hypervigilant and were not going to be left out of the discussions regarding the shapes, contours, and purposes of these hallowed spaces.

As we explain in more detail below, the NYPD and its supporters in the years before the opening of the museum constantly battled with those who seemed to forget about the terrorist dangers that confronted the citizens of New York City. What some might regard as fearmongering could be configured as prudential urban planning.

Those who lived in Lower Manhattan, and those who visited this space before 2014, could not help noticing that with the passage of years, it seemed as if there was even more policing of these sacred spaces and places. Architects and politicians talked about open skylines and spacious views, but locals who witnessed the construction of the National

September 11 Memorial viewed matters differently. One resident said, "We see ourselves surrounded by a 'fortresslike' environment with the creation of a security perimeter around the W.T.C. site."[3] To David Dunlap of the *New York Times*,

> much of the security apparatus we develop, it seems . . . is meant to project our strength. But what it says is, 'Yikes . . . Ultimately, both the Trade Center and the Stock Exchange will never be fully integrated because the physical barriers always say, 'This is a danger zone.' We're scared something really bad could happen here.[4]

This example of a material ontology—where the dingpolitik of the physical barriers spoke volumes—reinforced and reiterated the securitized messages coming from the NYPD.

From a poststructural vantage point, the absence of another attack on New York's Ground Zero spaces could be interpreted in a number of ways. It could mean that the probable risks of a similar attack by terrorists were always low, or that the securitized measures put in place by groups like the NYPD were efficaciously deterring would-be terrorists. How would all of this securitization impact the memorial spaces in and around the National September 11 Memorial?

For years, numerous residents wanted to return to a sense of normalcy and perhaps not have to obsess about the transition of the residential areas around the World Trade Center into something like the infamous "Green Zone" in Iraq. The WTC Neighborhood Alliance, for example, went so far as to advance arguments against the NYPD's master plan before the New York Supreme Court in 2013. While this moment could have restricted, if not annulled, the possibility that Ground Zero would be characterized as a perpetual terrorist target, the court ruled in favor of the NYPD's security apparatus, echoing the concerns of the police as it accepted the argument that these hallowed grounds had to be securitized for the prevention of future attacks.

From an argumentative point of view, this was a key rhetorical moment, since after the ruling, momentum grew as other observers thought that the NYPD had passed a critical test in legitimating their positions on necessitous security. The department would now have a great deal of discretion as its officers policed these memorial spaces.

Civil servants interested in local governmentality added to the hegemonic power of the NYPD. Cries for more public, and less securitized, space were drowned out as those who crafted rhetorics of insecurity now had the imprimatur of the New York court system. As Mayor Bloomberg noted on the tenth anniversary of the attacks, "[This] morning is an opportunity for us to reflect on the progress we've made downtown—and across our city—since that tragic Tuesday morning when we suffered what I think is fair to say is the most deadly [*sic*] foreign attack in U.S. history, and it is a chance to recommit ourselves to the work we've done to honor all those we've lost."[5] To Bloomberg, security officials kept New York City "safe from terrorism thanks to the strong partnerships the NYPD has forged with state and federal agencies, and thanks to investments we've made in creating the largest, most sophisticated counter-terrorism operation of any city. That's what's keeping us safe, that's what we have to continue."[6] This type of rhetoric emboldened members of the NYPD as they prepared to debate other stakeholders who may not have shared these views.

This kind of discourse illustrates what we call *argumentative ossification*, where select dispositifs become entrenched in ways that help naturalize and normalize the police states that might *presumptively* be needed to supplement military efforts during times of emergency. We mentioned the nascent development of that presumptiveness in the previous chapter, but new layers of symbolicity were added when the NYPD joined the fray.

In the same way the first responders would become heroes in 9/11 tales, the act of policing the 9/11 memorial performatively proved that local police forces were also patrolling the homeland. Is it possible that this ossification at home complemented what scholars elsewhere refer to as the "perpetual" war overseas? Comments like Bloomberg's helped craft and maintain the security assemblages that configured the World Trade Center as a key nodal point for countering potential terrorist attacks.

In this portion of the book we study all of this legitimation of necessitous civilian policing, and we focus on how the NYPD, and other allied policing communities, were able, between 2011 to 2014, to help turn this space and place into an essential rampart that would symbolically help aid American military forces who were fighting terrorist foes. Debates in courtrooms were just one part of these policing and securitizing assemblages, and how one responded to these NYPD efforts often depended on how one felt about the purposes of memorial commemoration, the role of local police, and even New Yorkers' responses to the militarization of their city.

Other scholars in communication studies have commented on the role that military forces, intelligence communities, nongovernmental organizations, peacekeepers, and others played in the formation of this taken-for-granted security apparatus, but as Philip Cerny argued in *International Politics* in 2015, we need to be attentive to the ways that the "civilianisation of security" in globalized contexts has also empowered many police communities.[7] Military forces sent to fight overseas "contingency" operations have been asked to tread lightly and act like police personnel to win "hearts and minds"(called "counterinsurgency" or COIN), and domestic police forces have in turn been empowered to weaponize in ways that helps local citizens feel more secure.

By extending some of the work produced by the growing ranks of interdisciplinary scholars interested in critical investigations of these morphing policing powers, we use this chapter to illustrate how the policing of memorials, exhibitions, monuments, museums, and other spaces of a nation's "civil religion" can contribute to the nationalistic production of securitized spaces during wartime.

As we noted in previous chapters, local, regional, and national audiences working in several public and elite venues after 9/11 had plenty of opportunities to turn Ground Zero into something other than a walled fortress, but in Lower Manhattan, institutional stakeholders, including the NYPD, succeeded in using days of commemoration, court appearances, interviews with journalists, and other events as rhetorical opportunities for commenting on the need for hypersecuritization of Ground Zero. Between 2011 and 2014 both mainstream and social media outlets were filled with commentary on the ways that the police who worked in and around the National September 11 Memorial and Memorial Museum were helping to prevent the next local terrorist attack. Was this unnecessary threat-inflation that stroked the egos of those who wanted to feel like civilian warriors, or did New York publics, jurists, and others believe that the NYPD was responding to actual, and persistent, terrorist threats?

Earlier we alluded to the ways that diverse texts and visualities were used before 2011 to help U.S. communities cope with feelings of loss, absence, and vulnerability, and many visitors who came to this memorial heard about the necessitous nature of security checkpoints, countless surveillance cameras, and on-guard military personnel. What type of subject position is assumed by the police or by the visitors who come to Ground Zero?

As critical scholars we are concerned with the ways that some policing practices and assemblages may contribute to the coproduction of counterterrorist formations that interact with terrorist histories and memories in dynamic ways. Bruce Janz, for example, has remarked that some "othered" spaces of surveillance can become "places in terror" that "do not alleviate this terror in place, but rather re-assert it."[8] Certain formations of bricks and mortar, along with political speeches and police actions, create the very terrorist scenarios that they argue they are preparing for. Has the NYPD policing of these particular grounds helped with the creation of one of those situations?

All of the realpolitik and dingpolitik that swirled around Ground Zero would be (re)produced by the presence of impenetrable gates, fences, and barricades that surrounded the National September 11 Memorial between 2011 and 2014. Is it any coincidence that movement through the "temporary" security checkpoints required tourists and other visitors to show security guards (that is to say, the NYPD) special tickets? Omnipresent security cameras aided those who appeared to be blurring the lines between policing and militarizing as they tried to securitize this site. For example, some defenders were carrying sniper rifles and radiation detectors.[9] These are the weapons of war, helping produce a strategic "politics of things."

Others have written about the fatal shooting of a young black man by a white police officer in Ferguson, Missouri, and the politicized meanings of police purchases of old military weaponry used during Operation Iraqi Freedom and other counterterrorist campaigns, but we display here how a nation's museums and memorials can be appropriated for a variety of military and policing functions. Those already predisposed to feel insecure after 9/11 now face reinforcing performances in Lower Manhattan that encourage many stakeholders to feel as if the war against terrorism will never end.

We are convinced that too many of those who studied the memorializing or historicizing practices of the National September 11 Memorial and Memorial Museum have assiduously avoided studying the ideological nature of the policing features of Lower Manhattan securitization. As noted in the introductory chapter, there are many studies of the healing, the feelings of patriotism, and the compassion that swirls around this edifice, but this focus on the uplifting features of this memory-work—while important—dodges the question of how the museum, and the policing of the museum, are also agentic.

In the same ways that airport screening, retinal detection, disposal of improvised explosive devices, and other forms of dingpolitik complement the realpolitik that is used to rationalize the use of drones, special raids, and even President Trump's MOAB ("Mother of all Bombs") strike at Taliban targets in Afghanistan, our policing of major tourist sites reinforces the dominant messages of those who want publics to continue to fund counterterrorist ventures.[10]

The remainder of this chapter advances the speculative argument that during this transitory period under discussion, many members of the NYPD tried to turn Ground Zero into an idyllic, securitized space as they debated those who were more comfortable with less policing of this memorial space. Did this NYPD intervention, aided by the public memories of 9/11, allow for the formation of *heterochronias* (similitudes of temporal differences) that were utterly different from anywhere else in New York and, for that matter, the United States? Or was all of this local policing a microcosm of more globalized security apparatus?

Since the introduction, we have been emphasizing the role that elite and public argumentation has played in many memorial and museological controversies, and here we display not only the efforts of the NYPD but also others who intentionally or unintentionally aided their securitizing efforts. Our critical security readings underscore the point that many social agents—the NYPD, court authorities, politicians—helped with the securitization of Ground Zero.

We support these claims by proffering analysis of the arguments that came from local residents who expressed concern about both the policing and the militarization of their neighborhoods, the NYPD counterterrorist bureau members who saw themselves as freedom fighters, and the politicians who talked about how security measures have helped America recover. We go so far as to claim that even members of the New York Supreme Court—who may not have viewed themselves as stakeholders—intervened and impacted the institutional legitimacy of all of this policing.

Later on in the chapter, as we provide an example of the critical participation we mentioned in the introduction, we take advantage of the personal insights that came when one of us traveled to the National September 11 Memorial and Memorial Museum on four different occasions in May 2012, September 2014, May 2016, and September 2017, but we begin by commenting on policing that took place on the tenth anniversary of 9/11/01.

Anniversaries and the Argumentative Ossification of Securitizing Memorial Space

When the National September 11 Memorial was first unveiled to the public on September 12, 2011, it was safeguarded by a phalanx of police and other personnel who became part of an extraordinary security apparatus. Make no mistake; this building up of security arsenals, checkpoints, and other accoutrements was incremental over some ten years. Armed security guards surrounded the site, the streets were "barricaded and closed off to traffic" while the memorial itself was "gated off" to the general public, and there were "layers of security checkpoints on some blocks."[11] It was "some of the tightest security in recent memory," said reporter Erik Ortiz, especially considering that the NYPD received "reports" of possible terrorist attacks.[12] This type of reportage—by both the police and the reporters who covered their actions—linked September 12, 2011, worries to the horrors of 9/11.

As far as the NYPD and their supporters were concerned, the threat of another terrorist attack was never far away, and it was especially evident on the tenth anniversary of the attacks, when the memorial's very opening contributed to the elevated symbolicity of the site. After all, if disgruntled members of al Qaeda, the Taliban, or other aggrieved parties from Afghanistan, Iraq, Pakistan, and elsewhere were looking for an opportune moment to strike at America's vulnerable spaces and places, was not this the day?

In the eyes of the NYPD, the tenth anniversary of 9/11 created the perfect storm that could aid those who wanted to carry out potential terrorist strikes. So when security officials received word from a CIA informant in Pakistan warning of a possible bomb plot by al Qaeda terrorists to avenge the death of Osama bin Laden,[13] the whole area was on lockdown. Admittedly, NYPD spokesman Paul Browne said this "may well be industry-savvy thieves looking to steal expensive construction equipment, but it's receiving greater scrutiny because of the threat environment."[14] Note the way this statement was referencing the social agency of equipment sales personnel but not the police.

Even though the conversation appears to be a mundane one about expensive construction equipment, notice how commentary on ordinary building equipment can quickly be linked to talk of exceptional or temporary emergency measures during precarious times. These links, in turn, have a way of influencing our nonemergency daily lives and the power of those who act in the name of public safety, health, and welfare. To the assistant commissioner of the Counterterrorism Bureau of the NYPD, the security measures that law enforcement and counterterrorism units were taking was all part of a routine. "The high state of readiness that you see is going to be maintained," he said.[15]

Commenting on the status of the threat, he stated, "Nothing has really changed."[16] At the same time, the NYPD was on alert about possible threats from a missing North Carolina man who was "addicted to pills," armed, and heading to Ground Zero.[17] "The importance of security at this site, which has seen two terrorist attacks in the last 20 years, cannot be overstated," a Law Department spokesperson said.[18] The contexts behind those attacks, and the talk of rarity of any actual attacks, was replaced with *possibilistic* argumentation.

While the police were on constant guard against potential terrorist attacks at any moment, New Yorkers and other stakeholders were coproducing rhetorics on the necessity and effectivity of securitizing spaces that would ward off what Peter Schuck calls "citizen terrorists."[19] After all, didn't the period between 2011 and 2014 also witness spikes in studies of domestic terrorists, vigilantism, lone wolves, and other threats that exacerbated the problems of police who were already having to anticipate dangers posed by network-centric foreign enemies?

In this intermediate temporal period, between the opening of the memorial and the opening of the museum, it could be argued that the views of the victims' families were not always taking center stage. Nor would it be the commentary about the architect's plans, or the cost of funding these Lower Manhattan projects, that preoccupied journalists. Instead, it would be the issue of individual and communal public safety that became the dominant topic of conversation in these social dramas, and the police became some of the protagonists in these securitization narratives.

Note the differences in tone and attitude of those who were no longer traumatized by the immediate aftermath of 9/11. The passage of years had altered the evolutionary nature of both rhetorics of insecurity and security. For some ten years, stakeholders had gradually—sometimes grudgingly—come to reason that places like London, Madrid, and Paris might have to worry about the next Jihadist terrorism, but the local police in New York were helping prevent the next 9/11 here at home.

For many of those who commented on all of this policing, the fact that only two attacks had occurred (1993 and 2001) was not evidence of contested knowledge or minimal risk but rather *positive proof* that vigilant policing was paying off for New Yorkers living in and around Lower Manhattan. On the tenth anniversary Luis Bautista could tell reporters that he felt "extremely safe," and even though out "there's like Halloween," and you "never know what to expect," you could still take comfort from all of the police protection.[20]

Others, however, were frustrated with all the extraprecautionary security measures put in place by the NYPD. Many local residents, in particular, were irritated with the way that (in)securitization was interfering with their day-to-day life. After ten years the absence of another attack could be taken as evidence that the 9/11 attackers had been lucky and could never have succeeded if minimal security measures had been put in place before 9/11. Was all of this continual security really necessary for those who simply wanted to walk by the memorial or pay their respects to the dead?

Many of these concerns had occasionally manifested themselves before 2012, but some image events magnified and amplified these worries. Although security matters had always been broached by those who spoke about the safety of the neighborhoods surrounding Ground Zero, the opening of the 9/11 memorial intensified matters and created new, proliferating concerns for NYPD officials. To Joe Coscarelli of *New York Magazine*, "even with the specter of September 11 hovering, there's nothing less New York City than a gated community."[21] Why were the police acting as if they were in Baghdad or Kabul?

It was not just the difficulties involved with the collection of trash that were frustrating local residents. Many were expressing general concern over what they might have perceived to be the police occupation of their neighborhoods. One resident of Manhattan, John Ost, commented in the *New York Post* that the "neighborhood in the area surrounding 1 Police Plaza looks like an occupied Third World nation. With all the existing video surveillance in that area, it is time for the NYPD to pull back from our neighborhood."[22] Another told CBS that the "police seem to be doing everything for the tourists at the expense of the community."[23] While the police may have felt that they were aiding counterterrorist efforts here at home, that was not the way others viewed this hypersurveillance.

In fact, security went so far that the NYPD identified local trash cans as objects of insecurity, as police officers argued that they could be used as storehouses for terrorist bombs. The resulting absence of public waste bins from the streets, of course, was met with frustration from local residents who complained about the piles of garbage stacking up on their doorsteps. One resident who lived on Cedar Street complained that it's "not like we have no garbage cans at all. . . . If someone wanted to drop a package or a bomb, they could use one of the existing cans. It doesn't make sense."[24] Another resident, John Gomes, who resided on Greenwich Street, expressed irritation over the way visitors polluted the streets with all kinds of trash, such as wrappers and soda cans. Without some sort of "*terrorproof* bins," "there's nowhere else to put" all of the garbage, he said. "Where does trash go?" he asked. "It's trash on top of trash."[25] Apparently, it is "better safe than sanitary!" commented Kate Briquelet of the *New York Post*.[26]

From a critical security vantage point, post-9/11 police skills, technologies, and dispositifs were simply not the same as they were before the attack on the Twin Towers, and what might have seemed as micromanagement could now be configured as efficacious police work. In response to some of the local criticism, Paul Browne of the NYPD Counterterrorism Bureau claimed that bombs are too easily made inconspicuous when mixed in with rummage. "It's a question of improved security by keeping a relatively small area free of trash and sweeping trash from streets as opposed to emptying trash cans."[27] The securitization of trash, then, is another example not only of Latourian dingpolitik but also of what Woolgar and Neyland have called "mundane governance" wherein governmentalities shape how "our lives are regulated and controlled by 'unremarkable objects and technologies.'"[28]

Public and institutional disagreements over objects as mundane as trash cans indicate the level of discomfort that many local residents were having amid the securitization of their neighborhood. While citizens across the nation were being regaled with metanarratives filled with talk of heroism and resilience, many locals just wanted their lives back. Meanwhile, Mayor Bloomberg was making national headlines with speeches reinforcing the importance of remembering the cost of 9/11 by claiming, "We will never forget those we lost. The Memorial and the Museum right here will help ensure that. And we must never forget the lessons of that day. . . . Freedom is not free."[29] The mayor had his supporters, but others questioned the costs of this messaging. The use of symbolic language might resonate with national and international audiences who were reading about NYPD activities or the mayor's speeches, but locals were complaining that they could not take out their trash because of perceived terrorist threats.

The legitimation of the NYPD policing of Ground Zero involved the discursive suturing together of many viewpoints, metaphors, allusions, and other figurations. It was no coincidence that many citizens not only heard some of these securitized rhetorics but also internalized them and recirculated permutations of these arguments as they witnessed the transformation of their neighborhood into an "armed bunker."[30] Some might come to ask, Is Ground Zero becoming more like a citadel, or even a fortress, than a therapeutic place for the living to grieve and recover? Is mourning even made possible for those trying to recover from the trauma of 9/11 when visitors are greeted with armed officers prepared for war? How much agency do local residents have in the security aesthetic of Ground Zero when many of them lived in the community most affected by the September 11, 2001, terrorist attacks?

These were the sorts of questions mulled over during mediated coverage of a 2013 New York Supreme Court case where a group of residents called the WTC Neighborhood Alliance challenged the NYPD's master security plan. As noted above, to many of them, Ground Zero had indeed become a "walled fortress,"[31] and that meant, perhaps, that the NYPD's securitization efforts had gone too far.

Legal Buttressing of Securitizing Ideologies

In the 2014 case *Mary Perillo v. Kelly*, plaintiff WTC Neighborhood Alliance asserted that the NYPD's security plan for the WTC complex not only was excessive but was turning a neighborhood into a "fortress-like isolation" as "impervious to traffic as the Berlin Wall."[32] Journalists and laypersons soon learned that the legal basis for the plaintiff's case involved not some traditional tort claim for damages but rather a charge based on problems with the NYPD's environmental impact statement (EIS) for the site.

For those who care about the Latourian aspects of these controversies, issues related to hazards or toxicity or debris were matters that occupied the attention of many during and after the 9/11 attacks. Füsun Türetken, writing in *Forensis* in 2014, explained:

> In the early hours of September 11, 2001, NYPD Detective James Zadroga arrived at Ground Zero in Lower Manhattan to take part in the recovery efforts. He stepped onto this debris and took his first breath on site. When breathing this debris pile, one inevitably inhaled the amalgamated toxicity of September 11: the building itself, the planes, the components and the trash that makes our daily environment, as well as the traces of human bodies. . . . With the body, buildings, objects, and other bodies intermeshed in this way, the source of any toxic element found in the "assembled" body became inextricable. The capacity to link the original evidence (the microfibers or molecules in the air) to the forensic evidence in order to make legal claims on the part of the "forgotten victims" of September 11 thus remains a difficult venture.[33]

This assemblage, however, would not be the only one posing challenges for police and legal forces.

Many other environmental junctures and fissures were features of these complex assemblages. For example, technical arguments about urbanization and traffic flows around the National September 11 Memorial became topics in texts required by the National Environmental Policy Act for actions "significantly affecting the quality of the human environment."[34] The plaintiffs' lawyers were interested in going after the police for failing "to explain and generally [suppressing] the N.Y.P.D.'s rationale for critical aspects of the plan based on a purported need for secrecy."[35]

The arguments advanced in this case tested the NYPD's rhetorical arguments that sustained the securitization of memorial space, especially in jurisprudential settings, because now they were having to discuss issues that, at first glance, may not have had anything to do with the usual constitutional or criminal rationales used by those with a great deal of discretion during times of emergency. Could the NYPD find a way of rationalizing the existence of that tightly knit security apparatus when they had to confront local citizens who could find creative ways of framing neighborhood needs?

Members of the WTC Neighborhood Alliance asserted that the NYPD overlooked the local effect of extensive security measures and failed to include public participation when crafting its security plan (see chapter 2). The plaintiffs could highlight the negative effects of closing off local streets to vehicular traffic, and requiring all vehicles to go through state-of-the-art security screening at the Vehicle Security Center, for instance, was detrimental to locals' quality of life by congesting their neighborhoods with millions of tourists, polluting the air, and mitigating public space. In other words, the case was a fissure that challenged the absolute securitization of space. As the main petitioner, Ms. Perillo, put it in her affidavit: "I live in the City of New York—not on campus or a gated community. I do not want to prove who I am to come home to my own apartment."[36]

The specific arguments enumerated by the petitioners included a laundry list of items that the NYPD failed to take under consideration when they crafted their EIS. This catalog of proposed amendments— sent to the NYPD on March 12, 2012—included nineteen proposals for consideration, among them not-so-veiled argumentative critiques of police practices. For example, the list mentioned increased "pedestrian flow into and out of the WTC site and surrounding area to . . . prevent the creation of a 'fortress' environment"; a more transparent perimeter; "unobstructed access for residents, workers and visitors to and from the Memorial Plaza"; diversion of pedestrian and vehicular congestion on local streets; the impacts of police, firefighters, emergency service personnel, parked vehicles, traffic, and security infrastructure around the WTC site, and other concerns.[37]

What the residents wanted, in sum, was *less securitization* of what was otherwise public and residential space. Because the NYPD implemented a federal EIS for the WTC's security plan without "taking a 'hard look' at critical areas of environmental concern" or adopting alternative proposals, the WTC Neighborhood Alliance could argue that the NYPD security plan should be annulled, since it does not comply with mandates of the State Environmental Quality Review Act (SEQRA) and the city's environmental review rules.[38] Those rules required state authorities to go through certain public procedurals before submitting the EIS, such as making it available to the public and taking into consideration comments made at public hearings.

This case seemed to serve as a judicial condensation symbol for all types of grievances that had been building up over the previous twelve years, not all of which had anything to do with al Qaeda or the financing costs of rebuilding in and around the voids at the memorial. Residents such as Perillo contended that the security plan "favors the concerns of tourists over those of the City Residents,"[39] and that the effect of implementing such a plan would create an "even more dramatic drop in quality of life in [their] neighborhood,"[40] which was already a place where residents were coping with tourists trying to get closer to Ground Zero. Another resident said in an affidavit, "With as many as 42 tour buses at peak hours at the height of the tourist crush in constant motion or gridlocked, along with car, truck and taxi traffic . . . the air quality will be worse than ever."[41] To the WTC Neighborhood Alliance's lawyer, Albert K Butzel, "these are people who know first-hand about the destruction that terrorism can cause . . . so they take security very seriously. But they also value quality of life, and fear that this is what will be destroyed by this plan."[42] Urban sprawl, environmental degradation, traffic control, property valuation, and quality of life were issues that became entangled in all of this judicial squabbling.

The petitioners also argued that the security measures implemented by the NYPD overlooked certain scenarios that it would not be able to prevent; thus, enforcing many of the NYPD micromanagement security measures could be deemed excessive and unnecessary.

We might imagine this argument would be one of the hardest-hitting on those who pride themselves on their police professionalism and their ability to stand shoulder to shoulder with others who wore uniforms in the service of their country. One affidavit, from the group's security expert, Richard Roth, an executive director at a security consulting, planning, and design firm called Counter Technology, said the underground Vehicular Security Center runs "counter to a fundamental criterion of security planning . . . because blast injuries and other effects are intensified by such spaces due to the enormous pressure and degree of focusing from the walls and ceilings."[43] This, to Roth, warranted off-site inspection. He asked, "What if there was a bomber[,] waiting in line for inspection, [who] panics and detonates the explosives while still outside the security campus? Disastrous!" To Ross, "the 'fortress-like defenses' proposed by the NYPD" could at least be "softened" with the use of alternative safety measures such as "head bangers" that serve as "height limit barriers."[44]

Obviously realpolitik and dingpolitik concerns were not just the province of police officers and local planners who built barricades and put up security cameras. Those who objected to what they viewed as unnecessary hypervigilance could take advantage of the discursive power of securitized rhetorics as they used contradictory arguments to put on display the lack of security that might have embarrassed those who took pride in their micromanagement of the spaces and places around Ground Zero.

As if the critiques of securitization were not enough, the WTC Neighborhood Alliance could also launch arguments against the NYPD security plan that had to do with references to pollutants from tour buses visiting the National September 11 Memorial and the dangerous health effects of x-ray, gamma, and neutron radiation from inspections. These arguments focused on police facilitation of increased tourist traffic, which contributed to poor air quality in and around the memorial.[45]

In response to the WTC Neighborhood Alliance's arguments, the

NYPD submitted affidavits from its authorities such as David Kelly, the assistant commissioner of the Counterterrorism Bureau, and Lieutenant Thomas Ferramosca, from the Threat Reduction/Infrastructure Protection Section of the bureau, who defended the securitizing of the WTC site. They explained how the security master plan allowed the NYPD to adhere to all of the public dimensions of policy that were stipulated by SEQRA.

Legal representatives of the NYPD noted how the master plan already went through various revisions, such as the 2005 amendment to include the Vehicular Security Center, and this revision had built on the work of those who arranged public comment periods by the Federal Transit Administration and the Port Authority, the agency responsible for developing and operating the center.[46]

As readers might imagine, after outlining their compliance with various public input requirements, the defenders of the NYPD decision moved toward a robust discussion of existential terrorist threats in New York. Ferramosca argued for preservation of the security plan due to its "robust[ness] in warding off 'vehicle-borne explosive devices'" similar to the one used in the 1993 WTC bombing and the 9/11/01 terrorist attacks, since the WTC site "continues to be a top terrorist target."[47] Even though Ferramosca understood the arguments for less security, to him, the security plan is designed to "balanc[e] the needs for security" with "the needs of commercial and retail enterprises, and the access needs by local residents and businesses."[48] In other words, the NYPD had heard these arguments before—they were simply advocating that the courts accept different hierarchies of needs and recognize that they had already done the "balancing" of rights and interests that was expected of those who cared about public safety.

In a somewhat crucial decision for the future of the WTC site, the judge, Margaret Chan, sided with the NYPD in ruling that its EIS for the security plan was neither "capricious" nor "an abuse of discretion"[49] and had been completed in accordance with the law. In technical legal parlance, the court was using the *legitimate state interest test*, one of minimal scrutiny of administrative decisions where institutional powers like the NYPD must show only that their actions are related to some "reasonable" state interest. In theory, as long as the decisions of the police were not arbitrary, capricious, or unreasonable, then Judge Chan was going to follow the traditional legal formalisms that deferred to the judgment of those who were tasked with public safety missions.

In this case, Chan found that the NYPD met all of the public requirements for implementing its security plan, and she seemed to be arguing implicitly that the security plan itself was necessary. In her opinion, Chan specifically addressed the plaintiffs' arguments about the closing off of streets and the isolation of the WTC from other areas. Was it true that some of this design unreasonably interfered with traffic flow?

Chan appeared to be recontextualizing some of the plaintiffs' arguments when she averred that the new plan provides *more* public spaces for pedestrians and cyclists than there were prior to September 11, 2001. "As many residents in Manhattan either walk or bike to neighboring areas, the design makes it easier to connect with other neighborhoods."[50] Regarding the proximity of security devices to neighborhoods, the court said the NYPD took into consideration the day-to-day public life in the area and so it was "not made in a vacuum."[51]

At the same time that Chan responded to these trafficking issues, she also weighed in on questions having to do with potential hypersecuritization. "The WTC site does not resemble a 'walled city' at all," the opinion stated. "To the contrary," she said, "there [is] plenty of open green space in the plan. There are no 'walls' to speak of that would isolate the WTC site from its neighboring areas. The only features that are somewhat uninviting are the security measures such as the sally ports and police security checkpoints" that she decided not only were necessary but "blend in with the streetscape."[52]

Judge Chan seemed to be wearing an architectural-design lens as she blended rhetorics of aesthetics, space and place, and securitization in her hagiographic depiction of an ideal way of carrying out unobtrusive urban planning. Was it possible that she was joining those who believed in the ontological existence of terrorist threats? Was she giving her warranted assent to the NYPD's epistemic framings of those threats?

Apparently dispassionate legal decision-making could mask judicial acceptance of hegemonic securitizing postures.

For those laypersons who accept the counterterrorist premises and warrants that were supplied by NYPD lawyers and Judge Chan, and for others not bothered by the hegemonic nature of these securitizing practices, this particular case may appear to be benign, commonplace, or even frivolous. However, from a more critical vantage point, these empowered actors were contributing to the argumentative ossification of a securitized memorial space that reproduces insecurities to justify the ubiquity of security.

While we grant that the WTC Neighborhood Alliance may have been trying to use procedural technicalities as a way to gain judicial interventionism that would help with more substantive law issues, this case does not hide the possibility that between 2011 and 2014, an increased number of stakeholders in New York, and throughout America, were feeling confident enough to rationalize controversial policing measures.

Judge Chan was not some neutral arbiter; she was a social actor who intervened and help reinforce the dominant ideologies of (in)security that were purveyed by institutional forces like the NYPD.

These securitizing arguments appeared to be so persuasive that even some of the plaintiffs involved in the *Mary Perillo v. Kelly* case seemed to express wonder regarding their own priorities and transcendent values. For example, not long after the case was decided, plaintiff Mary Perillo thanked the NYPD for their time and their consideration, claiming that she more or less now had a better understanding of their viewpoint. "I'd like to say first of all thank you," she said at a community board meeting. "I see the logjam moving, I see that you're seeing what it's like on the ground a little bit."[53] Other residents, too, "felt their voices were being considered . . . for the first time in over a dozen years."[54]

In fact, it could be argued that some of the residents understood the necessity for so much security all along, but they may have felt that tourist concerns were overriding local input about securitized planning. Consider, for example, how the plaintiffs' lawyer in this case claimed that the locals "know what terrorism means because they were exposed directly to it, they know and accept there has to be some type of security."[55] What began as a critique of securitizing practices was turned into an opportunity to further ossify already strong security assemblages.

Instead of interrogating and questioning the origins, argumentative validity, and warrants that went into the creation of typical security apparatus in places like New York, this court provided a venue for legitimating and calcifying sedimentations that were strong even before they received Judge Chan's imprimatur. This court decision would make it even more difficult to question assertions made regarding permanence of emergency states, and it could be argued that this type of legal decision also contributed to the (in)securitization of the National September 11 Memorial and Memorial Museum.

Obviously, we are not arguing that the NYPD, or Judge Chan's courtroom, was doing anything that was not being performed in other places, from Afghanistan to California, Yemen to Pakistan. The particular memorializations of this museum included added touches to the American exceptionalist template that was coproduced by many who supported hypervigilance.

Consider, for instance, how just about every terrorist threat or tragic event during this period was situated within rhetorical frames of aggressive post-9/11 counterterrorism, and how few questioned the potential militarization of police forces that often looked as if they were blurring the traditional lines between domestic law enforcement and foreign counterinsurgency. Mass-mediated coverage of the Boston Marathon bombing, for instance, was used as another terrifying example where local communities and cities could become entangled in nationalistic securitization. Fighting and victoriously foiling terrorist plots, and crediting police with those victories, became stock figurations.

In the wake of the Boston Marathon bombing NYPD officials stood on high alert, especially when New York prepared for its own races such as the 9/11 Memorial 5K Run/Walk, the Family Day nearby Ground Zero, and the New York City Marathon. The irony is that while some decision makers mentioned the elevated security levels throughout the city in preparation for the upcoming events, the NYPD commissioner and Mayor Bloomberg were telling people not to "give in to fear" and to stay strong and resilient. "That's what we have to do," said Bloomberg, who was speaking about the necessity of preventing similar attacks in New York. "Go about our day, keep the victims of this awful tragedy in our thoughts and our prayers. Go about our business." Amplifying the rhetoric of resilience, the mayor also said, "It's our intention to have a marathon and to have all of the other events that make America, the state and the city what they are."[56]

We will have more to say about this resilience in other chapters, but for our purposes here we point out the contingent nature of all of this naturalization of what could have been contested securitization frameworks.

Mayor Bloomberg would be just one of the many argumentative performers who underscored New York's preparedness. Elsewhere, other people were also helping with the reaffirmation of police decisionism. After a successful, terrorist-free 9/11 Memorial 5K Run/Walk, one participant, Julie Shull, said, "We can't live in fear."[57] Others, wanting to show support for Boston, wore T-shirts with phrases such as "I run for Boston" on them, taking what Vera Chinese and Barry Paddock of the *New York Daily News* called "the added security in stride" in an article titled, "In Races, Fear Finishes Last." Governor Cuomo, who dedicated the 9/11 run to Bostonians, said, "We know the feeling, we know the anger, we know the pain."[58] "We are with you," NYPD commissioner Raymond Kelly added.[59] National sentiments override provincial concerns.

At the same time that people in several cities were building this argument assemblage—with Boston survivors reinforcing the perceived necessity of security—there were moments of self-reflection when one sensed that at least some citizens were wondering about the possible instrumental nature of some of this race planning. "Even to get into the Port-A-Potty, you had to go through a security check,"[60] one said. Security checks at places as mundane as portable toilets might be considered outrageous, but these microissues could be symbolically linked to macroissues. This connection was understandable, given the nature and the scope of the security apparatus and the rhetorical force of the ideologies that were being instantiated. Responding to one of the few incidents that did occur during the race—the removal of a baby stroller unattended during a trip to the bathroom—the mother of the three-year old child who ran in the race said, "If they say it's for everyone's safety, then that's what they have to do."[61] Again, dingpolitik merged with realpolitik.

Securitized Pilgrimages between 2011 and 2014

To those who have visited the National September 11 Memorial during the interim operating period of September 11, 2011, and May 25, 2014, it was described as "highly secured, with fences, a heavy police presence, and—of concern here—significant access-control"[62] that "almost precisely replicates that required to board an airplane."[63] When Elinor Light looked over all of this policing, she thought that the memorial produced the subject position of a surveilling flâneur or a "security conscious consumer whose gaze is conditioned through practices of consumption and surveillance."[64] To Light, the memorial "promotes the sense that although one is 'secure,' one's body is also always also being watched for the deadly and invisible markings of terrorism."[65] Drawing from Foucault's book *Discipline and Punish*, she suggests that "technologies of security and discipline . . . turn [the] gaze inward, producing a visceral unease, a 'sense' of being watched, and an anxiety of (in) security."[66] What police might regard as necessitous counterterrorism, then, could be recontextualized as intrusive and excessive surveillance.

Those who were suspicious enough to question some NYPD practices were censured for their idealism or incredulousness. Consider the comments made by Michael Goodwin in the *New York Post*:

The misguided souls and professional whiners determined to keep the New York Police Department handcuffed, blind and silent need a refresher course on terrorism. There are lots of good articles and books on the topic, but for the most powerful reminder of why we must stay vigilant, I recommend a visit to the 9/11 memorial. . . . The irony is that security concerns may never allow that openness. The Islamic fundamentalism that created the need for [Arad's] memorial is far from extinguished. Which is why it is distressing that there is a movement to have the NYPD drop its guard. The loudest and most vicious attacks—mostly from *The New York Times* editorial page, a few professional-victim Muslim groups and extreme libertarians— make it seem as if thousands of Muslims have been rounded up and sent to internment camps. . . . The critics are wrong, profoundly and dangerously. To cure their amnesia, they should make a pilgrimage to the 9/11 memorial and remember those we must never forget.[67]

Critical security scholars might point out that this missive makes several assumptions. First of all, it creates the impression that everyone recognizes the dangers presented by "Islamic fundamentalism" and that the police have the situational awareness to deal with those threats. Second, the writer of this passage implies that most Americans understand the need for hypervigilance, where liberals who control outlets like the *New York Times* worry about threat inflation. This commentary on a "pilgrimage" to this site illustrates how becoming a tourist to this hallowed ground is supposed to be not only a reverential experience but an eye-opening one. The sacred and the secular merge. Who, after all, after going to the National September 11 Memorial, could doubt the existential nature of enemy threats?

This typical calling for the instrumental usage of the National September 11 Memorial as a didactic tool for educating the nation about the necessity of hypervigilant policing is yet another example of calling for the material securitization of memorial space.

In what follows, we offer a reading of the memorial based on a May 2012 visit that builds on the work of those who care about critical participatory rhetoric. To us, the National September 11 Memorial at this time was a highly controlled security apparatus—a claim echoed by other researchers such as Light and Forest and Johnson. What we add to this discussion, however, is a slight modification of what we have said elsewhere and reaffirm here: that this securitized space is a form of "dark tourism," that is, adapted to the presentist needs of melancholic, and terrorized, subjects.

The Return of the Repressed: Public Mourning and the Performative Policing of the 9/11 Memorial and Museum

Many visitors and commentators often talk about their traumas, their need to mourn, and their respect for the sacrifices of those who died on September 11, but they also have to navigate some of the more haunting features of this hallowed space, and regardless of their political proclivities, they too have to decide what to do when confronted by the tightly controlled security apparatus. Long before reaching the waterfalls of the memorial, visitors pace through a securitized pavilion that constantly reminds them that this is still a haunted place, a potential target for terrorism, and cameras watch travelers' every step in the name of law and order.

When one of the authors first visited the memorial during the summer of 2012, the memorial had just opened to the public and the museum was still under construction. At that time, there was an exceptional number of closed-circuit television boxes in the memorial's terminal, and a mandatory security checkpoint ensured that all visitors went through security screens. Here, police authorities guided people through metal detectors after visitors waited in long lines protected by the NYPD. These authorized figures served as visual reminders of the continued importance of security, safety, and decorum. During this period, visitors were forced to walk through a narrow postsecurity corridor to the memorial's entrance, with cameras tracking every move.

Visitors are then presented with a wealth of acoustic and visual registers as they hear the tranquil sound of moving water. While the Towers' "footprints" (once "voids" before the addition of pools of water) cannot be seen for part of the walk, the sound of flowing water notifies people that they are near the two massive reflecting pools. The names of those who died on 9/11 are etched on bronze parapets that surround the voids.

The communal space that the architect Michael Arad once envisioned now covers a total of about sixteen acres, and a giant plaza includes the North and South Pool and the National September 11 Memorial Museum. While the North Pool contains the names of victims from the North Tower, the 1993 bombing, and Flight 11, the South Pool has the names of those from the first responders, the South Tower, Flight 93, Flight 77, the Pentagon, and Flight 175. This naming underscores the potential magnitude of past and present terrorist dangers.

The shimmering pools with the names are stunning, but before visitors get that far they walk across an enveloping space filled with four hundred swamp white oak trees. These trees are also natural symbols of devastation, because many came from the Washington DC and Pennsylvania locales hit by the 9/11 attacks. According to the 9/11 Memorial Commission website:

> [The trees] remember life with living forms, and serve as living representations of the destruction and renewal of life in their own annual cycles. The result is a memorial that expresses both the incalculable loss of life and its consoling regeneration.[68]

The design of the plaza theoretically "conveys a spirit of hope and renewal and creates a contemplative space separate from the usual sights and sounds of a bustling metropolis."[69]

Trees are everywhere, but cement walkways direct visitors to one of the main features of the memorial: the footprints. The footprints are the hollowed-out remains of the former World Trade Center. Here, in their vacancies, they are a key part of "reflective absences," the massive architectural counters that channel the symbolic water. For many commentators and visitors, this water is said to be a healing feature of the memorial, a material reality that influences how one contextualizes 9/11. Roger Denson, for example, argues that the falling water "is the embodiment of the gravity to which all things must submit," signifying key parts of "Arad's heightened sense of the theatrical virtuosity of minimalism and the 'truth to materials' functionalism."[70] Yet one wonders what happens when this minimalism in juxtaposed with other functionalist efforts.

While families of the dead may want to view this site as a place that needs more than minimalism, others may view the memorial in more therapeutic and cosmopolitan ways that have everything to do with surviving traumatic events. Institutional state forces may focus on preventing terrorism, but the metaphorical nature of water at least allows for the possibility that for a time, visitors can adopt interpretative frames that have little do to with security rhetorics.

Water flows may be viewed as polysemic and polyvalent in that they can convey many diverse messages, including pacifist ones, for numerous religious organizations. While the capacity to withstand physical immersion is an important sacrament within Christian doctrines, the primal ritual washing function of water is also relevant to Hinduism, Buddhism, Sikhism, Judaism, Shinto, Taoism, and Islam. Visitors of all ascetic backgrounds may identify with the rhetoric of rebirth associated with these water flows, inciting careful thought to the redemptive capacities of "reflection pools." Roger Denson remarked that the "waterfalls and reflecting pools are hypnotic, inducing the calm necessary for contemplation and spirituality."[71] Could these types of vantage points be used to critique the counterterrorist policing of these grounds?

There is no shortage of commentaries from visitors who write or talk about the potential healing power of the National September 11 Memorial. A visitor who lost her nephew in the World Trade Center commented that the water "is stunning, like Niagara Falls, and yet calm. It is serene, and we are at peace."[72] Another, who never found his son in the 9/11 wreckage said, "They did a fantastic job. . . . To me it's very peaceful."[73] Colum McCann puts it quite simply: "the falling water, beside the reflecting pools, spoke volumes."[74]

Yet, in many ways, visitors may still be melancholic because of the aura of absence and the memories of the missing Twin Towers. Arad's "voids" were so large that the sheer size of each footprint reminds one of the massive destruction that took place on 9/11 and the fragility of America's collective psyche (figure 8). For example, to Phillip Kennicott, the memorial "recalls ancient and deeply embedded connections among water, memory and death."[75] These conscious or unconscious worries about past deaths and future worries—along with the loathing of omnipresent and omnipotent enemies—overpowers the water's soothing rhetorical effects as we think back to the fires and dust of that tragic day.

It would obviously be a mistake to think that most members of the NYPD might view the water's soothing effects in pacifist ways. Local police authorities have even raised concerns about potential suicides at the memorial due to its "layout and its powerful relationship to the terrorist act of Sept. 11, 2001, and because those who lost loved ones that day may still have unresolved issues of loss."[76] Could all of this evocation of emotions lead to a spontaneous attack that might escape the attention of those not listening to the police?

Indeed, we would argue that both the texts and the contexts of the 9/11 memorial are filled with spatial contradictions that reflect and refract the macrotensions of 9/11 public memory. The memorial's reflection pools offer solace, but its physical absences may demand a retraumatization. The rhetoric of absence is traumatic because it displays the horror of nothing to see and the repetitive memory of loss. This trauma is supercharged because it is contrary to the promise of closure displayed by the water. These two affective feelings become combustible when we think of the center of the pools where all hope for therapeutic access dribbles into an unknown abyss. As Edward Helmore put it, the water "cascades down the sides toward a giant drain, creating the disconcerting feeling of being sucked into earth."[77] Roger Denson, who wondered whether Arad had planned on evoking sentiments that brought together "architecture, culture, holocaust and mysticism," was convinced that "no one critic can make proclamations concerning whether a memorial site succeeds in mitigating the lingering trauma and loss of an act of war for the public."[78] Again, these forces touch on myriad securitization concerns.

The absence of the Twin Towers and the materiality of the memorial's securitized spaces remind us of the difficult nature of what it takes to work through traumatic memories during times of war. In this particular case, the palpable presence of insecurity is confirmed in three ways.

Fig. 8. Water feature at the National September 11 Memorial.

First, the cameras and the security guards constantly watch all bodies, which emphasizes the insecurity of this place of remembrance. Although the bordered security checkpoint was eventually removed and relocated to the museum, the memorial's cameras, security guards, and security booths on its periphery ultimately put the visitor in a panopticon-like securitization complex.

Second, although visitors are allowed to touch the names on the slabs of granite, they cannot touch the voids' absence, leaving them estranged from the healing powers of mourning that were offered acoustically. Mourning can be heard, but it remains physically inaccessible.

Third, the slanted angle of the parapets forces the viewer to take a downward, melancholic visual perspective as they view the names of the 9/11 victims. Anne Hilker calls this perspective an "absent gaze,"[79] because the visitor remains mentally absent from the rest of the world as he or she can only downwardly gaze in a lethargic, nonengaged optical manner at the names of those who were lost. Unlike the viewing of the Vietnam Veterans Memorial, there is no visual verticality to access at the 9/11 Memorial; there is only a horizontal spread of absence through descent. This craning of one's neck may even leave the visitor uncomfortable while standing (see figures 8 and 9).

It might be said, therefore, that this memorial's material rhetorics of absence and loss produce a unique materialist ontology, a commemorative form of melancholia that spatially undermines much of the mourning needed for the ending of conflicts. While visitors can touch the names of loved ones that have passed, their physical *presence* pales in comparison with the physical *absences* displayed in the one-acre pits of hollow spaces inscribed by granite borders (see figure 9). Effectually, security becomes the very thing that is memorialized.

Simply stated, the absence of the towers, and the traumatic public memory associated with the violence that created their absences, have prevented psychological and social closure and necessitated object-oriented spatial securitization. This lack of closure serves as one more example of how the "accident of art" can be used to invite select performances of melancholia,[80] where even comfort can be sacrificed in the name of national security.[81]

The performative framing of portions of the National September 11 Memorial cannot help reminding visitors of the wars with al Qaeda in Iraq and the Taliban in Afghanistan. Thus the heightened security at this memorial constantly repeats the "aesthetics of dematerialization" that has dominated these uncertain times.[82] These violent securitized references—often added by the presence of police or surveillance cameras—materially undercut the peaceful feelings that came from being surrounded by the water around the voids.

In sum, the National September 11 Memorial uses its rhetoric of absence to hold visitors in a constant state of uncertainty about how to live at peace, while knowing that unknown terrorists may always be lurking around the next corner. Visitors themselves are nearly treated as potential terrorists, in that closed-circuit television cameras and

Fig. 9. The melancholic gaze at the National September 11 Memorial.

on-site security personnel carefully monitor their activities to make sure 9/11 never happens again.

The hypervigilance and the policing of the National September 11 Memorial and Memorial Museum (discussed more in the following chapter) mean that millions of visitors are involved in becoming a part of securitized commemorative practices. Now, even those who did not actually witness the attacks on the Twin Towers can still recall—and be haunted by—past and present terrorist dangers. However, even though the specters of the dead are haunting, terrifying, and gruesome, they may also create a sense of community engagement that is uniquely melancholic. The rhetorical effect of this securitized memorial space is that 9/11 is treated not as some past historical incident but as a lingering cultural presence that reminds visitors that the American homeland is always under the threat of terror. Both the memorial and the museum recall the precarious lives of family members, architects, and tourists, and the omnipresence of police helps many remember that they live in a twenty-first century that is filled with doubt, uncertainty, and anxiety.

Conclusion

This chapter has argued that the National September 11 Memorial evokes a sense of securitized commemoration that depends on aesthetic displays of absence to remind visitors of their nationalist obligations of upholding, if not performing, counterterrorist practices. Some of these obligations include the support of the NYPD, who are doing their best to make sure that risky objects such as trash receptacles do not become another terrorist opportunity. While many observers talked and wrote about this memorial's curative powers and the importance of mourning for a "working-through" of traumatic memories, this goal has been undermined by those who demand eternal reverence for those who lost their lives during the terrorist attacks.

We have argued that the materiality of security at the National September 11 Memorial was the result of a series of argumentative exchanges that legitimized the perceived necessity to securitize Ground Zero space. Although some civilians questioned the necessity of securitization, it was eventually decided by many police supporters that Ground Zero's security apparatus was necessary to prepare for the believed inevitability of another attack. For instance, citizens who lived near Ground Zero complained about the excessive securitization of public space in their neighborhoods when things as mundane as trash bins had to be made "terrorist proof." Securitized trash interrupted day-to-day life by contributing to piles upon piles of unattended trash in front of residents' doorsteps. These issues came to the fore in the 2014 case *Mary Perillo v. Kelly*, which tested the legitimacy of the NYPD Counterterrorism Bureau. The effect of this legitimation was a calcification of securitization at Ground Zero.

We have explained how even cosmopolitan renderings of this hallowed ground have to be juxtaposed with dreary reminders of absences and global violence. Susan Sci may be right when she argued that some public memorials serve as places for public eulogizing and aesthetic negotiation, but there are also times when the reverence for the dead is used to warrant counterterrorism during heightened states of securitization.[83]

Our own experiences and research support Simon Stow's claims that the National September 11 Memorial is a topographical manifestation of *alaston penthos*, of mourning without end, a phenomenon that encourages the circulation of a kind of "pornography of grief," where emotional responses are deliberately cultivated in ways that are "a confirmation of the viewer's own victimhood."[84] When memorial sites are used for these types of affective purposes, visitors experience insecurity and loss, especially in sacred places where an "enigmatically abstract pair of abyss-like pools" are used in a "sobering, disturbing, heartbreaking, and overwhelming masterpiece."[85] From a critical rhetorical, and critical participatory, vantage point, all of this reminds us that monuments, museums, memorials, and archives can be used for a host of politicized purposes, including policing functions that totally securitize space.

5

Holocaust Memories and Counterterrorist Practices at Ground Zero

The very notion that an American site of memory—especially the National September 11 Memorial and Memorial Museum—might have anything to do with Nazi pasts may raise the ire of those who worry about too much universalization of traumatic memories. Over the years, however, this subject has been broached by a variety of elite and public social actors. For example, in both his recent book *The Stages of Memory* and a public lecture about the stages of memory,[1] James Young—one of the world's leading scholars on memory studies and Holocaust remembrances[2]—recalled a reporter's question about the progress of the design of the National September 11 Memorial. Young had served as one of the jurors for deciding its design, and the reporter asked, "Knowing that you have written much about Holocaust negative-form monuments in Germany and that you were also on the jury that chose Peter Eisenman's design for the Berlin Denkmal (for Europe's murdered Jews), it seems that you've basically chosen just another Holocaust memorial. Is this true?"[3] Young says the question initially caught him "off balance" and he was "somewhat offended,"[4] so he responded with a curt denial of this possibility. The reporter, however, continued to press Young, who became reflective about possible parallels:

But is it possible that Jewish architects are somehow predisposed toward articulating the memory of catastrophe in their work? Would this explain how Daniel Libeskind [original site designer of the new World Trade Center complex], Santiago Calatrava [designer of the new World Trade Center Transportation Hub abutting Ground Zero in Lower Manhattan], and now Michael Arad [designer of the memorial at Ground Zero] have become the architects of record in post-9/11 downtown Manhattan?[5]

In both his lecture and his book, Young recalls that he contemplated the difficult, multilayered question and responded by observing that there is no way to get around the point that the National September 11 Memorial has been influenced by "the forms of postwar architecture [that] have . . . inflected . . . an entire generation's knowledge of the Holocaust."[6] He says he told the reporter that "Michael Arad and Peter Walker's 'Reflecting Absence' is not a Holocaust memorial . . . but its formal preoccupation with loss, absence, and regeneration may well be informed by Holocaust memorial vernaculars."[7] In other words, this might be a situation where the new National September 11 Memorial served the purposes of multidirectionality, where Holocaust remembrances influenced the reception of 9/11 memories.

This relationship made sense in that the aftermath of World War II was experienced by those who suffered through the carnage of massive tragedies, and Young was forced to acknowledge that it was quite evident that the National September 11 Memorial and Memorial Museum symbolized a related period of "irredeemable, inconsolable loss."[8]

Drawing parallels between the National September 11 Memorial and Memorial Museum and the representations of the Holocaust is just one of many ways to conceptualize these hallowed spaces and places, but it is certainly among the most controversial. One never knows when the drawing of some parallels might contribute to competitive memory formations.

In previous chapters we presented readers with a variety of ways to conceptualize the spatial securitization of these grounds, and in this chapter we augment earlier analyses by underscoring how some actors, such as the curators and designers of the National September 11 Memorial and Memorial Museum, were interested in portraying these institutions in more universalist, cosmopolitan, or globalized ways. Was it possible, in the same way that the U.S. Holocaust Memorial Museum (USHMM) has become a didactic site for the intellectual study of many genocidal memories (of, for example, the Armenian and the Rwandan genocides), that the National September 11 Memorial and Memorial Museum could be linked to other tragedies?

As we noted before, the idea of having multicultural messages circulated alongside antiterrorist messages had not resonated with some of the empowered decision makers during reconstruction planning stages, and some voiced similar objections to Holocaust memorialization at Ground Zero.

There is no doubt that some of these attempts to broaden the potential transnational symbolism of the National September 11 Memorial and Memorial Museum has to run against the grain of attempts to focus exclusively on American suffering, in addition to American exceptionalist behavior during the Global War on Terrorism. Consider, for example, how at various times, this site of memory has been called a reminder of Osama bin Laden's terrorist barbarism, a place of commemoration for rescue efforts, a symbol of national resilience, a mausoleum, and a site for local rejuvenation of Lower Manhattan. When President Barack Obama came to this place to help dedicate the museum at its opening on May 15, 2014, he stated, "Here we tell their story, so that generations yet unborn will never forget.... A nation that stands tall and united and unafraid—because no act of terror can match the strength or character of our country."[9] No wonder that the expression of nationalist sentiments like these led Holland Cotter of the *New York Times* to wonder whether this particular museum was going to be "a historical document, a monument to the dead or a theme-park-style tourist" attraction.[10]

All of this was taking place as some victims' family groups were trying to use a rhetoric of American innocence[11] as a way of understanding these traumatic events in monolithic, utopian, and idealistic ways (see chapter 3).

While countless journalists and bloggers were convinced that a dominant *American* story was being told by those who designed, developed, and maintained this site, the complex nature of these particular places, as well as the competing goals of various stakeholders that had been expressed for more than a decade, ensured that many other narratives would shadow these hallowed spaces. Long before the opening of the museum, local, national, and international audiences had witnessed conflicts over how to grieve, endless debates over designs, partisan rancor, and even some physical inundation from Hurricane Sandy.

In this chapter we ask whether Holland Cotter is right when he comments that "the 9/11 story" is being told at Ground Zero, and we are intrigued by the rhetorical features—and limits—of the negotiated ideological boundary-work that has gone into the development of this intriguing site of memory.[12] More specifically, we ask the following question: Are there more globalized, more cosmopolitan features of the U.S. September 11 Memorial and Memorial Museum that can be fruitfully linked to broader concerns regarding Holocaust or genocidal memories?

In previous chapters we focused on the memorial in general, but these last two chapters will focus on the realpolitik and dingpolitik nature of the argumentation that shadows the actual museum.

This chapter begins by providing a brief rhetorical history that explores whether the architects, designers, funders, and other stakeholders in the debates over these sites' trajectories have shared Young's interest in seeing parallels between the museum's securitizing antiterrorist messages and the Holocaust. At the same time, we wonder whether these Holocaust linkages presented by scholars, journalists, and other social actors have impacted the ways that visitors and commentators try to police museological memories.

In fascinating ways, these attempts to recontextualize this memorial and museum as another "dark tourist" Holocaust site differ from the ways that some other American sites of memory have taken international incidents and made them "our" own. As Peter Ehrenhaus once noted in his own study of the "American Holocaust," different U.S.

generations use selective interpretations of historical mass-mediated events that may take place elsewhere as they form their own memories.[13] What happens when observers symbolically and materially link the commemoration of 9/11 events with pasts and presents of other nations? When observers write or talk about the National September 11 Memorial, do they ever argue that there are historical parallels that should *not be* drawn, or that specific types of comparisons with other museums should not be made? When theorists, planners, and laypersons are trying to respect and revere "the" American story that is being told at the National September 11 Memorial and Memorial Museum, is their room for discussion of other, more polysemic tragedies, other historical horrors?

At first glance, one could argue from an affective standpoint that a visit to the National September Memorial or Memorial Museum triggers some of the same reflective, dark thoughts that one gets from a visit to the USHMM due to the presentation of irredeemable loss and stories of human loss and suffering. In fact, the director of the National September 11 Memorial Museum—Alice Greenwald—who is also the former associate museum director of the USHMM, said she has recognized that memories of the Holocaust have informed her decisions about how to curate ways of remembering at the National September 11 Memorial Museum. In an essay about the lessons of planning the museum, Greenwald says that the National September 11 Memorial Museum is "not unlike the USHMM,"[14] where she worked for almost twenty years, since the USHMM set a "paradigm" of museology by speaking "directly to conscience, and ultimately, to the need to act in the face of genocide."[15] For Greenwald, this lesson from the USHMM has "directly informed the development of the 9/11 Museum."[16] One of the major issues, of course, is *how* that has informed the development and how visitors and others react to those linkages.

As we mentioned in the introduction, some memorializing practices involve *thanatopolitics*—the political mobilization of death—and for our purposes here, we view the object-oriented similitudes between the Holocaust and 9/11 as an affective form of thanatopolitical maneuvering.

Curators and others involved in this process can appropriate, and channel, feelings of death and disaster to justify post-9/11 securitizations across the nation and at Ground Zero itself. As such, the dingpolitik functions of the objects in and around the National September 11 Memorial and Memorial Museum open up spaces of temporal discontinuity by juxtaposing two separate histories of mass murder: 9/11 and the Holocaust.

This kind of historical coupling—despite profound differences in both time and space—may be understood as a spatial *heterochronia*, which is broadly understood as a sort of "break" from traditional or canonical ways of thinking about the temporal features of cemeteries, museums, memorials, libraries, and prisons. We hold that the appropriation of memories of death and disaster at the National September 11 Memorial and Memorial Museum functions as a heterochronia that is used for the potential multidirectional remembrances of both the Holocaust and the destruction of the Twin Towers.

The securitization of the National September 11 Memorial and Memorial Museum has created an alluring potential dark tourist site for tourists across the world. According to one 2015 end-of-the-year report, more than twenty-three million tourists have visited the memorial since it opened in 2011, and over four million visited the museum since it opened in 2014.[17] By July 2017 some ten million people had visited the museum.[18]

We wonder, then, how these parallels between 9/11 and the Holocaust have rhetorically impacted the evolutionary development of this hallowed ground, and whether U.S. audiences—who are used to hearing narratives about American exceptionalism[19]—would respond when they heard observers making comparisons with other catastrophic events. More specifically, are patriotic American audiences comfortable when they hear historical comparisons between the deaths that occurred during the terrorist attacks of 9/11 and other massive loss of life? When New Yorkers and other Americans visit this site and mourn the more than twenty-nine hundred who died during the attacks on the Twin Towers, the Pentagon, and elsewhere, are they interested in joining Professor Young and linking together 9/11 commemorative acts with World War II Holocaust remembrances?

As Michael Bowman and Phaedra Pezzullo note in their study of thanatopolitical dimensions of travel sites, the critical investigation of dark tourism is an increasingly popular academic approach to the study of tourist sites because it invites researchers to pay attention to the politicized role that the "disgusting, the abject, and the macabre" play in places that also include the "picturesque, the romantic, and the sublime."[20] These haunting places of abject suffering have everything to do with thanatopolitical reasoning.

In this particular case, we are convinced that tales of American victimization and talk of the need for constant securitization of this site aid the cause of those who find parallels between the Holocaust and 9/11. Rife with contradictions, similitudes, and fissures, these parallel memories provide excellent examples of what Michael Rothberg calls multidirectional memory-making and "competitive" memorialization. In theory, because of its capacity to take into account the traumas of others without eclipsing other memories or histories of suffering, a multidirectional memory does not have to involve the erasure of other memories. This is why, to Rothberg, memory is "subject to ongoing negotiation, cross-referencing, and borrowing; as productive and not privative."[21] Yet there are times when Rothberg's idealism needs to also be juxtaposed with more "competitive," more mutually exclusive memory-work that he deems to be problematic.[22]

Some of the parallels between 9/11 and the Holocaust that have appeared in hundreds of newspapers, journal articles, popular magazines, and websites—lead us to conclude that sometimes commentators even appropriate phrases like "never again" as they use this sacred site to comment on the continuing dangers posed by al Qaeda and other organizations. Although local communities living next to this memorial have often complained about all the gates and fences that surrounded the site (see chapter 4), many other commentators have viewed Ground Zero as a place that could still be targeted by terrorist extremists, groups that can be characterized as contemporary Nazis.

A review of much of the architectural and public debates that circulated between 2001 and 2014 illustrate how talk of the World War

II Holocaust impacted everything from the choice of architectural designs to the curatorial decisions that were made about what to display in the National September 11 Memorial Museum.[23] To museum director Alice Greenwald, decision makers at the National September 11 Memorial and Memorial Museum, like the ones at the USHMM, "have an opportunity and an obligation to remember well, so that the intense and immediate particularity of 9/11 can speak to bigger concerns."[24] What are those bigger issues?

This move toward linking 9/11 to the Holocaust may involve a broadening of twenty-first-century securitization concerns. Articulation of the constant worries about potential future terrorist attacks has made it easier to draw symbolic and historical linkages with Holocaust events, sites, and remembrances. From a tourist standpoint, there is no doubt that this connection transforms the architectural and geographic landscape of memory into a place of remembrance that commodifies death and disaster. As Alan Lew once noted in an editorial reflection, 9/11 has "probably damaged the global travel and tourism more than any other single economic sector."[25]

Now that several years have passed since the National September 11 Memorial and Memorial Museum opened to the public, we are also interested in investigating how this centerpiece of 9/11 memory has itself become a place for dark tourism; and as such, we wonder how Holocaust analogies and securitization concerns have produced unique and affective objects of commodification. As we intend to demonstrate, a substantial amount of anecdotal and other evidence indicates that more than a few are now connecting 9/11 with the Holocaust, and this in turn creates a tourist subject who is attracted to death and disaster.

All historical comparisons and memorialization parallels have their limits, and those who seek to connect the horrors of the World War II Holocaust with the tragedies of 9/11 have to always be mindful that many visitors to the renovated areas around Ground Zero may want to prioritize the traumas and the losses that were suffered by Americans on September 11, 2001. In other words, families of the victims, and first responders, for example, don't mind hearing stories about other tragedies like the Shoah—as long as they feel that none of this detracts from the display of individual heroism and the uniqueness of the "American" 9/11 tragedies.

We continue our critique in this chapter by providing readers with a summary of the theoretical importance of dark tourism and thanatopolitics, and then we apply some of those conceptual insights as we write about how social agents have circulated counterterrorist securitization rhetorics that have invited us to link the horrors of the Holocaust with the tragedies of 9/11.

Considering the Role of Thanatopolitics in Practices of Remembrance

The concept of thanatopolitics provides a heuristic way of understanding select American usages of the National September 11 Memorial's securitized spaces.[26] As we noted in the introduction, many classical architectural forms of monuments and museums provide us with uplifting, epic messages about a nation's civil religion,[27] but more postmodern and poststructural ways of thinking about memorial designs—as displayed in places like Daniel Libeskind's Jewish Museum, Berlin—often showcase a darker, more brooding way of conceptualizing memorialization.

Thanatopolitics thus refers to the way that contemporary audiences memorialize their dead in *strategic and deadly ways* that often illustrate the ideological usages of the symbols associated with dark bodies and other abject objects.

When Michel Foucault[28] and Gorgio Agamben[29] used the term "thanatopolitics" they often underscored the ways that the living used recollections of death as a way of reminding us of the importance of coping with unpunished killing. Unlike discourses of "biopolitics" that referenced the need for recording births or the monitoring of the reproductive habits of populations, thanatopolitics is understood as an appropriation of grief, death, and disaster that helps with the governance of communities.[30]

All of this dark tourism has destructive as well as constructive features. John Lennon and Malcolm Foley note in their book *Dark Tourism* that visitors are drawn to places associated with death and disaster, in spite of the commodification of knowledge and the doubts that might be produced by those visits.[31] Work done on frightening or unsettling geographies of tourist spaces such as the Korean Demilitarized Zone[32] and Jim Crow–era tourism[33] remind us that dark tourist sites attract attention because anxieties or fears are commodified affects that are consumed by the tourist visitor.

At the National September 11 Memorial and Memorial Museum visitors do not only see uplifting images of patriotic rebirth. They also see horrific signs of devastation—displays of mangled cables that broke during the attacks on the Twin Towers—while they hear the recorded voices of victims who left messages for their loved ones just minutes before they died. All of this provides examples of what Philip Stone and Richard Sharpley called an encounter with some of modernity's failures.[34] Like other places of remembrance that offer thanatopolitical feelings as well as products, people will come from near and far to feel connected with the 9/11 victims who were targeted for their ideological belief in the system of capitalism.[35] Failure to appreciate the American way of life is linked to misunderstandings of U.S. cultures.

If one focuses on the trees, the open spaces, the water around the famous voids, one might conclude that the developers of the National September 11 Memorial and Memorial Museum are inviting New Yorkers and others to think about the importance of biopolitical rebirth and rejuvenation, but we contend that all of this needs to be juxtaposed with the darker, more haunting spaces of remembrance that also remind visitors of the terrorist dangers that have continued to exist since 9/11/01. The dark tourism of some of the underground spaces below the Pavilion, for example, distributes an affective force of victimage that faithfully represents the entire nation's worries. While some critics argue that this re-creation of worry creates "neurotic subjects"[36] who sustain a "productive economy of fear,"[37] others contend that all of this display of abject objects helps visitors remember what Ground Zero was really like on September 11, 2001. Yet, as Marieke De Goede noted in another context, all of this talk of death and destruction constitutively creates a problematic "subject of risk," a person "who is governed through 'anxieties and insecurities,' striving to attain the impossible in 'absolute security [and] . . . absolute safety.'"[38]

"Never Again": The Sacred and Secular Dimensions of the 9/11 Memorial and Museum's Security Apparatus

We are convinced that when Professor Young wrote and spoke about some of the striking resemblances between the remembrances of the Holocaust and recollections of the events of 9/11, he was taking a stance that reflected the arguments of many of those involved with this site's planning and development. For example, consider the discussions in chapter 2 about the Lower Manhattan Development Corporation's failed proposal to create an International Freedom Center (IFC) between 2005 and 2006 that was intended to contextualize 9/11 within linear historical trajectories of genocidal pasts. Explicit linkages were made to the wiping out of Native Americans in America, the horrors experienced by African Americans during the Jim Crow years, and the destruction wrought by the Nazi Holocaust.[39] So, why, given these earlier worries, were curators and others able to continue to draw parallels with the Judeocide?

As we noted earlier, some of the groups representing the surviving family members who lost loved ones on 9/11 considered the plans for the IFC to be politically motivated activities, and they articulated their belief that these globalization plans would detract from the reflection and the reverence that they felt must be reserved for those who died on 9/11.[40] Perhaps what happened here is that those who objected earlier to multicultural efforts became convinced that some forms of Holocaust thanatopolitics involved not politics but pedagogy.

Many supporters of the IFC and some of the other cosmopolitan projects were convinced that early planners were signaling how they felt about the architectural representation of trauma and the processes of mourning, but left out was the fact that many drew linkages between the Holocaust and the National September 11 Memorial when they chose two Israeli Americans, Daniel Libeskind and Michael Arad, as the chief architects. Calev Ben-David of the *Jerusalem Post* argued that

Libeskind was being lauded as chief architect of the reconstructed World Trade Center master plan in large part because of his Jewish background. His parents, after all, were Holocaust survivors, and he had already received accolades for his proposed "Holocaust tower" that would be a part of the displays at the Jewish Museum, Berlin.[41] Form and substance came together in the minds of some journalists, and Ben-David went on to argue that Ground Zero's plan for "thematic links to Libeskind's Holocaust-related work was duly noted, for the most part in approval."[42]

These types of arguments invited readers and potential visitors to think about how the National September 11 Memorial and Memorial Museum might be able to reference some of the lingering traumas of second and third generations of European and Israeli audiences. More than a decade after the attacks on the Twin Towers, as millions of Americans prepared themselves for the emotional opening of the National September 11 Memorial Museum, Barbara Sofer recalled, "How fitting that both of the major architects in this project are Israeli citizens. Israeli-American architect Daniel Libeskind, son of Holocaust survivors, has created the master plan for reconstruction. . . . As heirs to our national experience of survival, they might have had an advantage."[43] The resilience of New Yorkers, as well as that of the American nation, could now be reconfigured as newer examples of survival in the face of mounting international threats and risks. This reconfiguration allowed for sequential multidirectional memory-work.

American resilience meant no appeasement and no let-up in the Global War on Terrorism, a lesson that had been learned by those who watched Hitler's minions march through Czechoslovakia and then Poland. As Benjamin Forest and Juliet Johnson note, there may be a not-so-hidden motive operating behind this securitizing agenda, in that these securitization measures put on display the endurance of New Yorkers as well as the perseverance of the nation.[44]

Homeland security takes many forms, and the securitization of the National September 11 Memorial could be linked to many transcontinental nationalistic acts of defiance. The Americans, unlike the British

with Chamberlain, had the chance to avoid appeasement and compla-
cency. Forest and Johnson get to the emotive power of some of these
rhetorical linkages when they explain:

> Strict access-control at the WTC site provides atonement for security
> personnel and police, as proxies for airport checkpoint screeners.
> The conscientious application of an airport-like security protocol is a
> chance to symbolically "get it right"; to implement security measures
> conscientiously that might have prevented the September 11 attacks.
>
> In Radzik's terms, such atonement seeks to repair the social contract
> between security and society: that in exchange for inconvenience,
> limits on certain liberties, and reduced personal privacy, society will
> be protected from violent harm.[45]

Given these psychological and sociological linkages, we can readily
understand why planners, curators, and visitors who were worried about
atonement would put up with security price tags of approximately $12
million of the $60 million annual operating costs of the memorial.[46]

We would go so far as to argue that some promoters of securitization at the National September 11 Memorial and Memorial Museum
have found a way of ensuring that the trope "never again" can have an
American inflection that particularizes the horrors of 9/11. Securitization
practices thus become didactic acts of commemoration that allow New
Yorkers to rationalize and justify high levels of security. As Forest and
Johnson elaborate, securitizing the National September 11 Memorial
assumes that social agents "have the moral responsibility to act" in
ways that counter perpetrators' deeds.[47] In sum, post-9/11 heightened
levels of security can be understood as a means of atoning sins wrought
by forces of evil that have "slipped under the radar" during times of
appeasement or insecurity. Those who once failed to patrol the skies
over New York or Pennsylvania had another opportunity to make sure
that this time there would be no Pearl Harbor type of sneak attack.

The heightened levels of security at the National September 11 Memorial and Memorial Museum have led some to question whether these
measures are actually necessary, and in some cases, critics wonder

whether all of this securitization makes visitors feel any safer. Mark Vanhoenacker, for example, argues that while the security may be comforting
for the 9/11 family members and survivors, "it's time for a freedom-loving
people to consider the purpose and impact of such security measures."[48]
Interviewing a number of people who have researched the topic, he
noted that some contend, as counterterrorism fellow Max Abrahms
does, that "although the memorial's 'extra psychological importance'
warrants heightened security, 'it's now clear that sleeper cells are not
infesting our country. . . . al-Qaeda can hardly generate any violence
at all.'"[49] In other words, these types of securitized messages were
needed in places that suffered from terrorist infestation, but they were
not necessarily needed in New York if domestic surveillance sufficed.

But, for others, these trials and tribulations revive memories of
more globalized historical tragedies. Clearly, talk of "never again" raises
implicit or explicit references to other atrocities, the Holocaust, or other
genocides, and their ideologically charged thanatopolitical dimensions
refute the claims of skeptical viewers or listeners.

Observers who worry about all of this dark talk of renewed attacks
or who want to critique the need for counterterrorism in Lower Manhattan often complain about the politicization of a site that is supposed
to be set up for commemoration of the dead. Some go so far as to argue
that treating the National September 11 Memorial as a security fortress
does little to aid the cause of those who actually fight the Taliban or al
Qaeda. John Mueller, a counterterror expert, argued that the threat of
another terrorist attack on New York City is greatly exaggerated and
that all of this wasteful spending "produce[s] widespread and unjus-
tified anxiety."[50] A year later, Mark Sedgwick complained that local
politicians were using "terrorist events as excuses to do what [they]
wanted to do anyway."[51]

These have been lingering concerns. As early as 2003, for instance,
Bruce Schneier characterized all of the performances of the guards
and checkpoints as a type of "security theater"[52]—a term that we talk
more about in the following chapter—and he criticized these activities
as intrusive, pointless, or ineffective (figure 10). "The best memorial to

Fig. 10. Security screening sign in front of the National
September 11 Memorial Museum.

the victims of 9/11," according to Schneier, would be to "forget" most
of the "lessons" of 9/11. "It's infuriating," he noted to Charles Mann,
author of an essay titled "Smoke Screening" in *Vanity Fair*.[53] In other
words, the didactic or pedagogical functions of the museum needed
to take a back seat to the reverential functions of these sacred grounds
to help traumatized publics move on with their lives. Whether these
terrorist threats were real or imagined, we can appreciate why Bruce
Janz characterized some of this as evidence of the nation's post-9/11
"topophobia."[54]

   Is it possible that these affective displays of fear and anxiety have been
commodified in such a way that they have become part of the attraction
itself? Indeed, as our evidence in the following section reveals, many
have made sense of the 9/11 tragedy through the mnemonic frame of

the Holocaust. What might be called the "transnationalization of the Holocaust"[55] provides a unique, if startling, instance of dark tourism.

The Transnationalization of the Holocaust:
Rethinking the Boundaries of Commemoration

Although most commentary has focused on the American features of 9/11 horrors, there has always been a vocal minority of observers who presented us with more generalizable, or more universal, messages. "This is like the Holocaust," a witness told a *Toronto Sun* reporter the day after the attacks.[56] A week later, *Washington Post* columnist Richard Cohen found rays of hope for the nation's future by recalling "the people who survived the Holocaust and made a life for themselves."[57] Like those imprisoned in Adolf Hitler's death camps, an Ohio newspaper observed, Americans could not control the enormity that had befallen them, but they could control their response to it.[58]

Our study of securitization and the parallels that have been made between the Holocaust and the events of 9/11 indicates that these symbolic linkages can take many forms, and that all of this speaks to the ways that select usages of historical memories can be appropriated and deployed for prescient needs. As Peter Ehrenhaus once noted, "Holocaust memory has a crucial role in American national identity that extends beyond American Jewish community to the larger, predominantly Christian population."[59]

For our purposes here, there is no shortage of commentators who have implied that Nazi extremists share commonalities with Jihadist extremists, and this comparison allows some to see how Jews around the world and New Yorkers were victims of terror that could only be explained as "pure evil."

Is it possible that other social actors and audiences want to supplement these types of messages by going beyond American national interests in representations of 9/11? We are convinced that it is fair to argue that the National September 11 Memorial and Memorial Museum may have become a Judeo-Christian site of secular and sacred memory, a place of reverence that also has more polyphonic dimensions that need to be explored.

This relationship, which sutures together shared histories of victimage, has established a Manichaean good-evil dichotomy used to justify controversial agendas, policies, and wars. This dichotomy builds on earlier figurations. In one key portion of his book *Good Muslim, Bad Muslim*, Mahmood Mamdani reflected on some other historic parallels:

> The lesson of Auschwitz remains at the centre of post-9/11 discussions in American society. An outside observer is struck by how much American discourse on terrorism is filtered more through the memory of the Holocaust than through any other event. Post-9/11 America seems determined: "Never again." Despite important differences, genocide and terrorism share one important feature: both target civilian populations.[60]

Steven Carr went even farther and averred that 9/11, much like the Eichmann trials, became an iconoclastic "modern media event"[61] that helped publics make sense of this thanatopolitical horror by juxtaposing it with something else that some felt was comparable in nature.

These mnemonic frameworks, filled with related traumatic tales, similar villains, and readily identifiable victims, can be thought of as examples of what Daniel Levy and Natan Sznaider have titled *Erinnerung im globalen Zeitalter: Der Holocaust*, or "Holocaust memory in the global age," a phenomenon that Andreas Huyssen translated as "the transnationalization of the Holocaust."[62]

In some situations, the Holocaust becomes both a particularized, unique event as well as a more universal and mobile yardstick for measuring unmitigated evil.[63] For instance, just days after the attacks on the Pentagon and Twin Towers, Charles Krauthammer, in a short article in *Time* magazine titled "The Greater the Evil, the More It Disarms" complained about Americans' lack of vigilance against demonic antagonizers. "The [hijacked airplane] passengers' seeming passivity is reminiscent of the Holocaust," Krauthammer intoned, and "not since the Nazi rallies of the 1930s has the world witnessed such celebration of blood and soil, of killing and dying."[64] The alleged celebration among jihadists over the deaths of rich Americans in the Twin Towers allowed readers to be transported back in time, where some too easily looked away when confronted with the dark, brooding omnipresence of earlier Nazi years.

Oftentimes, scholars who write about the planning and development of the National September 11 Memorial and Memorial Museum realize that some of the affective nature of this place has to do with the ways that visitors or pundits think about the role of evil in the world. To Jack Holland, some representations of 9/11 events have become "somatic markers" for pure evils that are similar "to the Holocaust,"[65] and all of this has come about because of the "elevated" framing of 9/11 to a "position of Absolute Evil."[66] Holland, among others, appears to be inferring that 9/11 is connected with the Holocaust in metaphysical, as well as existential, ways. Bülent Diken and Carsten Bagge Lausten similarly remark that "9/11 is a sacralized event; it is sublimated and elevated to a level above politics, dialogue, and humor in a way reminiscent of the Holocaust."[67]

The Holocaust is of course not the only World War II event that reminds Americans of the dangers of appeasement or the need for vigilant surveillance. Gregory Wallance has remarked that "only a major terrorist strike on American soil will convince the public to accept the kind of intrusive surveillance that, in the first instance, might have prevented the attack."[68]

America's post-9/11 security measures on prominent display at the National September 11 Memorial and Memorial Museum can be viewed as part of complex textual and visual horizons that historically link America's entry into World War II, Auschwitz, and Ground Zero. No wonder some contend that the rhetoric about the dangers of contemporary terrorism is a "language of apocalyptic and holy war" that is also "nostalgic in its appeal to WWII through appeals to both Pearl Harbor and the Holocaust."[69]

For those who would like to form even earlier historical linkages, the horrors of 9/11 can be used as mnemonic markers for remembering the centuries of struggles of Jewish communities in the Middle Eastern Holy Land, where Zionists fought their own terrorists and dealt with the age-old religious conflicts between Israel and Arab Palestinians. Churches, states, and other institutions can use a host of securitization permutations to explain why both the American and Jewish nations need to remember their common, transnational bonds and struggles. David MacDonald averred several years ago that

> "America-as-victim" was not a popular image until after 9/11, when stories of Holocaust survival helped make sense of American vulnerability and anger. . . . That Israel and the USA are innocent of any wrongdoing, and possess special unique characteristics, is taken-for-granted.[70]

The secular and the sacred blur together as members of several nation-states use their political and geographical imaginations to contextualize 9/11 in select but politicized counterterrorist ways.

We have also found that Ground Zero has become an incredibly emotive site for some because it allows the personal to become political as various individuals explain their own connections with the Holocaust and 9/11 through image events. In a recorded entry written in autobiographical form just days after the 9/11 Holocaust, scholar and professor Elizabeth Baer remarked:

> So many sad stories, so many eerie parallels to the Holocaust in terms of the consequences of hatred, racism, and religious fanaticism. . . . Trauma at home. Women standing on the street in New York City with photos of their missing husband or son or daughter. Such a low-tech approach to finding the missing after such high-tech terrorism, reminiscent of the searches conducted for loved ones in displaced persons camps in the aftermath of the Holocaust.[71]

Some of those who had lived through the horrors of the Holocaust also came forward and acted as contemporary witnesses who could speak to the problems associated with fighting existential evils. Eli Wiesel, for example, in February 2002, taught these pedagogical lessons to an audience at Eckard College in Florida:

> I know what it means to face danger. . . . It takes so little if we are not careful for terrorists to annihilate all that we who believe in civilization have tried to build. . . . Now we know that evil has power and we now know that power must be countered.[72]

Although perceptions regarding the similarities between Israel and the United States may have been below the surface prior to 9/11, the lingering emotional turmoil wrought from this "day of terror" may have triggered new affective identifications between these two supporting nations. Consequently, this emotional identification is being used to justify heightened security measures in the Middle East and abroad, in airports, and at the National September 11 Memorial and Memorial Museum. If one looks at this renewed identification from a thanatopolitical, geopolitical vantage point, one could argue that the security measures taken at Ground Zero are not so different from the way that Israel is protecting its borders and air spaces from non-Jewish nations.

Many academics, perhaps sensing that some elites and publics are willing to "see" 9/11 through the lens of Holocaust remembrances, disagree about whether this point of view is a constructive way to think about reverence, collective memory, and victimage. Steven Carr, Keith Jenkins, and David Sterritt, for example, warn readers of the potential problems that come from overlooking key existential differences between the World War II Holocaust and 9/11 events.[73] Besides the obvious point that the 9/11 terrorist attacks killed about three thousand people and the Holocaust killed somewhere between six million and eleven million people, other issues of representation have been raised. Sterritt argues that while visual footage from the Holocaust wasn't released until after World War II, the images of 9/11 were *immediately circulated* in a host of mass-mediated venues, offering viewers "instant access" to the horrors of this day.[74] This difference might indicate that collective traumas for different historical periods might not be that related. Sterritt, however, concedes that in spite of these reservations, many continue to see these symbolic linkages:

> Both atrocities, the protracted one of the Holocaust and concentrated one of 9/11, produced widely seen images, and both did so despite limitations of visibility built into their material conditions—the concealment and secrecy with which the Holocaust was carried out, and the suddenness and localness of the Twin Towers' destruction. Once put into circulation, the images have proved enduring.[75]

We would also argue that the *reactions* to all of this apparent concealment have also been enduring, as we witness how all of the thanatopolitical worries at Ground Zero have manifested themselves in so many securitizing ways.

By now readers may be wondering: how do the objects that are displayed in the National September 11 Memorial Museum create the same type of affective feelings that one gets during a three- to four-hour tour of the USHMM? Below, we offer a short, performative analysis of the National September 11 Memorial Museum so that readers can see some of the influences that help with the spatial juxtapositions of these multidirectional memories.

Thanatopolitical Spaces at the National September 11 Memorial Museum

When the National September 11 Memorial Museum opened to the public in 2014, it was met with a host of emotive commentators on various struggles and accomplishments involved in the museum-making process. According to the National September 11 Memorial and Memorial Museum Foundation, the underground museum's 110,000 square feet of exhibition space "serves as the country's principal institution for examining the implications of the events of 9/11, documenting the impact of those events and exploring the continuing significance of September 11, 2001."[76]

The way that the museum is organized—spatially, visually, and aesthetically—makes it impossible for visitors not to experience some form of post-9/11 grief. When one of us visited this site in 2014, and another time in 2016, that person could not help noticing that the architecture, the pictures, the videos, the holograms, and the recordings produced a ghastly experience that reminded guests of cadaverous objects and haunting spectacles (figure 11). There were firefighter helmets, fire trucks, cellphones, shoes, wallets, bicycles, and fragments of metal shrapnel, all of which told dingpolitik stories about 9/11 horrors. Most of all, these abject museum artifacts produced thanatopolitical structures of feeling that recalled the crimes perpetrated by perfidious terrorists. These haunting presences invite visitors to view themselves as traumatized subjects still living in an exposed and vulnerable world of death and disaster after 9/11. This emotion-evoking display is consistent with Bradford Vivian's description of the rhetorical act of witnessing as the ensemble of "words, images, or other precious remainders of those who endured appalling oppression and injustice" that "endow historical accounts with auras of factual and emotional authenticity."[77]

Witnessing the luridness of these ghoulish objects has thus served as an obligatory act of citizenship for the post-9/11 melancholic citizen-subjects who now perform commemoration by taking this pilgrimage while they show that they have internalized the admonition—"Never forget."

In this particular case, the witnessing that "rhetorically evokes and shapes collective perceptions of time so as to commend appropriate historical, political, and moral judgments"[78] has mandated continued vigilance and counterterrorist displays.

Even journalists—trained to use an objectivist, dispassionate lens in their descriptive accounts of museological visits—could not help themselves as they too wrote about the darkness they witnessed during their early visits. Holland Cotter, for example, characterized the National September 11 Memorial Museum as a place and space that was simultaneously "a historical document, a monument to the dead [and] a theme-park-style tourist attraction."[79] Cotter went so far as to claim that the "prevailing" story in the museum, "as in a church, is framed in moral terms," where "the angels are many and heroic, the devils few and vile, a band of Islamic radicals" who "are identified in a cut-and-dried,

Fig. 11. Holograms of the "missing" posters at the
National September 11 Memorial Museum.

contextless and unnuanced film called 'The Rise of al Qaeda' seen at
the end of the exhibition."[80]

Artifacts like that six-minute video on the rise of al Qaeda help
coproduce the fragments into the production of master narratives that
frame the 9/11 attacks as if they could be compared to the beginning of
the rise of the Nazism that was the prelude to the Judeocide. As visitors
walk through various parts of the museum they are confronted with
dingpolitik objects that function as testaments to American victimage: wrecked ambulance cars, devastated fire trucks, and left-behind
vernacular items. It is no coincidence that some of these artifacts were
taken from the makeshift memorials that once painted the streets of
New York—teddy bears, unopened letters, piles of shoes, and firefighter
helmets (figure 12).

Fig. 12. Lady Liberty at the National September 11 Memorial and Memorial Museum.

"Stuff"[81] was arranged in such a way as to expose visitors to underground halls of terror, where people were encouraged to get to know the victims by reading their biographies and gazing at their pictures so that they could *feel* an attachment with their stories of victimage, much like the way objects function at the USHMM.[82]

Holland Cotter gave us an uncanny description of a typical visitor's experience when he characterized the museum as a place that offered a "descent into darkness" where "the stuff of suspense"[83] took center stage. A spatial tour of the museum began at the plaza stage, where visitors were confronted with "steel trident columns that were the signature features of the twin tower facades."[84] Then this typical journey took visitors seventy feet below ground, "where the foundations of the towers met raw Manhattan schist."[85] After visitors walk past the atrium and travel below the plaza, they are "out of the range of natural light, and not so neutral in feeling."[86] Visitors can now hear the recordings of the 9/11 narratives that gave "urgent accounts of catastrophe" that "crowd the air."[87] And of course, there is the exposed slurry wall, which was built as a foundation to the WTC and prevented the Hudson River from flooding Ground Zero (figure 13).

This movement underground is contextualized by commentary about "Missing" posters and vernacular objects that coated the city before the official memorial was ever constructed. One museum tour ended "at bedrock," where visitors have the option of visiting the galleries of those who died, something that Cotter regarded as "a disturbingly vivid evocation of the events themselves."[88] Adjacent to the commemorative exhibition is another room—a repository of some 7,930 remains that have not been identified by experts.[89] The choice of this repository as the final resting place for the unidentified victims conjured up even more thanatopolitical horror.[90]

It is quite obvious that the museum has produced a surplus of traumatic meaning about 9/11, and some objected to the way that curators represent 9/11. One group, called the 9/11 Parents and Families of Firefighters and WTC Victims, argued that they were not properly consulted during the museum planning stages, and they have been

Fig. 13. The slurry wall at the National September 11 Memorial Museum.

particularly vocal about their opposition to the on-site repository (figure 14). During the May 10, 2014, ceremonial transfer of the remains, a few dozen families protested the event on the grounds that they were not consulted about the decision to store the unidentified remains in the museum. In an article titled "The Worst Day of My Life Is Now New York's Hottest Tourist Attraction," one family member revealed that his "sister is among the many for whom there have been no remains recovered whatsoever. Vaporized. So there's no grave to visit. . . . Just this theatrically lit Ikea warehouse behind a panel of glass."[91] Many wore black gags over their mouths to symbolize their alleged marginalization, and a seventy-seven-year-old retired deputy chief in the fire department said, "We had no say in what was going on here. . . . You can't tell me that tour guides aren't going to be going inside that building and saying, 'Behind that wall are the victims of 9/11.' That's a

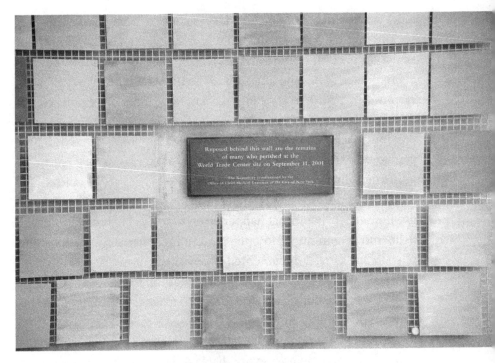

Fig. 14. Repository of the 9/11 victims at the National
September 11 Memorial Museum.

dog and pony show."[92] Charles Wolf, however, who was on the Families Advisory Council that worked with the Lower Manhattan Design Corporation in helping to design the memorial, responded by claiming that this organization was contradicting itself and was creating much ado over nothing.[93]

Regardless, it can be stated that for some, the National September 11 Memorial Museum blends American exceptionalist feelings with cosmopolitanism in complex ways. Affective feelings of grief and gruesomeness were used to signpost the individuality of death, trauma, and disaster at the same time that the museum invited national and international visitors to grieve collectively about terrorism. Adam Gopnik of the *New Yorker* similarly concluded, "The attempt to fill the museum with personal ephemera—the vitrines are stuffed with relics and mementos of the dead; even tapes of final phone calls play on a perpetual loop—seems merely macabre by comparison."[94] In an earlier portion of the same essay, Gopnik compared the National September 11 Memorial Museum to the USHMM, and he wrote about various similarities in style and design. For example, he pointed out that the director of the museum is Alice M. Greenwald, someone who previously served as the associate museum director for museum programs at the USHMM. Gopnik, however, was trying to make sure that his readers did not conflate the horrors of 9/11 with the Shoah, and he noted that the National September 11 Memorial and Memorial Museum is different because "what happened on 9/11, by contrast, was a crime deliberately committed in open air as a nightmarish publicity stunt, one already as well documented as any incident in history. We can't relearn it; we can only relive it."[95] One question that needs to be asked is whether museum visitors are forced to make this connection in the name of performing American antiterrorism.

The National September 11 Memorial Museum is yet another component of post-9/11 memory-work that is still only beginning to develop. The museum fleshes out the details of the hypersecuritized feeling of being watched that one felt while visiting the giant voids of the aboveground memorial.

In many ways, the museum takes collective national victimage one step farther by commodifying anxieties about death and disaster in near carnival fashion.[96] Alan Feuer commented on how local New Yorkers felt about the museum, and he surmised that handfuls would stay away until the rush of tourists calmed down, if ever. One survivor who was interviewed by Feuer argued that the museum "was made for people who don't really know what 9/11 is about."[97] Another blithely stated that he "won't visit it anytime soon" because "it promises to be filled with gawking, ghoulish out-of-towners who will overwhelm the New Yorkers, who lived through the sorrow of those days and will have a hard time getting in."[98] While many New Yorkers were simply waiting for a quasi-return to normalcy during the opening ceremonies, the National September 11 Memorial and Memorial Museum was attracting tourists drawn to the permanent suspension of relief and closure as they thought about terrorist dangers.

In a few years, we will know whether this talk of Holocaust analogies and dark tourism at the National September 11 Memorial Museum will resonate with diverse American audiences. In one *New York Times* article, titled "As 9/11 Museum Opens, These New Yorkers Will Stay Away," Alan Feuer noted that "some people said they did not need a public exhibition to remind them of a personal tragedy that they could not forget. Others simply said they would not find healing or relief at the memorial—only more pain."[99] Yet for millions of potential visitors, traveling to this site was almost obligatory, a vicarious—and nationalist— way of recalling the horrors of that day and revering the dead.

Regardless, there is no question that the past and present darkness that continues to haunt this famous place has roused complicated, multidirectional memories between the Holocaust and 9/11. At first glance it may appear to be irrational to make analogous arguments about the loss of approximately three thousand lives versus at least six million, but we need to remember the magnitude of traumas that we described in the first few chapters of this book. Perceptions matter, and such is the nature of argument assemblages that take on securi-tized functions, especially when they involve darker, posttraumatic remembrances. Thanatopolitical affects, after all, are not quantifiable. This is why emotive public memories are just as important as rational, realpolitik claims-making.

Conclusion

It is our hope that this chapter's transglobal reading of the National September 11 Memorial Museum informs readers about how affective displays of fear and anxiety are appropriated to sustain biopolitical and thanatopolitical motives. Future researchers may want to build on our work by questioning how terrorist dark tourist attractions produce particular kinds of subjects and events. As we have demonstrated, the 9/11 tourist, and the post-9/11 subject, provide supportive examples of Marieke De Goede's securitized subject who is controlled by those who produce insecure imaginaries filled with traumatic pasts and uncertain futures.[100] This may provide us with a more detailed example of what Lennon and Foley call dark tourism[101] because it is here we are dealing with multidirectional memory-work that involves both Holocaust consciousness-raising as well as 9/11 edification. This melding of different horrific memories supplies a materialistic, spatial heterochronia that breaks linear time by comparing events from different periods.[102]

We therefore encourage future researchers who analyze this emerging phenomenon to consider the thanatopolitical dynamics of space at other places of tourism, so that they can trace the production and maintenance of subjects within their historical, and sometimes transnational, assemblages. For example, they may want to compare and contrast some of the dingpolitik and realpolitik that swirls around the Holocaust and the Stalinist genocides that have become part of the multidirectional and competitive memories of museology and commemoration in the former countries that were part of the pre-1989 Soviet Union. As Egle Rindzeviciute argued in 2011, "knowledge about the Soviet deportation of people, to use the expression of Bruno Latour, was produced in public and used to shape a new public around it."[103] Rindzeviciute speculated that while scholars seem to assume that nation-states control the archives and the knowledge production and "assembling and representing" of things that become the "material settings for stabilizing knowledge" about topics like the Holocaust or Soviet rule, perhaps researchers might profit theoretically or methodologically from approaches that pay attention to the "highly messy and complex" forces that are linked to perceived consensus or even governmental strategies.[104]

Others may find that post-Holocaust consciousness-raising takes many of us in unanticipated rhetorical directions.

Conclusion

How the National September 11 Memorial and
Memorial Museum Functions as a Political Platform
for Legitimating Future U.S. Interventionism

Others have written about how securitizing and militarized rhetorics have been used to invent real and imagined enemies for initiating wars, legitimating lethal strikes by drones, justifying extraterritorial incursions by special forces to "get" bin Laden, and using enhanced interrogation, but in this concluding chapter we illustrate how tourist sites can also be used as epideictic forums. We display how some dark tourist "terrorist museums" become venues that allow certain arguers to advocate for never-ending counterterrorism.

To maintain a perpetual war that has to be fought against a growing list of al Qaeda, the Taliban, ISIS, and other foes, various American and coalition publics must be convinced they are living in twenty-first-century states of emergency, exception, or insecurity. At times, a nation's commander in chief may issue an executive order, a congressional leader may present a speech in some legislative forum, or an investigative journalist may write a persuasive essay that contributes to the metaphoric beating of war drums on the Potomac, but those are not the only performative acts that help produce, and reproduce, securitizations.

American liberals and other critics of U.S. counterterrorist policies make a mistake when they blame single rhetors like George W. Bush,[1] Colin Powell, and influential media pundits for leading America into some counterterrorist "quagmire."[2] The otherwise excellent work of someone like Mark Danner blames empowered figures for "Rumsfeld's War,"[3] but as we have argued since the introduction, all of this focus on the intentionality of single individuals misses the constitutive coproduction of larger ideological formations.

Focusing on the securitizing or militarist discourses of some single great or influential leader underestimates the vernacular nature of the counterterrorist rhetorics that are coproduced by millions of elites and citizens who share the motives and interests of their leaders. The disputes over everything from the representation of the Smithsonian's Enola Gay to the reinterpretations of the Vietnam Veterans Memorial remind us of the symbolic importance of collective actions that can sometimes produce what James Young and others call "counter-monument."[4]

If James Young, Marita Sturken, and many other interdisciplinary scholars who study both architectural forms and cultural memorial contexts are right, then it behooves us to study not just the contentious nature of architectural disputation but also the militarized and securitized demands of publics who want their histories, monuments, and museums to represent their own counterterrorist solutions.

Again, these states of insecurity are not simply produced by those who pass laws, execute those laws, or judicially interpret texts like the Patriot Act of 2001. Many of those who helped elect Donald Trump now talk about terrorist threats at the Mexican borders and the need to build figurative and literal walls, and Washington DC is no longer the only potential epicenter of counterterrorist responses. States of insecurity are therefore not just the topics that occupy the attention of academics, Pentagon generals, Washington senators, or supporters of "unitary executive" powers.[5]

These days, when trillions of dollars are willingly spent by elites and public communities for counterterrorist efforts, even visitors to the National September 11 Memorial and Memorial Museum can feel as though they too have participated in fighting the enemy. Evocative patriotic sentiments, existential feelings of perpetual victimhood, and traumatic states of (in)securitization have helped influence the formation of what we have called "terrorist museums."

Granted, we do need to keep track of situations where former presidents like George W. Bush pay "surprise" visits to these grounds,[6] but as we noted in previous chapters, this focus on empowered rhetors should be balanced with studies of larger post-9/11 ideological forces.[7] How laypersons, as well as museum curators, tourists, and others react to the speeches of those who visit this site after the 2014 opening of the museum has much to tell us about the a nation's collective willingness to maintain states of counterterrorist preparedness.

We contend it is no coincidence that many rhetors asked to present major speeches at the National September 11 Memorial and Memorial Museum help legitimate, amplify, and echo some of the same securitizing messages that appear in museum videos, interactive materials, and captions of many artifacts strategically selected by curators or journalists writing about this space. The dingpolitik of fire trucks, columns, and bandannas can be symbolically linked to realpolitik speeches about future counterterror or counterinsurgency efforts.

Many of the luminaries who visit this securitized site of public memory link their own decision-making to the material artifacts that appear at the memorial and museum. For example, in December 2014, when former president George W. Bush visited the museum, he appeared to be overcome with emotion as he touched the Fifth Column, the exhibit that displayed the last steel beam removed from Ground Zero, in 2002.[8] The Bush administration, after all, made the momentous decisions that ushered in the Global War on Terrorism (GWOT), and even though former president Bush did not join then-president Obama at the opening, he sent along a statement thanking "all those who played a role in creating this inspiring tribute."[9]

Another popular visitor to the museum is ex–Navy SEAL Robert O'Neill, who unexpectedly met with 9/11 families as he explained that he was the soldier who came face to face with the man who "masterminded" the killing of their loved ones.[10] An even broader audience was allowed to performatively become a part of what might be called "security theater" when *Fox News* decided to capture this "breaking the silence" moment on video and air it. One surviving wife of a 9/11 victim told O'Neill that he didn't "close a chapter" but "closed the book,"[11] but this speaker may have underestimated the persistent needs and the motives of those who did not want the same type of closure. Killing bin Laden may have been an important milestone, but this particular exhibitionary complex and securitized war machine needed other, invented enemies. Recall the families of the victims talking about the need to go after low-level fighters and all of the Saudis who may have aided and abetted terrorists.

Instead of being a hallowed place for burying contentious pasts or commemorating the acts of those who became the unwitting victims of a war with al Qaeda, these securitized grounds have been used to satisfy an assortment of other political needs that take us far away from what happened on September 11, 2001. For example, O'Neill's visit conjured up images of events taking place thousands of miles away. This was a geographical imaginary filled with tales of famous snipers, remarks about participants in Operation Neptune Spear to capture or kill bin Laden in Pakistan, lectures by FBI agents lauding the efforts of their agency around the globe, speeches by diplomats about securitizing embassies, and those who insisted that efficacious counterinsurgency required stricter immigration restriction.

This constantly expanding list of topics that can be linked to the GWOT and the securitization of the National September 11 Memorial and Memorial Museum resonates with countless local and national visitors to these secular and sacred spaces and places. It is not unusual on anniversaries of the 9/11 attacks, for instance, to find members of the FBI's New York field office mingling with citizens who participate in a "9/11 Memorial RunWalk." Dozens of participants in these activities gather in front of 26 Federal Plaza, and while some carry commemorative 9/11 flags, others lead the group past the Police Memorial at Liberty Street and South End Avenue before they head toward the New York City firehouse Engine 10/Ladder 10.[12]

On the fourteenth anniversary of 9/11, more than a thousand of the victims' relatives, recovery workers, and survivors traveled to Ground Zero "to keep the toll front of mind as years pass."[13] Tom Acquaviva told reporters that it seemed as though the crowds have diminished over time, but this eighty-one-year-old said that as long as he was breathing he was going to be there.[14] A CBS writer used the occasion to remind readers that the fourteenth anniversary was coming in the wake of news that a "Florida man" was being charged with plotting to set off an explosive at a 9/11 event in Kansas City. The same reporter noted that the FBI joint terrorist task force had arrested a suspect after someone tried to tell an online informant how to make the bomb he wanted.[15] These anecdotal examples of what we would call *populist securitization* allow visitors to the memorial and museum to treat their pilgrimage as an act of resistance.

These types of patriotic and popular commemorative practices have turned travel and tourism into securitized actions of participatory deliberation that help ratify, and legitimate, the counterterrorist decisions of empowered U.S. civilian and military leaders. In this "new" global war on terrorism the conflict does not end with the death of Osama bin Laden, the dismantling of the major cells made up of high-value al Qaeda detainees, or the reduction of the power of the Taliban in Afghanistan or Pakistan. As Robert Ivie and Oscar Giner explain in *Hunt the Devil*, America's "national psyche" demands constant U.S. deployments that are a part of a cycle of mythical projects,[16] and in this case it is the complex and multidirectional nature of tourism to patriotic sites that becomes a key part of securitizing war cultures.

Here, unlike the Korean War or the Vietnam War, commentators and visitors do not talk and write about discernible beginning and endpoints. The strategic ambiguity that has become such a key feature of this perpetual war against terrorism ensures that many different speakers—who can provide primary, secondary, and tertiary links to "what happened" on 9/11—will get a hearing if they travel and speak at this venue.

The recursive nature of public and elite securitized rhetorics, and the protean features of these counterterrorist rhetorics, have paved the way for the presentation of public addresses at this hallowed ground that helped turn the National September 11 Memorial and Memorial Museum into a venue for defending U.S. governmentality and private outsourcing of key parts of what detractors call the "American war machine." This is not a site for any detailed interrogation of why American military forces were in Central Asia or the Middle East before 2001, nor is this a public arena for debating the wisdom of foreign interventionism, lethal drone strikes, night raids in Afghanistan, or the use of Special Forces by U.S. Africa Command. Instead, mainstream journalists, milbloggers, and many others who read and talk about this place want to hear more and more uplifting stories about the heroism of diverse social agents who collectively know the importance of fighting "America's Way of War." More than a few want to congratulate aggressive members of the nation's Special Forces, CIA operatives who tried to "get" bin Laden, the conventional forces who joined overseas contingency operations, and anyone else who can publicly align themselves with the first responders and the victims of 9/11.

We realize these are contentious claims, but the rest of this chapter displays the varied ways that visiting crowds, and mainstream journalists, laud the efforts of presidents, congressional leaders, diplomatic dignitaries, military leaders, celebrities, and others whose neoliberal messages have everything to do with securitizing twenty-first-century America.

We begin this concluding chapter by providing myriad examples of how U.S. supporters of the GWOT have used these spaces and places for epideictic purposes since the 2014 opening of the National September 11 Memorial Museum.

The National September 11 Memorial and Memorial Museum's Futuristic, Twenty-First-Century Securitized Activities

There is little question that many visitors to the memorial and museum expect that speakers invited to this venue will help with the commemoration and preservation of the memory of those who died on September 11, 2001. Yet it is not always easy to predict the trajectory of some of these commemorative practices.

When Pope Francis spoke at an interreligious prayer service at Ground Zero on September 25, 2015, he described how the water that flowed at the memorial reminded many of the "thousands of lives that were taken in a senseless act of destruction."[17] Unlike many others who spoke about the need for perpetual counterterrorist violence in the name of retribution, revenge, or preventive deterrence, Pope Francis provided a more cosmopolitan critique of international violence in general:

> The flowing water is also a symbol of our tears. Tears at so much devastation and ruin, past and present. This is a place where we shed tears, we weep out of a sense of helplessness in the face of injustice, murder, and the failure to settle conflicts through dialogue. Here we mourn the wrongful and senseless loss of innocent lives because of the inability to find solutions which respect the common good.[18]

The pope was able to contrast the existence of some metropolis that might seem "impersonal, faceless, and lonely" with the mutual support, solidarity, and sacrifices of those who died on September 11, 2001, without regard to "race, nationality, neighborhoods, religion, or politics."[19]

Candidates for major offices have also ventured to these sacred grounds, and a few want listeners to focus on their own "get tough on terrorism" plans. When Donald Trump was campaigning for the 2016 presidential election, for example, he brought along an entourage of media personnel during his visit to the National September 11 Memorial and Memorial Museum, and some posted photographs of Mr. Trump on Twitter that showed him standing in front of a wall of portraits of 9/11 victims.

Not everyone approved of this politicizing of public memory at the memorial and museum. "Of the tens of millions of people from all over the world who have come to the place where so many people have died, and where so many heroes sacrificed their lives to save others, Mr. Trump may be the only one to bring along the press to chronicle his first visit," noted Debra Burlingame.[20]

Some visitors come to talk about small programs that need broader journalistic coverage, and these events help broaden the reach of the museum's free evening program series. For example, retired special agent Mary Galligan was invited to speak on her supervision of the 9/11 investigation. She explained to visitors of the memorial and museum's website that as soon as she heard that a commercial airliner had crashed into the World Trade Center, she knew that al Qaeda was responsible. Her experiences in Yemen, where she had spent months as an on-scene commander who investigated the attack on the USS *Cole*, and her service in Tanzania during the time of the U.S. embassy bombing, had led to her appointment as the supervisor of PENTTBOM, the FBI's 9/11 investigation.[21]

These types of FBI stories appeal to veterans and their families who know all about the USS *Cole* or President Clinton's orders regarding the firing of Tomahawk missiles in Tanzania, and it gets a hearing from those who believe that these behind-the-scenes narratives provide situational awareness that cannot be understood by those who object to the carrying out of the GWOT.

Yet for readers to more fully understand some of the realpolitik that swirls around these visits, they need to see more detailed critical rhetorical analyses of some of the speeches that helped with the securitization of the National 9/11 Museum. As you read our critiques, keep in mind the claims we made about the *production*, and not just representation, of real and imagined threats. It matters how speakers who visit these sites of public memory frame domestic and international issues.

A Close Reading of William Brennan's CIA Storytelling at the National September 11 Memorial and Memorial Museum

One of the most telling examples of American exceptionalist bully-pulpit speeches at the National September 11 Memorial Museum was delivered when the former CIA director John Brennan visited this place on September 26, 2016. Elsewhere, Brennan had been one of the leading spokespersons for former president Barack Obama's administration, and he had supplied journalists and laypersons with many oratorical defenses of America's "just war" against terrorism and stories about precision drone warfare, but when he visited the National September 11 Memorial Museum in New York City, he seemed to be motivated by the desire to mainstream CIA securitizing activities.

Like many of the speakers who traveled to this hallowed ground, Brennan mentioned the sacrifices of those who died on September 11, 2001, but what made his presentation especially memorable, and positively unique, was the way he used the occasion to help establish parallels between the efforts of the 9/11 first responders and the activities of the CIA during the GWOT. Unlike the CIA's detractors who had complained about the alleged torturing of high-value detainees, the extraterritorial lethal strikes in Pakistan, and other potential abuses of executive authority, Brennan characterized the CIA in his 2016 address as being among the first to "man" the ramparts against foreign foes. For example, he regaled listeners with stories of how fifteen years before his visit—on that very same day—a team of CIA officers had boarded an "unmarked, Soviet-made Mi-17 helicopter that landed in the Panjshir Valley of northern Afghanistan."[22] In his framing of affairs, seven Americans stepped out of their lumbering aircraft and were greeted by members of Afghanistan's Northern Alliance, who were "eager to meet with the Americans and join forces with the United States against al-Qa'da."[23]

Brennan then presented a narrative about a CIA mission called "Jawbreaker" as a way of explaining the importance of mounting early missions to go after and kill Osama bin Laden.[24] Jawbreaker, explained Brennan, was going to be the "first salvo in a global counterterrorism campaign that continues to this day," and he underscored the point that this was used to "unleash America's response to the 9/11 attacks."[25] Temporal and geospatial distance is removed as actions in faraway lands are linked to perceived threats in the homeland.

As he talked about Jawbreaker, Brennan could not help dwelling on his personal role in this affair when he served as the CIA's deputy executive director, and he implied that senior agency officials and operatives in the field knew about mounting al-Qaeda threats long before 9/11. He remembered, after all, exactly where he was when the second enemy aircraft crashed into the South Tower on live TV, and he averred that he was one of many who, for many months, had been "following the increased drumbeat of threat reporting."[26] Here there is little mention of the embarrassing fact that at one time the CIA helped fund the efforts of bin Laden and other mujahideen forces. Instead, Brennan's chronology focuses on events just before and after 9/11. This was a time when the CIA seemed to be ahead of the curve, based on their mosaics and the human intelligence gathering that helped them keep track of morphing al Qaeda threats.

In Brennan's telling of how the CIA responded to bin Laden's threats on domestic shores, director George Tenet and the CIA's entire leadership team are configured as heroes who packed into conference rooms as they pieced together thousands of bits of information that came from their questioning of individuals like Ramzi Yousef, the "convicted mastermind of the 1993 World Trade Center Bombing."[27]

Brennan sutured together past, present, and future national security threats in a monologue that mentions the chartering of the CIA after World War II and recognizes the need to confront the "painful reality that our country was enduring another Pearl Harbor."[28] This popular linking of members of the "greatest generation" to contemporary audiences is a popular rhetorical strategy in twenty-first-century commemoration, and it gained even more resonance when Brennan explained that Director Tenet's swift actions—including the checking of passenger manifests—helped validate the national security adviser's beliefs that Osama bin Laden and al Qaeda had orchestrated the attacks. This validation was treated as an intelligence coup that played a major role in waging America's continued fight against terrorism.

In a host of metaphoric and metonymic ways, the description of Direct Tenet's efforts is used to paint hagiographic pictures of the CIA's relentless pursuit of the nation's number one enemy. For example, in Brennan's temporal punctuation of time, the CIA "had already been at war with al Qaeda since December 1998," and the director had sent out members to "Agency principles declaring as much."[29] The CIA's declarations on this "war" thus become pronouncements that stand for the views of the entire United States.

Rhetorical commentaries like these are used to popularize, legitimate, and normalize the use of extreme violence in the name of national security, and it is the professional skills of CIA operatives working overseas that become the focal point of John Brennan's address at the National September 11 Memorial and Memorial Museum. At the same time that he implies that the Northern Alliance represented the majoritarian public will in Afghanistan, he explains to his listeners that CIA officers traveling to this part of the world knew all about what military scholars call "hearts and minds" counterinsurgency tactics. Here it would be unthinkable that the Taliban or Afghan insurgents represented the views of the millions of Afghan citizens who may not have needed American interventionism.

Perhaps his listening audiences expected to hear some American exceptionalist remarks, and if so, they were not disappointed. Brennan lauds the CIA officers who had a "thorough grounding in the culture, knew the players, and understood the rivalries."[30] Unlike the British imperialists or the Soviet occupiers who quickly found that this was the "graveyard of empires" the American forces who populate Brennan's works know how to deal with Taliban enemies.

In Brennan's telling of the tale, American heroism, dedication, and technical prowess are underscored in this peroration.

During the second half of his address, Brennan argued that in those early months and years after 9/11/01, CIA agents put aside their petty squabbles, cut through red tape, and ended their turf wars as more and more volunteered for "counterterrorist assignments." An obviously proud Brennan elaborated by noting:

> It was a snapshot of the Agency at its best—a relatively small and agile organization that serves as the Nation's overseas troubleshooters. In combatting al-Qa'ida, just knowing the identity and location of the enemy was well over half the battle. And no other group was in a better position to lead the charge.[31]

Any members of intelligence communities in the audience would know he was implying that the FBI's criminological way of handling terrorism would not have prepared them for the challenges that the CIA handled with skill and grace.

In fascinating ways, an agency that had once been accused of being involved in coups, assassinations, foreign intrigue, and avoidance of congressional oversight and accountability was rhetorically transformed into an organization that fielded needed "agency paramilitary teams." This GWOT was clearly going to involve much more than the criminal trials of a few al Qaeda operations who might have aided and abetted the 9/11 hijackers.

John Brennan did not simply dwell on past threats—he also focused on present dangers and potential future catastrophes. He deftly celebrated the decimation of key enemy cells while magnifying persistent and morphing terrorist threats:

> The core al-Qa'ida organization that attacked this city is now a shadow of its former self. It was pushed out of Afghanistan, largely dismantled, and is now scattered around South Asia. Much of its cachet and influence among the extremist terrorist community died with bin Ladin. . . . Regional al-Qa'ida affiliates that have sprung up since 9/11 also pose serious challenges—groups like al-Qa'ida in the Arabian Peninsula; Jabhat al-Nusra in Syria, and al-Qa'ida in the Islamic Maghreb. . . . they remain capable of mounting external terrorist operations to this day. And, of course, what used to be al-Qa'ida in Iraq morphed into Daesh, or the so-called Islamic State in Iraq and the Levant. . . . It is also a younger group as well as more sophisticated and more dangerous in its use of the digital domain.[32]

Brennan, like the NYPD officers who wanted to secure the part of Lower Manhattan around the World Trade Center, was sure America faced continual terrorist threats.

Brennan is able to recognize the gains that came from the bin Laden raid without having to say that that his death "ended" the GWOT. Brennan's comments on the omnipresence of new enemies, who are allegedly capable of carrying out similar attacks, transforms this site from a sort of mausoleum to a place continuously under threat from future attacks in the GWOT. His comments also broaden the range of enemies—and the list of potential CIA interventionist practices—to include anything that can be labeled a threat to an embassy, a friendly country, or even any portion of the "digital domain" that some CIA officer deems a threat.

From poststructural vantage points, this is not some social scientific exercise where a leading terrorist expert simply represents preexisting terrorist realities. What he is doing here is an exercise in knowledge production, in which the podium at the National 9/11 Memorial is used strategically to defer, for the foreseeable future, any "end" to this type of irregular warfare. As our critical participatory colleagues are fond of saying, "place matters," and Brennan is asking his listeners—who are social-media-savvy—to think how dangerous it is to have a "younger group" recruited by terrorist foes. Brennan, the CIA, and this museum become a part of that terror exhibitionary complex that we discussed in previous chapters.

We can guess that Brennan, who seemed to view himself as an Orientalist expert on the "Middle East," would vehemently disagree with our critique, and parts of his peroration do sound as if he were presenting rebuttal arguments in a heated debate about "the facts" behind some of the public claims made by CIA spokespersons. Perhaps sensing that his geographical imagination has taken him far away from 9/11, Brennan uses the rest of his address to establish myriad links between the CIA and what he calls "national security elements"—law enforcement, the military, the intelligence community, "overseas partners," and a "sense of common cause among our citizens."[33] Was he on point when he implied that the NYPD and other security officials took for granted that the CIA needed to be involved in tracking down so many omnipresent enemies? Or was he trying to use the rhetorical technique of identification to broaden his constituency and make them feel that they too would have put together the same mosaics if they had been in his shoes?

Activating both dingpolitik and realpolitik topoi, Brennan also focused on some of the material objects that helped the CIA create symbolic bridges between the CIA's memorialization and the National September 11 Memorial Museum:

Thirty-three stars of the 117 on [the] CIA's Memorial Wall attest to the lives of Agency women and men lost in the line of duty since September 2001. The first of them was Mike Spann, a remarkably brave and dedicated officer who came to us from the Marines and was the first American to die in Afghanistan in the aftermath of 9/11, on 25 November 2001. We will always remember Mike—and all our colleagues who died combatting terrorism—for their valor and supreme skill. . . . The same holds true for the firemen, police officers, and paramedics who died here in Manhattan 15 years ago, along with the innocents they tried so hard to save—all of whose stories are lovingly preserved and retold by this wonderful museum.[34]

It would be for these reasons that Brennan had little trouble unabashedly celebrating the "American exceptionalism" that he argued came from the Constitution, the nation's natural resources, U.S. economic power, and America's diverse "melting pot." These characteristics, he averred, meant that the United States. also had exceptional responsibilities and thus had to take the lead in countering perceived international threats and instability around the globe.[35]

If listeners had any doubts regarding the reach of U.S. power and the extraterritorial jurisdiction of the CIA, they would be erased by Brennan's laundry list of places he thought posed dilemmas that required American attention. Items on the list amounted to a responsibility-to-protect call to help "millions of innocent citizens" in Syria, those threatened by a destabilized "North Korea," and even the "hackers, terrorists, and governments" that exploited unregulated cyberspace as they try to "steal wealth and intellectual property, indoctrinate followers, and subvert democratic institutions."[36]

The CIA's hot-button topics meant that civilians who cared about their safety should defer to the judgment of CIA officials who were collecting information on all of these existential threats.

Is it any coincidence that Brennan's 2016 cataloging of CIA concerns seemed to reflect and refract the populist views of many of the visitors who traveled to the National September 11 Memorial and Memorial

Museum? As we alluded to earlier, this type of rhetorical strategy may be considered a populist securitization tactic that casts narratives of continual threats to national securities that members of the public, like the CIA, can read about. They may not have access to the secret "mosaics" produced by members of intelligence communities, but they can use their own common sense as they think about everything from North Korean threats to the stealing of commercial information.

After listening to Brennan, who could doubt that the CIA was doing essential work that helped with containment of terrorist foes? Invoking memories of heroism and resilience against the tragedy of 9/11 at Ground Zero in situ, Brennan uses the National September 11 Memorial Museum as a platform for turning contingent, partial, and controversial information into irrefutable factual information about "real" terrorist threats.

Security Theater: Robert O'Neill and the Spectacle of American Heroism

When Robert O'Neill visited the National September 11 Memorial Museum on May 1, 2011, he did not intend to deliver a speech about his 2011 assassination of Osama bin Laden to a group of about thirty families of 9/11 victims. Rather, he planned on just taking a private tour of the museum itself, which made sense due to his anonymous donation of the T-shirt he wore when he made the kill shots on that fateful night in bin Laden's Abbottabad compound. Strangely, though, he wanted to be recorded, which is why he asked *Fox News* to document his journey to bedrock. When he was introduced to the families of 9/11 victims in the private room mentioned in chapter 4, the words just poured out of him, and he felt he found a new purpose in sharing his story about Operation Neptune Spear to as many Americans as possible in the years to come. More than that, he saw it as his patriotic duty.

O'Neill's story, told during his spontaneous visit to the museum, was full of tropes of sacrifice, heroism, and resilience. It was a textbook example of post-9/11 patriotism, and as it turns out, it was exactly the kind stuff that families of victims wanted to hear. There was talk, for instance, about how he gained personal motivation to fulfill the mission from the memories of all of those who perished on 9/11, how he and his team of Navy Six were prepared to sacrifice their lives for the mission, and the satisfaction that came from carrying out the execution of America's public enemy number one. O'Neill's impromptu speech provided the families with levels of comfort and security that could only be attained from encounters with the man who came face to shadowy face with the enemy and who shot him two times in the skull. And once more "in the head" for "insurance,"[37] he later explained. One of the family members, Monica Iken Murphy—who lost her husband on 9/11—told O'Neill, "I feel a little bit safer because of you . . . and the work your men do and the women. . . . I'm just grateful."[38]

Consider the way O'Neill talked about how the memories of 9/11 gave him the courage and inspiration to carry out his duty despite great odds of surviving a trip that was dubbed "a one-way mission" to Abbottabad. "I remember talking to the guys," he is quoted saying on the National September 11 Memorial Museum website—one of the only platforms that has transcriptions of O'Neill's private conversation with the families.[39] "There was never a hesitation. We're going now, were going to do this for . . . the single mom that went to work on Tuesday morning [on 9/11] and then decided it's better to jump to her death than burn alive. We went for her. We went for the firefighters who were running up as everyone was running down. We went for everybody."[40] The photographs and the television coverage of these events and the daily activities of survivors were all a part of security assemblage.

O'Neill has also talked about how he gained motivation from the recollection of something former president George W. Bush once said when O'Neill and his team were on that dreadful ninety-minute helicopter ride through the Pakistani night to bin Laden's compound. "On the flight on the way to kill Osama bin Laden," O'Neill explained to Steve Doocy of *Fox News* in an interview, "Out of nowhere I said the quote from George W. Bush on 9/11. He said, 'Freedom itself was attacked this morning by a faceless coward and freedom will be defended.'"[41]

After the Abbottabad mission O'Neill tattooed those words on his left arm, an example of embodied rhetoric.

O'Neill went on to tell the families of 9/11 victims that he and his crew were prepared to sacrifice their lives for the greater good, and they all understood the risks involved. "We accepted it; we weren't' afraid," he said. "We had been fighting since 9/11 . . . to get to a spot of preparedness to be good enough to get this mission done. This was a means—a proof of concept [that] 'we're going to be able to do this,' and we're not coming back."[42]

Then came the climax of encountering bin Laden when O'Neill said the next thing he knew, the mastermind of 9/11 was "a foot and a half in front of me. And I shot him twice, and then once more."[43] After the deed, O'Neill admitted, "it didn't really sink in." He then recounted the momentary quandary of what to do next:

> The wife [of bin Laden] sort of came at me and there was like, [a] two-year-old kid there. So I pulled her over to the bed and grabbed the kid. And I remember thinking to grab the kid because he had nothing to do with this. I [didn't] want him to be afraid. So I picked him up, put him with the wife.[44]

A moment of humanity that heroes, and those who revere heroes, would understand.

In this telling of the tale danger was omnipresent. Reflecting on the killing of bin Laden, O'Neill later said, "Standing over him in that moment, looking down on him, hearing him exhale his last breath—I could hear it, it was quite a moment." Getting to that moment of satisfaction was no easy feat. Even still, "there was never a moment of hesitation," he told *Fox News* at the National September 11 Memorial Museum. "The team not only not feared . . . [but knew] . . . this needs to happen." It was a feeling of, "We'll do this. We're going to die doing this but it's worth it."[45]

After his meeting with the 9/11 families, O'Neill realized that it was part of his duty to share his heroic tale with as many people as possible to help them heal from the traumatic wounds of 9/11. In an interview at the bedrock of Ground Zero, he told reporters that one grandfather told him that he had "killed the devil," and that made him realize that all of this was "bigger than the team."[46]

By the time he finished speaking, everyone "in the room was crying," O'Neill later explained. "They couldn't hold the tears back. That was the first time I publicly told the story. I thought: if I can do it for these people, I can do it for more people."[47] His visit to the National September 11 Memorial and Museum had helped him find peace and another mission in life.

Now that O'Neill has gone public with his story, he says his "life is on airplanes," because he is so busy sharing his inspirational story with so many Americans across the country. Traveling "five or six days a week,"[48] O'Neill feels like he is doing his part to help post-9/11 America heal.

> I travel around the country. I talk to Americans every day. . . . I get a call or an e-mail from a 9/11 family member who lost a husband, a wife, a son, or a daughter and saying "thank you for coming forward with this because your helping with the process." . . . The assumption of risk is worth it again because . . . we're healing as a nation.[49]

In this securitization rhetoric, the National September 11 Memorial Museum becomes an epideictic forum, a place of praise and blame, where there is little question of the existential nature of terrorist evil or the rectitude of those who killed bin Laden. Here there is no discussion of "extrajudicial" killings, no mention of Pakistani sovereignty. The exclusive focus is on the bond between the 9/11 family members and one of those who carried out the revenge that brought them "justice." From a Foucauldian standpoint, performing a thanatopolitical task had biopolitical consequences. The United States, and the world, now had one less "high-value" terrorist to worry about. Society had to be defended.

O'Neill is now perhaps as close as a Navy SEAL can get to having celebrity status. With his retired Navy SEAL T-shirt framed at the base of the National September 11 Memorial Museum, and with the circulation of a newly released book titled *The Operator: Firing the Shots That*

Killed bin Laden, we can understand why Internet visitors might flock to see his public-profile website that contains numerous interviews and statements about Operation Neptune Spear.

O'Neill has become a poster boy for the GWOT. At times his public iconicity rivals that of Chris Kyle, the Navy SEAL who was immortalized in *American Sniper,* the popular film directed by Clint Eastwood. Kyle would be remembered in military and civilian circles for his record of 160 kill-shots during four tours in Iraq. In fact, just before Kyle was tragically killed by a deranged veteran he was trying to help, he sent O'Neill a copy of his book, *American Sniper,* with a note that said, "Good shot."[50] These welters of cultural fragments link spaces and places to objects and events that only add to the securitization of this site of public memory.

It is stories like O'Neill's that amplify the populist appeal of post-9/11 securitization practices, as the glories of the GWOT are recounted for audiences who want them to take center stage. Some might argue that twenty-first-century warfare has entered a "post-heroic age,"[51] but O'Neill's reception at the National September 11 Memorial and Memorial Museum showed that some still need heroes.

Perhaps this search for heroes, as well as storytelling about good triumphing over evil, explains, in part, some of the nostalgia for World War II memorabilia and the desire to Americanize the Holocaust we discussed in the previous chapter.[52] Regardless, O'Neill's testimony on the killing of bin Laden not only has proved consoling to the families of 9/11 victims but also renders legible parts of an invisible Special Forces war that is affectively materialized at this securitized space of public remembrance. In the same way that Brennan was able to humanize the CIA and connect with first responders, O'Neill treated the Special Forces as the avengers who had set things right.

In his own way, O'Neill also concretizes the otherwise abstract rhetorics of securitization. After all, did some of the 9/11 family members say they felt more security?

Popular culture has, of course, had much to do with this this securitization dispositif—from *Saving Private Ryan* to *American Sniper* and

Zero Dark Thirty.[53] These films become part of what Roger Stahl has called "Militainment Inc.," a term used to describe how media and popular culture "revel in the suspense and excitement, and inevitably the violence and suffering, of combat."[54] To Stahl, the production of Militainment, Inc., showed "that this state violence is not of the abstract, distant, or historical variety but rather an impending or current use of force, one directly relevant to the citizen's current political life."[55]

Visitors to the National September 11 Memorial and Memorial Museum thus become part of the GWOT's securitized imaginary as they listen to Brennan and O'Neill and hail them as some of today's most successful counterterrorist warriors.

When O'Neill mentions his personal memories of 9/11 and ties them to the heroic killing of bin Laden, he does so at a special place that brings together the realpolitik of White House situation rooms with the dingpolitik of shirts, guns, helicopters, and bin Laden's body parts.

Sadly, O'Neill's image events, which could have been turned into a moment of possible traumatic closure or provided an opportunity to discuss the potential "end" of the GWOT, were turned into epideictic moments that blamed foreigners for America's vulnerability. This is the affective and cerebral material that helps coproduce the post-9/11 security assemblage and counterterrorist imaginaries. In this way, members of Navy SEAL Team 6 are no longer the only ones who can relish in the phantasmagoria of bin Laden's death, as this structure of feeling is also made accessible to all of those who visit this site of public memory.

Robert O'Neill's almost apocryphal tale of the killing of bin Laden made it nearly a foregone conclusion that any number-one enemy of the United States was not going to be captured and interrogated. This type of spectral evil was so extraordinary that it could only be fought by the best of America's fighting forces. Not only the telling of O'Neill's tale but the media coverage of his storytelling led to the theatrical staging of a retributive story that comes full circle, where the protagonist family members get to see the killing of their antagonist, bin Laden. The personal becomes political as O'Neill and his comrades finished the job that eluded those who witnessed Enemy Number One escape from Tora Bora.

In this way, O'Neill is not only serving in the capacity of what Bradford Vivian would call a rhetorical witness who did his part for historical remembrance[56]—he becomes a willing condensation symbol of American vengeance.

All of this brings to life the events that are presented on walls or on videos inside the National September 11 Memorial Museum, which becomes a sort of security theater that dramatizes the acting out of revenge and puts on display the *jouissance* of those who become vicarious witnesses to the death of bin Laden. In other words, the National September 11 Memorial Museum has provided O'Neill with a platform for telling his palatable story of retributive justice that just so happens to also legitimate the United States' GWOT efforts. Even after he finishes his tale and leaves, the objects he left behind speak volumes.

O'Neill's storytelling comes alive when he can prove the authenticity of his experiences and account by referring to the objects—his Navy SEALs T-shirt—that can then be linked to the impact steel from the former World Trade Center. This is an example of what Eyal Weizman calls forensic architecture, where truth telling depends on things as well as events.[57]

Consider the affective force of O'Neill's interview with *Fox News* that was carried out in front of the Ladder 3 fire truck at the base of the National September 11 Memorial Museum (figure 15). The visual context of this scene alone is striking, because the truck shows the signs of being bludgeoned by falling detritus on 9/11/01 and is in utter disrepair. Viewers can see that the cab has been sheared off by falling masonry, in addition to other visualities that help with the retraumatizing of those cued to recall 9/11 horrors. The news cameras circulate representations of wiry steel tentacles that flare out toward the front half of a vehicle, and viewers can see that the rest of the truck is mangled, battered, and charred. Its tires are flat and side cabinets are broken and ajar.

If we viewed these objects as mere museological artifacts, or simply interesting but mundane curatorial materials, we would miss the symbolic nature of this juxtapositioning, where it matters how we contextualize O'Neill's storytelling. Rather, as a dingpolitik object of securitization, the truck is active as an agentic, something that supplements O'Neill's act of killing as an argumentative warrant that points to the necessity of retribution. The Ladder 3 fire truck thus becomes more than a stage prop; it is an object that helps explain the very motivations behind O'Neill's story of hunting and killing.

All of the thousands of securitized dingpolitik objects at the National September 11 Memorial Museum are part of the complicated security assemblage that O'Neill mobilizes when he uses this site as a platform for justifying the necessity of continuing the GWOT. Consider O'Neill's comments while standing directly in front of the fire truck: "I was fortunate to be with a great group of guys. . . . They're fighting the same ideology that cut this fire truck in half. Still out there. It's not over yet. This is a constant reminder that our nation needs to have."[58]

This is what we mean when we talk about knowledge production. "It's not over yet" is not just some one-off remark but a phrase that clearly works to remind listeners of the need for hypervigilance. Many parts of this security assemblage would make no sense without these museological artifacts that become part of a complex "politics of things."

O'Neill uses the rhetorical force of the museum's in situ argument (the attacks happened here, and here is the proof of our collective suffering) as support for his contestable claim that the GWOT is not over. In this way, O'Neill's "surprise" visit to the National September 11 Memorial Museum has become a choreographed, touchstone example of forensic architecture and dingpolitik at this securitized space (which has itself become an agentic thing).

All of this, of course, reiterates the point that the National September 11 Memorial Museum has been turned into a securitized space of public memory that uses objects, memories, and storytelling to support the continued counterinsurgency and counterterrorism efforts. Consider O'Neill's closing comments on the role of the National September 11 Memorial and Memorial Museum in post-9/11 society:

Fig. 15. Ladder 3 fire truck.

It brings me personally back to 9/11. . . . This is by no means a happy place. . . . This brings you back to probably the most important day in American history. . . . But it's a reminder. . . . It stokes it again. This is an uncut display memorial of what happened. This is not politically correct. This is what evil did to us. It's a reminder of how everyone felt that day. And even for the kids that weren't born yet . . . this can bring them to a place and time that they didn't get to see. It's also a reminder of what we will do in response. Again, this is American exceptionalism leading the rest of the world.[59]

In this comment, O'Neill is explicit about his conviction that the National September 11 Memorial Museum serves as a dark tourist type of repository for militarized memories, to the point he thinks that 9/11/01 is the most important day in American history. Not the Revolutionary

War, not the signing of the Emancipation Proclamation, but the day when nineteen attackers brought down the Twin Towers. The museum thus is turned into a secular place of civil religion, a space and place that are expected to relay the stories of American exceptionalism for years to come.

Even though many of the families of 9/11 victims indicate that they have gained much relief from O'Neill's story of his state-sanctioned killing, some still feel that it is not enough to compensate for their pain. Note how Debra Burlingame reacted to the news of bin Laden's death:

> We saw the crowd celebrating when the mission was announced by the president. . . . I know a lot of families did not feel celebratory. . . . There was a sense of remembering the loss again because bin Laden was dead but my brother wasn't coming home.[60]

The existence of traumatic memories of loss, in this situation, begets unremitting quests for justice. And since the National September 11 Memorial and Memorial Museum permanently display melancholia and insecurity from the terrorist attacks, the GWOT can never end, geopolitically or mentally.

The fact that O'Neill's "coming out" party began at the National September Memorial Museum, and was performed before a handful of families of 9/11 victims who found gratification in O'Neill's sometimes gruesome description of splitting bin Laden's skull, demonstrates that the museum itself has become a type of soapbox and militarized venue. This is a place where theatrical stories of retributive justice can be told even if they are not "politically correct," but they nonetheless serve the objective of advancing the cause of those who want to go after all terrorists. In this way, feelings of personal loss and suffering are mobilized once more, and in many directions, for asymmetrical warfare.

All of this provides additional support for Judith Butler's thesis that the politics of mourning—which parses distinctions between those who have "livable" lives with "grievable deaths" and those who live "unlivable lives" "whose legal and political status is suspended"[61]—can help explain key features of the United States' post-9/11 governmentality and its wielding of sovereign power that is "lawless and unaccountable."[62]

As Dwight Conquergood once asked before his own passing:

> What does it mean when the rituals of state killing are conflated and enfolded within rituals of mourning and bereavement? In the wake of the September 11, 2001[,] terrorist attacks, with its massive trauma to the national psyche, we can expect to see the death penalty figure prominently in the politics of grief as executions are argued for and justified as necessary therapies of collective healing and closure.[63]

Conquergood would not live to see some of the defenses of execution-style killings, but he seems to have anticipated the rhetorical power of this type of mourning.

It is also the body rhetorics of some of those who are missing that helps poststructuralists suture together the rhetorical memory-work that would unite portions of Brennan's public argumentation with O'Neill's confessions. To O'Neill, the reason why no photos of bin Laden were taken by the Special Forces had everything to do with the fact that his body was simply too pulverized for public viewing, due to the hundred rounds of bullets that Navy SEALs pumped into his body. Mangled from head to toe in bullet wounds, bin Laden's body was a "sickening sight to behold."[64]

Is it possible that his body was so mutilated that it could have produced sympathy, the kind of sympathy for a figure who had lost so much power that al Qaeda may have abandoned him to Pakistani or American forces, and who was living in a compound much easier to identify than we could imagine?

We are reminded of what Christine Harold and Kevin DeLuca have written about the rhetorical force of Emmitt Till's maimed body and what it did for the Civil Rights Movement,[65] and we are led to wonder if images of bin Laden's abject body would have produced a parallel effect on the GWOT by calling into question its nature, scope, and purpose when its trophy is a body so brutalized that it is unrecognizable.

Altogether, Robert O'Neill is another example of a spectacular all-American soapbox hero who uses the National September 11 Memorial Museum as a platform for advocating rhetorics of securitization. Despite some controversy regarding the veracity of his claims—Navy SEAL Matt Bissonnette[66] provides a different story of the bin Laden raid—O'Neill's testimonies become an example of how truth effects, rhetorical fragments, and objects can be used to tell the monolithic stories that so many Americans want to hear.

The commentary regarding O'Neill's visit to this museum would not be the last time image events could be used to try and alter American domestic or foreign policy.

Soapbox Arguments, JASTA, and the Search for the "Saudi" Aiders and Abettors

In chapter 3, we studied some of the activism of 9/11 family members who got involved in debates about memorial designs and museum planning, but readers should also consider survivors' ties to some of the most recent developments having to do with post 9/11 governmentality on Capitol Hill: the passage of the Justice Against Terrorism Act (JASTA) by the 114th Congress on the cusp of the 2016 general election. Introduced by Senators John Cornyn (Republican of Texas) and Chuck Schumer (Democrat of New York), JASTA was intended to soften the doctrine of sovereign immunity in ways that would empower individual American citizens who wanted to press legal charges against foreign nationals who may have sponsored terrorism.

As noted earlier, since September 11, 2001, many survivor families told members of the press that they were not enamored with the findings of the 9/11 Commission, but they did not stop there in their lamentations. They have now gone on to make clear to both mainstream newspaper audiences and blog visitors that they are also interested in getting to the bottom of what happened during 9/11—even when such discovery creates discomfort for U.S. diplomats. For example, for more than a dozen years they have expressed interest in going after potentially culpable parties living in places like Saudi Arabia, where money and support for Islamic fundamentalism supposedly helped the cause of the nineteen 9/11 attackers.

The passage of JASTA was thus viewed by 9/11 families as responsive to their argumentative claims regarding what "really happened" back in 2001. It was said that this law opened the door to the "truth" about nefarious forces helping shield the Saudi government or private corporations that might have ties to American interests. What if bin Laden was only a small part of more complex terrorist networks that had everything to do with Islamic proselytizing?

From a technolegal vantage point (see chapter 1), JASTA amended the Foreign Sovereign Immunities Act and portions of the Anti-Terrorism (1976) and Effective Death Penalty (1996) Acts—all of which posed restrictions on federal courts who needed the jurisdiction to hear cases involving civil claims against foreign states.

For our purposes, JASTA also served the realpolitik needs of those who wanted to allow 9/11 family members to seek justice against foreign nationals (viz., Saudi Arabia) who may be aiding foreign terrorism. For many years before the passage of this legislation, family members of the victims of 9/11 wanted action against Saudi Arabia, and it was no surprise to some when it was received with almost unanimous bipartisan support in both the U.S. Senate and the House of Representatives. One of the several recurring arguments made by proponents of JASTA was that fifteen of the 9/11 attackers were from Saudi Arabia, proof enough to the families of the 9/11 victims that Saudi Arabia had an active role in the plotting of the 9/11 attacks.

To these supporters, the bill was a necessary measure for paving a safer, securer America, because it equipped civilians with the ability to bypass a longstanding precedent (the Sovereign Immunities Act) so that they could act as vigilantes against terrorism. In theory, JASTA would strengthen 9/11 families' ability to press charges against the Saudi Arabian government for "unspecified monetary damages" due to their perceived role as coconspirators in the 9/11 attacks based, in part, on the supposedly novel (and hidden) findings of the infamous "twenty-eight pages." These pages were an investigative report from a 2002 congressional joint inquiry on the 9/11 attacks and selective readings of portions of a letter from former CIA director George Tenet.

The twenty-eight pages are a fascinating text some 9/11 family members consider to be a type of ontological smoking gun that reveals collusion between Saudi Arabia and the cabal of the 9/11 terrorists. But the intelligence community contends that its own mosaics, which take into consideration multiple texts and sources, show no verifiable evidence linking the Saudi government to the terrorist attacks. The controversial report states, "While in the United States, some of the September 11 hijackers were in contact with, and received support or assistance from, individuals who may be connected to the Saudi Government."[67] It also says that information indicates "Saudi Government officials in the United States may have other ties to al Qa'ida and other terrorist groups."[68] The report also indicates, however, that much of the obtained information "remains speculative and yet to be independently verified,"[69] qualifiers the 9/11 families have dismissed as mere caveats that have little to do with actual empirical terrorist realities.

Despite the conspiratorial or dubious nature of the arguments that swirl around these infamous twenty-eight pages, 9/11 families and certain congressional leaders have used this disputation as evidence that publics and legislators should lobby in favor of strict enforcement of JASTA. The cavalier way that intelligence analysts have treated the amateur interpretations of the twenty-eight pages adds fuel to some family members' belief that too many administrators and investigators had something to hide, raising questions about whose discourse and interpretations would hold sway in the dispute over counterterrorism.

These are not just matters of 9/11 historiography that involve chronicling debates about whose epistemic knowledge should matter. They are also conversations that involve lawfare, or the judicial politicization of the courts.[70] Fragments like the twenty-eight pages can be used strategically by lawyers to seek financial redress by suing the Saudi Arabian government in the Southern District of New York. After recently hearing the case in federal court, U.S. district judge George Daniels dismissed Saudi Arabia's attempt to have the lawsuit rejected, saying that the plaintiff's claims "narrowly articulate a reasonable basis" to enforce JASTA.[71]

The plaintiffs claim that Saudi Arabia supported al Qaeda in a myriad of ways: it created charities that served as "alter egos of the government" and operated terrorist camps in Afghanistan; it funded Osama bin Laden's terrorist group and specifically supported hijackers with passports for travel; and it allegedly provided the hijackers with "money, cover, advice, contacts, transportation, assistance with U.S. culture, identification, access to pilot training and other material support and resources."[72]

Due to the perceived apolitical nature of these particular American tropes, politicians of all stripes rallied behind JASTA so they could bolster their appeal to constituents who could now be told that they stood behind the families' efforts to seek retributive justice. Who did not want to find the true "facts" about 9/11, and who did not—after learning about the nationalities of the attackers—want to end speculation about Saudi involvement?

The borderline conspiratorial nature of some of these arguments did not stand in the way of politicking and the resonance of these claims. For instance, to Senator Richard Blumenthal (Democrat of Connecticut), the case against the Saudi government is getting stronger and stronger with time, and this knowledge justified the passage of JASTA to better enable families to seek rightful compensation. "We are still learning the facts," he said, "but there is mounting evidence that the Saudi government—or at least operations and operatives within the Saudi government—aided and abetted one of the most massive crimes in the United States."[73] Senator Chuck Schumer said "it was important in this case that the families of the victims of 9/11 be allowed to pursue justice . . . even if that pursuit causes some diplomatic discomforts."[74]

Many members of the executive branch and intelligence agencies agreed with Schumer that the bill would upend a legal precedent that, for many years, has safeguarded the United States from foreign nationals filing litigation against the homeland for its activities abroad. For this reason, when the bill reached the Oval Office for executive approval,

President Obama swiftly vetoed it because of the legal and political risks involved for future American interventionists.

Obama said publicly that the bill is "a dangerous precedent. . . . If we eliminate this notion of sovereign immunity, then our men and women in uniform around the world could potentially start seeing ourselves subject to reciprocal loss."[75] While this standpoint was surely rooted in intelligence briefings objecting to the bill—CIA director John Brennan said JASTA would have "grave implications for the national security of the United States"[76]—Obama was nonetheless rebuked by congresspersons such as Republican Ted Poe of Texas, who found the bill necessary in achieving justice for families of 9/11 victims. This, Poe averred, was not a time for "diplomatic niceties."[77]

The widespread support of JASTA by elected officials, 9/11 families, and the American public led to a deafening blow to Obama when, for the first time in his presidency, the legislative branch overturned one of his vetoes, and with astounding numbers (97-1 in the Senate, with Harry Reid being the only opposition, and 348-77 in the House).[78] The override was a clear defeat for the executive branch, especially considering it occurred when Obama was ending his second term as president. White House press secretary Josh Earnest commented on the defeat by saying, "This is the single most embarrassing thing the United States Senate as done possibly since 1983. . . . To have members of the United States Senate only recently informed of the negative impact of this bill on our service members and our diplomats is in itself embarrassing."[79]

Despite warnings from the president about possible security repercussions from enactment of the bill, Congress nevertheless felt the individual sufferings of 9/11 families were more important than any possible diplomatic fallout. To Senator Cornyn, "this legislation is really about pursuing justice. . . . The families have already suffered too much. They've already suffered untold tragedy, of course, and they deserve to find a path to closure that only justice can provide."[80]

The rhetorical authority of family members played a significant role in the congressional overriding of Obama's veto, especially considering that JASTA was passed on the cusp of the 2016 election. When the bill was on Obama's desk, for instance, family members used their moral standing to lobby against a possible veto with picket signs, American flags, and pictures of perished loved ones. One family member—Sylvia Carver—said, "I don't believe them one bit," referring to some of the early concerns raised by a few congresspersons, such as Lindsey Graham, before the bill was introduced to the floor. "Graham was one of the first signers, and I think he's allowing himself to be influenced by the Saudi government. . . . All of a sudden he's been wavering. . . . So I'm just hoping he and the president stand strong with the American people and not with the Saudi government."[81]

Others, such as Sean Passananti, carrying a picture of his father, who died in the 9/11 terrorist attacks, were more vehement in their protest remarks: "Obama is showing he's on the side of the Saudis instead of the 9/11 families and the American people," he told a reporter. "And (Graham and Corker) had both signed off on it, and now it looks like the Saudis got to them trying to delay the bill. . . . So we're going up against big Saudi lobbyists."[82]

Standing alongside other protesters who were carrying more photographs of fallen family members and signs saying "Stop Protecting Terrorism," "Pass JASTA Now," "Stand With Us," and "President Obama, You Can't Hide, We'll Get Congress to Override," Carver and Passananti represented the viewpoint that justice could be served to family members only if they were allowed to take legal matters into their own hands and heroically disallow Washington from putting "politics before people."[83]

In the same way survivors alleged in 2014 that crassness infected some of the displays of items for sale in the National September 11 Memorial Museum, now money and diplomacy were becoming entangled in the pursuit of 9/11 truths. "It's money," said Francine Gallagher, who lost her husband on 9/11, leaving her with an eight-week-old son. "At the end of the day it's money, and money shouldn't motivate justice. . . . It's very frustrating because it feels like [Obama] is letting us down, and it breaks my heart that the president of the United States would allow this to happen."[84] Eddie Bracken, another protester who lost a family member in the attacks, said, "After 15 years the memories are still raw, because we didn't get no justice, and our own government is undermining us. . . . [Obama] ain't doing right by us. My family's mad, upset and hurt that our president of the United States of America is not helping us. . . . How could it harm them if they didn't do anything wrong?" he added. "Let the proof be known. If they're not guilty, why do they need to have all these lobbyists here?"[85]

Some sixteen years after 9/11, the families were now finding new instrumentalist ways of levering their status as victims, and they were willing to adopt variations of conservative antigovernment sentiments in their campaigns to win support for JASTA. Instead of viewing their groups as collections of a few aggrieved individuals who wanted to become claimants in lawsuits, they posed themselves as truth seekers demanding justice for all patriotic Americans. Moreover, they used their identification with the National September 11 Memorial and Memorial Museum to help them appear to be the real authorities who were not compromising national security. Their stock arguments and assemblages allowed them to act as speakers at podiums that are typically reserved for the U.S. Department of State.

From the point of view of many intelligence analysts and administrators, the reality of JASTA is that it simply creates new scenarios of risk for the United States, because it potentially allows other foreign national countries to seek interpretations of justice in court systems outside the United States. In a recent interview with CBS, Obama said, "If we open up the possibility that individuals and the United States can routinely start suing other governments, then we are also opening up the United States to being continually sued by individuals in other countries."[86] Imagine how Iraqis, Afghans, or Pakistanis would like to see the United States tried in The Hague for its alleged use of torture, night raids, and drones.

The president thus had to be circumspect in the ways he discussed some of these securitization issues. In a convincing letter to Senator Harry Reid, Obama wrote, "JASTA sweeps more broadly than 9/11 or Saudi Arabia, and its far-reaching implications would threaten to undermine important principles that protect the United States, including our U.S. Armed Forces and other officials overseas, without making us any safer."[87]

In fact, while families were protesting the White House, Saudi Arabia and the United Arab Emirates (UAE) were warning Congress that if it did not kill the bill, it would receive less critical military intelligence on terrorist-related activities in the Middle East. According to a May 11, 2017, Associated Press release, the UAE and Saudi Arabia were paying American veterans thousands of dollars to appeal to Congress to vote "no" on JASTA in the name of national security. Some of these veterans, such as David Casler and his brothers—Dan and Timothy Cord—were disgruntled with news that their four-day protest trips to Washington DC were funded by Saudi Arabia. Casler, a former Marine sergeant, said, "It was very evident that they weren't forthcoming; they weren't telling us the whole truth. . . . They flat-out lied to us on the first day with the statement: 'This is not paid for by the Saudi Arabian government.'"[88] Timothy Cord told the *New York Post*, "I joined the Marine Corps as a direct result of 9/11, so to be wined and dined by the very people I joined to fight against, that was sickening."[89]

Others, however, such as former Air Force major general Chuck Tucker, understood the ambiguous and contradictory nature of fragile diplomatic work. He said he was indeed well aware that Saudi Arabia funded the trip to protest Congress. "We have allies," he said. "They're not perfect, we're not perfect. . . . It's not like it was blood money. We're taking money from somebody who is our friend and ally helping us around the world."[90]

Meanwhile, recent news organizations have reported that Pakistani banks owned by the UAE royal family sent money to the UAE to help finance not just the 9/11attacks but also the 26/11 terrorist attacks in Mumbai, India.[91] In the wake of these surfacing allegations, and amid clamor for renewed vigilantism, the UAE has warned the United States that it risks losing crucial "bilateral intelligence cooperation" if it allows families to take legal actions against the UAE or Saudi Arabia.[92] For instance, in leaked emails, Yousef Al Otaiba, the UAE ambassador to the United States, warns that the United States would lose "crucial information and intelligence" related to 9/11 and other international terrorist attacks across the world. While understanding "the desire to provide justice for those who were affected by 9/11," says Otaiba, passing JASTA presents "a large risk to the U.S. and its allies."[93] The effects of the act, he added, would directly trade off with GWOT objectives. We quote at length:

> JASTA would also have a chilling effect on the global fight against terrorism. In order to effectively fight the scourge that is terrorism, the US needs reliable, trustworthy international partners. If a foreign sovereign nation is at risk of being sued in a US court, even if it's an ally, that nation will be less likely to share crucial information and intelligence under JASTA. Why risk alienating key allies at a time when their cooperation is absolutely necessary?[94]

Additionally, Saudi Arabia threatened to rescind on a multibillion-dollar arms deal with the United States if it allowed families to take legal action for allegations of 9/11 involvement. But the Saudi government may be reconsidering after President Trump, a huge supporter of JASTA, visited Riyadh to strike a successful $100 billion arms deal with Saudi Arabia,[95] which, just to add to this complicated argument assemblage, would allow the Saudi government to perpetuate its asymmetrical warfare against Yemen, specifically the Houthis, who, as part of a Shiite insurgency, were charged with receiving financial assistance from Tehran, explaining U.S. support of the war.[96]

One of the 9/11 families' attorneys—Jim Kreindler—thinks that the arms deal may inevitably force Saudi Arabia to settle. "I believe this engagement helps," he told the *Tehran Times*. "If they are going to make billions of dollars out of infrastructure deals and the Royal family is preserved, maybe some wise person is going to say 'we have to get out of this 9/11 mess.' Because it's not going away."[97]

We conclude our discussion of future securitization at the National September 11 Memorial and Memorial Museum with considerations of how museological framings of political issues such as JASTA impact the production of future securitization rhetorics.

Platform Arguments and the Advancement
of Securitization in a Post-9/11 World

This chapter has argued that various actors have been using the National September 11 Memorial and Memorial Museum as a staged platform for executive, forensic, and deliberative arguments about future (in) securities. We began with a discussion about how different clusters of actors have utilized this site to speak about different degrees of necessity to securitize our post-9/11 world. This discussion was followed by a close reading of Brennan's address to publics about the imperative of continuing our GWOT to fight the unseen enemy at the National September 11 Memorial Museum. We also discussed how Robert O'Neill's story of heroism—and his invocation of museum dingpolitik—feeds the believed necessity of the never-ending war at home and abroad. To us, O'Neill's tale of retributive state justice at this place of memory in situ is characteristic of what we call *security theater*, which dramatizes individual and collective roles in resecuritizing the homeland through hunting and killing the unseen enemy. We then introduced a developing story that is literally getting more and more national attention as we write this concluding chapter regarding the widespread support for and the passage of JASTA. We call all of these argument encounters *platform arguments* because of their invocation of 9/11 securitization— especially ones delivered at the National September 11 Memorial and Memorial Museum—that mobilizes hosts of political, legal, and financial arguments in securitization contexts.

At least within the context of the National September 11 Memorial and Memorial Museum, this kind of argumentation displays the recursive nature of populistic securitization rhetorics that not only are tied to Ground Zero dingpolitik but also can be used by decision makers like Brennan and publics who support the congressional leaders that helped pass JASTA. They all become post-9/11 coproducers of a securitized space that extends beyond the confines of the National

September 11 Memorial and Memorial Museum, in the same way that the USHMM intervenes in debates about other modern genocides besides the Holocaust.

Through their own social agency and through the reception of their arguments by the public and the elite, the surviving family members who interject themselves into these security debates become empowered citizen-subjects who can impact more than just our historiographies or 9/11 public memories. These performers mobilize rhetorics of space-based securitization to affirm their own victimhood and participate in national security policy making through populist appeals to the nation about loss, insecurity, and mourning.

This is also why numerous security and military experts are regularly invited to speak to both immediate and mediated audiences at the National September 11 Memorial and Memorial Museum, and often why their securitized messages appeal to the geographical imaginations of Americans who constantly worry about homeland security and the adequate funding of counterterrorism. From a critical memory standpoint, visiting these hallowed grounds means tourists are invited to believe it is their individual civic duty to stay on alert, be watchful, and show gratitude for "freedoms" brought to them from the GWOT. This is especially the case on national holidays—such as the Fourth of July, Memorial Day, Veterans Day—and anniversaries of the terrorist attacks, with heightened symbolism that breeds unfettered nationalism, if not nativism.

Congress's passage of JASTA, despite President Obama's veto and security experts' admonitions, demonstrates that these perceived threats, coupled with the believed necessity of perpetual justice for families of 9/11 victims, illustrate the realpolitik potency of the blurring of word and deed in places like the National September 11 Memorial and Memorial Museum.

Critical participatory studies, combined with critical rhetorical analyses, enable us to see the persuasive force of objects and events that cannot always be discerned when we assume that well-reasoned arguments, advanced by single rhetors or small groups, always drive the passage of policy. Rather, there are many times when networks, assemblages, and coalitions composed of clusters of persons and things in the current Anthropocene create rhetorical flows that impact policy and social change, especially within densely populated spaces and places such as the National September 11 Memorial and Memorial Museum.[98]

Congressional leaders, of course, probably thought they were doing what was in the nation's best interest when they overruled the president's veto of JASTA; their prioritization of individual memories of loss and trauma sustained by families of those who perished, however, may have interfered with the securitization and diplomatic efforts of the Obama administration.

Moreover, the passage of JASTA makes the United States susceptible to future litigation against U.S.-sponsored activities in other countries. One has only to consider the level of U.S. involvement with countries such as Iraq, Syria, and Yemen, in addition to historical interventionism in places like Afghanistan, Vietnam, Iran, Iraq, Venezuela, Chile, and Guatemala to realize the risks of eroding international precedents for sovereign immunity.

That said, we also understand the vernacular appeal of pro-JASTA rhetorics at Ground Zero celebrations: the idea that citizen-subjects must uphold their duties as freedom fighters by participating in epideictic, deliberative, or judicial forums. This type of securitized lawfare ensures that the provision of justice after terrorist acts is no longer an institutional matter that involves only the decisions of a few elites. Now, instead, ordinary citizens become part of a governed milieu that "creates indefinite series of mobile elements" and individualizes post-9/11 governance through security apparatuses' objects, ideas, and arguments.[99]

In the case of populist support for JASTA, local communities and amateurs, not traditional members of institutions (e.g., Congress, courts, the military) become the freedom fighters—new types of first responders—who demand that Congress and White House authorities follow the public will. In other words, JASTA instantiates a governmentality logic that holds that citizens, and not just governments, are responsible for securitizing the homeland. This is especially the case in situations where that government has been accused of hiding the "real" causes of 9/11—a point that future researchers may wish to study from a neoliberal, or even cosmopolitan, governmentality standpoint.

Although the effects of JASTA have not yet been fully realized on an international scale, we believe that that the celebration of this legislation will add new layers to the structural and affective (in)securities linked to the National September 11 Memorial and Memorial Museum. As matters of post-9/11 spatial securitization continue to surface litigiously and judiciously, we believe the strategic use of the memorial and museum as a soapbox for populist harangues will gladden the hearts of many Trump supporters. Meanwhile, the perpetual war continues apace, as we are invited to forget about the trials and tribulations of millions in Afghanistan, Iraq, Pakistan, and elsewhere who do not understand all of this securitization and all of the investments in what scholars call, following Rudyard Kipling, the "savage wars of peace."

We end this chronicling of the 9/11 dispositifs at Ground Zero with more questions than answers. If we are right about the building and maintenance of this "terrorist museum," will we see the funding and building of other structures that mimetically mirror parts of the USHMM or the National September 11 Memorial and Memorial Museum? Will communities in places like Afghanistan and Iraq build their own countermemories so that they can critique the securitized messages we have identified? Will the veterans of the "perpetual war" have their own memorials, separate from the National September 11 Memorial and Memorial Museum? If so, will they be in Lower Manhattan or somewhere along, or nearby, the National Mall? What form would such memorials take, and what story would they tell? Would they be didactic and hail American resilience that fought the "good fight" against those who plotted the greatest attack on American soil, or would they tell a more postmodern, abstract story closely related to the Vietnam Veterans Memorial?

Regardless of the possible future directionality of possible multidirectional or competitive memories, we hope readers have gained an appreciation of the heuristic value of critical rhetorical studies and the rhetorical fieldwork methodologies of participatory critical rhetoric communities. At the same time, we hope our extension of Latour's work on the "politics of things" encourages others to question some of the claims, warrants, and conclusions reached by so many who helped securitized Lower Manhattan landscapes.

SOURCE ACKNOWLEDGMENTS

Portions of this manuscript previously appeared or are forthcoming in the following publications:

M. Hasian Jr. and N. Paliewicz, "Thanatopolitical Spaces and Symbolic Counterterrorism at the National September 11 Memorial and Museum," in *Global Dialectics in Intercultural Communication: Case Studies*, ed. J. A. Drzewiecka and T. K. Nakayama, 119–41 (New York: Peter Lang, 2017).

Nicholas S. Paliewicz and Marouf Hasian Jr., "Popular Memory at Ground Zero: A Heterotopology of the National September 11 Memorial and Museum," *Popular Communication* 15, no. 1 (2017): 19–36, http://www.tandfoline.com.

N. S. Paliewicz, "Bent but Not Broken: Remembering Vulnerability and Resiliency at the National September 11 Memorial Museum," *Southern Communication Journal* 82, no. 1 (2017): 1–14. © Southern States Communication Association, www.ssca.net, reprinted by permission of Taylor & Francis Ltd, http://www.tandfoline.com, on behalf of Southern States Communication Association.

N. S. Paliewicz and M. Hasian Jr., "Mourning Absences, Melancholic Commemoration, and the Contested Public Memories of the National September 11 Memorial and Museum," *Western Journal of Communication* 80, no. 2 (2016): 140–62. © Western States Communication Association, www.westcomm.org, reprinted by permission of Taylor & Francis Ltd, http://www.tandfoline.com, on behalf of Western States Communication Association.

N. S. Paliewicz and M. Hasian Jr., "The 9/11 Families, the Passage of the Justice Against Sponsors of Terrorism Act (JASTA), and the Pursuit of <Justice> in the Saudi Legal Cases," *Communication and Critical/Cultural Studies*, August 13, 2018. © National Communication Association reprinted by permission of Taylor & Francis Ltd, http://www.tandfoline.com on behalf of the National Communication Association.

NOTES

Throughout the book, we refer to the above-ground memorial as the National September 11 Memorial, the underground museum as the National September 11 Memorial Museum, and the entire ground site as the National September 11 Memorial and Memorial Museum.

INTRODUCTION

1. Young, *Stages of Memory*, 127.
2. Zelizer, *About to Die*, 307.
3. Douglas, *Purity and Danger*, 2, 35.
4. Wenner, "Unbearable Dirtiness."
5. Walters, "Drone Strikes."
6. Douglas, *Purity and Danger*, 119.
7. Yaeger, "Rubble as Archive," 188.
8. For a fine overview of some of the biopolitics involved with the public formations of these security dispositifs, see Muller, "Securing the Political Imagination."
9. As Jacques Derrida famously said during a lecture at the University of Chicago, "We do not recognize or even cognize that we do not yet know how to qualify, that we do not know what we are talking about." Borradori, *Philosophy in a Time*, 86.
10. For Agamben's take on the Foucauldian production of dispositifs, see Agamben, *What Is an Apparatus?*
11. Duvall and Marzec, *Narrating 9/11*.
12. Steven Brill, "Are We Any Safer?," *Atlantic*, September 2016, https://www.theatlantic.com/magazine/archive/2016/09/are-we-any-safer/492761/.
13. Brill, "Any Safer?," paragraph 34.
14. National Commission, *9/11 Commission Report*, 346. See Salter, "Risk and Imagination."
15. Brill, "Any Safer?," paragraph 241.
16. Fagan, "The Next Wave of Terror," *San Francisco Chronicle*, paragraph 1, https://www.sfgate.com/news/article/The-next-wave-of-terror-Scenario-planners-2865787.php.
17. Brill, "Any Safer?," paragraph 93.

18. Brill, "Any Safer?," paragraph 6.

19. Heath-Kelly, *Death and Security*, 28.

20. Heath-Kelly, *Death and Security*, 28.

21. Heath-Kelly, *Death and Security*, 28.

22. David W. Dunlap, "Residents Suing to Stop 'Fortresslike' Plan for World Trade Center," *New York Times*, November 13, 2013, paragraph 4, https://mobile.nytimes.com/2013/11/14/nyregion/residents-suing-to-stop-fortresslike-security-plan-for-world-trade-center.html.

23. Vanhoenacker, "Do You Have a Photo ID, Young Man?," *Slate*, September 10, 2012, paragraphs 1, 11, http://www.slate.com/articles/life/culturebox/2012/09/sept_11_memorial_does_the_world_trade_center_site_really_need_so_much_security_.html.

24. Dunlap, "Residents Suing," paragraph 19.

25. Foucault, *Security, Territory, Population*.

26. Janz, "Terror."

27. Blair, Jeppeson, and Pucci, "Public Memorializing."

28. Latour, "From Realpolitik to *Dingpolitik*," 14.

29. Latour, "From Realpolitik to *Dingpolitik*," 15.

30. See Latour, *Inquiry into Modes*.

31. "Assemblages" are the combination of material and symbolic constructions that occupy the attention of critical scholars interested in dingpolitik, the Anthropocene, and feelings of (in)security, and the old antiquated or monumentalist edifices now give way to more emotive, ambiguous, indeterminate, and polysemic objects and heterodox creations. These are what Latour calls the "missing masses."

32. Latour, "From Realpolitik to *Dingpolitik*," 15–16.

33. See, for example, Simons, "Parliament of Things."

34. Rickert, *Ambient Rhetoric*, 25.

35. See Bennett, *Vibrant Matter*.

36. Rickert, *Ambient Rhetoric*, 25.

37. Deleuze and Parnet, *Dialogues*, 69.

38. Nora, "Between Memory and History," 7.

39. Toom, "Whose Body Is It?"

40. See Agamben, *Homo Sacer*.

41. Latour, "War and Peace."

42. Latour, "From Realpolitik to *Dingpolitik*," 16.

43. Latour, "From Realpolitik to *Dingpolitik*," 16.

44. Latour, "From Realpolitik to *Dingpolitik*," 16.

45. Law, "Actor Network Theory."

46. Ringle, "What the Death Machine Could Not Kill: Review the Holocaust Museum, an Album of Agony," *Washington Post*, April 22, 1993, https://www .washingtonpost.com/lifestyle/style/what-the-death-machine-could-not-kill -review-the-holocaust-museum-an-album-of-agony/2013/04/22/6db5d7e0 -ab6c-11e2-a198-99893f10d6dd_story.html?utm_term=.e802050c444e.

47. Ringle, "What the Death Machine."

48. See Williams, *Memorial Museums*.

49. Young, *At Memory's Edge*.

50. Shields, Laurendeau, and Adams, "Logic of Memory."

51. Latour, "Missing Masses?"

52. Young, *Stages of Memory*.

53. Sagalyn, *Power at Ground Zero*.

54. Sturken, *Tourists of History*.

55. Doss, *Memorial Mania*.

56. Rothberg, *Multidirectional Memory*.

57. For more discussion on thanatopolitics see Murray, "Thanatopolitics"; Kuljić, "Thanatopolitics and Thanatosociology"; Ali Nasir, "Biopolitics, Thanatopolitics"; Kelly, "It Follows"; Chouliaraki and Kissas, "Communication"; Brager, "Selfie."

58. Examples of this growing body of work include Heath-Kelly, *Death and Security*; Williams, *Memorial Museums*; and parts of Parr, *Deleuze and Memorial Culture*. Also see Lennon and Foley, *Dark Tourism*, for more discussion on dark tourism and thanatopolitics.

59. Heath-Kelly, *Death and Security*, 13, 51, 120.

60. See Duvall and Marzec, *Narrating 9/11*.

61. Weizman et al., "Forensic Architecture."

62. Paliewicz and McHendry, "When Good Arguments."

63. Mitchell, *Strategic Deception*.

64. See Paliewicz and McHendry, "When Good Arguments."

65. Edkins, "Forget Trauma?," 248.

66. Edkins, "Forget Trauma?," 248.

67. See Forest and Johnson, "Security and Atonement."

68. Heath-Kelly, *Death and Security*, 5.

69. Heath-Kelly, *Death and Security*, 5, 57–92.

70. Laclau and Mouffe, *Hegemony and Socialist*.

71. Rothberg, *Multidirectional Memory*.

72. Phillips, *Framing Public Memory*.

73. Young, *Stages of Memory*.

74. Middleton et al., *Participatory Critical Rhetoric*; McHendry et al., "Rhetorical Critic(ism)'s Body.

75. Middleton et al., *Participatory Critical Rhetoric*, 18.

76. Middleton et al., *Participatory Critical Rhetoric*, 19.

77. Blair, "Reflections on Criticism"; Dickinson, "Joe's Rhetoric"; Dickinson et al., "Memory and Myth"; Hasian, "Remembering and Forgetting."

78. Blair, "Reflections on Criticism."

79. Hasian, "Remembering and Forgetting."

80. Blair and Michel, "Reproducing Civil Rights."

81. Vivian, *Public Forgetting*.

1. AMBIGUITIES AND INSECURITIES

1. Rothberg, *Multidirectional Memory*.

2. Sitaraman, "Counterinsurgency."

3. See Senie, "A Difference in Kind," paragraph 16; Biesecker, "No Time for Mourning."

4. Doss, *Emotional Life*, 15. See also Doss, *Memorial Mania*.

5. Mitchell, *What Do Pictures Want?*

6. Toom, "Whose Body Is It?, 698.

7. National Commission on Terrorist Attacks, *9/11 Commission Report*.

8. Associated Press, "NYPD Transformed Since 9/11 Attacks," *New York Daily News*, September 10, 2008, paragraph 3, http://www.nydailynews.com/news /crime/nypd-transformed-9-11-attacks-article-1.322395.

9. New York State Division of Homeland Security and Emergency Services, "Ten Years After 9/11: An Overview of New York State's Homeland Security Accomplishments," New York State Division of Homeland Security and Emergency Services website, 2011, http://www.dhses.ny.gov/media/documents/Ten -Years-After-9-11-NYS-Accomplishments.pdf.

10. Associated Press, "NYPD Transformed," paragraph 8.

11. Associated Press, "NYPD Transformed," paragraph 15.

12. Sciulo, "Ghost," paragraph 14.

13. Biesecker, "No Time for Mourning."

14. Sciulo, "Ghost," paragraph 15.

15. Sciulo, "Ghost," paragraph 16.

16. Trigg, *Topophobia*.

17. Janz, "Terror," 191.

18. George Bush, "The State of the Union," *New York Times*, last modified January 30, 2002, http://www.nytimes.com/2002/01/30/us/state-union-president -bush-s-state-union-address-congress-nation.html.

19. Dan Balz and Bob Woodward, "A Pivotal Day of Grief and Anger," *Washington Post*, last modified January 30, 2002, http://www.washingtonpost.com/wp-dyn/content/article/2006/07/18/AR2006071800696.html.

20. Ken Wiwa, "In America, Afterwards," *Globe and Mail*, October 6, 2001, paragraph 24.

21. Edkins, "Forget Trauma?," 248

22. *CNN* staff, "Public Viewing Platform Opens at Ground Zero," *CNN*, last modified December 30, 2001, http://www.cnn.com/2001/US/12/30/rec.viewing.platforms/http://edition.cnn.com/2001/US/12/30/rec.viewing.platforms/index.html.

23. Low, "Memorialization," 329.

24. See Taylor, *Archive.*

25. See Redfield, "Virtual Trauma," 69.

26. Taylor, *Archive*, 342.

27. Rudolph Giuliani, "Giuliani, Go Shopping," ABC, filmed September 2011, *YouTube* video, 0:17, posted July 2, 2008, https://www.youtube.com/watch?v=6jxlQZskGFg.

28. George W. Bush, "At O'Hare, President Says 'Get On Board," *White House Archives*, September 27, 2001, https://georgewbush-whitehouse.archives.gov/news/releases/2001/09/20010927–1.html.

29. Taylor, *Archive*, 244.

30. Redfield, "Virtual Trauma," 69.

31. Ilya Baranikas, "Ground Zero Revisited," *Moscow News*, last modified September 10, 2003, paragraph 5, http://www.lexisnexis.com/hottopics/lnacademic/?.

32. Baranikas, "Ground Zero Revisited," paragraphs 42, 43.

33. Doss, *Memorial Mania.*

34. Latour, *We Have Never*, 55.

35. *CNN* Staff, "List of World Trade Center Tenants," *CNN*, accessed January 29, 2018, http://www.cnn.com/SPECIALS/2001/trade.center/tenants1.html.

36. Naudet, Naudet, and Hanlon, *9/11.*

37. Sturken, "Aesthetics of Absence."

38. Toom, "Whose Body Is It?"

39. Toom, "Whose Body Is It?" 688.

40. Harold Evans, "Review of the Year: 11 September," *Independent on Sunday* (London), last modified December 23, 2001, paragraph 3, Lexis Nexis.

41. Patrick Rhoades, "At Ground Zero Devastation 'Incredible,' Denver Firefighter Attests," *Denver Post*, last modified January 13, 2002, paragraph 25, http://www.lexisnexis.com.echo.louisville.edu/hottopics/lnacademic/?.

42. Ben White, "Cleanup Hazards at Ground Zero an Ongoing Worry," *Washington Post*, last modified October 16, 2001, https://www.washingtonpost.com/archive/politics/2001/10/16/cleanup-hazards-at-ground-zero-an-ongoing-worry/.

43. Tom Leonard, "Is the Dust Lady's Death from Cancer Proof 9/11 Could Kill Thousands More? Thousands Caught Up in Terror Attacks Have Been Diagnosed with the Disease," *Daily Mail*, last modified August 26, 2015, http://www.dailymail.co.uk/news/article-3212239/Is-Dust-Lady-s-death-cancer-proof-9-11-kill-thousands-Thousands-caught-terror-attacks-diagnosed-disease.html.

44. J. Freedom du Lac, "9/11 'Dust Lady' Marcy Borders, featured in a Haunting Photo, Has Died of Cancer," *Washington Post*, last modified August 26, 2015, paragraphs 15, 16, https://www.washingtonpost.com/news/morning-mix/wp/2015/08/26/911-dust-lady-marcy-borders-featured-in-haunting-photo-dies-of-cancer/.

45. Anita Gates, "Buildings Rise from Rubble While Health Crumbles," *New York Times*, last modified September 11, 2006, http://www.nytimes.com/2006/09/11/arts/television/11dust.html?_r=0.

46. Dehncke-Fisher, *Dust to Dust: The Health Effects of 9/11*.

47. Ashley Portero, "9/11—The Dust That Refuses to Settle."

48. Portero, "9/11—The Dust."

49. Ellen Barry, "Lost in the Dust of 9/11," last modified *Los Angeles Times*, October 14, 2006, paragraph 7, http://articles.latimes.com/2006/oct/14/nation/na-cleaners14.

50. Barry, "Lost in the Dust," paragraph 3.

51. Qtd. in Barry, "Lost in the Dust," paragraph 16.

52. Harriet Alexander, "Marcy Borders 'The Dust Lady' of 9/11 Dies of Stomach Cancer," *Telegraph*, last modified August 26, 2015, paragraph 13, http://www.telegraph.co.uk/news/worldnews/september-11-attacks/11824581/Marcy-Borders-The-Dust-Lady-of-911-dies-of-stomach-cancer.html.

53. CNN, "Ex-EPA Chief Rejects Criticism Over 9/11 Workers' Illnesses," last modified June 26, 2007, paragraph 21, http://edition.cnn.com/2007/POLITICS/06/25/ground.zero/.

54. See Latour, *Pasteurization of France*.

55. Nyers, "Moving Borders," 2.

56. See Nyers, "Moving Borders."

57. Doss, *Emotional Life*, 15.

58. Johnson, "Savage Civil Religion."

59. Haskins and DeRose, "Memory, Visibility," 383.

60. Stephen Buckley, "24 Hours at Ground Zero," *St. Petersburg Times*, last modified December 6, 2001, paragraph 32, http://www.sptimes.com/News /121601/Worldandnation/24_hours_at_ground_ze.shtml.

61. Johnson, "Savage Civil Religion," 308.

62. David W. Dunlap, "A Round Symbol of Resilience Rolls Out of Public View," *New York Times*, last modified May 4, 2012, paragraph 12, http://query.nytimes .com/gst/fullpage.html?res=9404E3D9103BF937A35756C0A9649D8B63.

63. Low, "Memorialization."

64. Low, *Behind the Gates*.

65. Low, "Memorialization," 333.

66. Low, "Memorialization," 333.

67. Low, "Memorialization," 333.

68. Low, "Memorialization," 333, 335.

69. Dewan, "Closure? A Buzzword Becomes a Quest," *New York Times*, last modified November 25, 2001, paragraph 11, http://www.nytimes.com/2001 /11/25/nyregion/closure-a-buzzword-becomes-a-quest.html.

70. Edkins, "Absence of Meaning."

71. Rick Hampson, "Americans Rush to Build Memorials to 9/11," *USA Today*, last modified May 22, 2003, paragraph 14, http://www.lexisnexis.com.echo .louisville.edu/hottopics/lnacademic/?.

72. Hampson, "Americans Rush," paragraph 23.

73. Doss, *Memorial Mania*.

74. Foote, *Shadowed Ground*; Young, *At Memory's Edge*.

75. Zelizer, "Reading the Past."

76. Low, "Memorialization," 335.

77. Low, "Memorialization," 336.

78. Low, "Memorialization," 336.

79. Greg Gittrich, "Victims' Kin RIP Church 9/11 Memorial Service Was Called Off," *Daily News*, last modified January 24, 2002, paragraph 1, http://www .nydailynews.com/archives/news/victims-kin-rip-church-9-11-memorial-se rvice-called-article-1.476479.

80. Gunn, "Mourning Speech."

81. Low, "Memorialization," 335.

82. Low, "Memorialization," 335.

83. Low et al., "Battery Park City," 656.

84. BBC staff, "Outrage at Ground Zero Visitor Platform," BBC, last modified January 17, 2002, http://news.bbc.co.uk/2/hi/americas/1766687.stm.

85. Johnson, "Civil Religion," 295.

86. Johnson, "Civil Religion," 303.

87. Johnson, "Civil Religion," 304.

88. Joshua Burstein, "Pushcart Wars," *Gotham Gazette*, last modified March 22, 2004, http://www.gothamgazette.com/criminal-justice/2366-pushcart-wars.

89. Clyde Haberman, "NYC; The Sacred and the Tacky, Inseparable," *New York Times*, last modified May 6, 2003, paragraph 14, http://www.nytimes.com/2003/05/06/nyregion/nyc-the-sacred-and-the-tacky-inseparable.html.

90. Haskins and DeRose, "Memory, Visibility," 383.

91. Hauser, *Vernacular Voices*.

92. Doss, *Memorial Mania*.

93. Kirshenblatt-Gimblett, "Kodak Moments."

94. van Toor and Ronnes, "Reflecting Absence."

95. van Toor and Ronnes, "Reflecting Absence."

96. See Johnson, "Civil Religion."

97. Haskins and DeRose, "Memory, Visibility," 392.

98. Balmori Associates, "Ground Zero Viewing Wall," *Balmori.com*, accessed January 29, 2018, http://www.balmori.com/portfolio/ground-zero-viewing-wall.

99. Balmori, "Ground Zero," paragraph 1.

100. Weizman, *Least*.

101. CNN Staff, "You Are Either with Us or against Us," *CNN.com*, last modified, November 6, 2001, http://edition.cnn.com/2001/US/11/06/gen.attack.on.terror/.

102. Senie, "A Difference in Kind," paragraph 16, http://www.sculpture.org/documents/scmag03/jul_aug03/webspecial/senie.shtml.

103. Johnson, "Civil Religion," 303.

104. See Gunn, "Mourning Speech."

2. REBUILDING GROUND ZERO

1. Taylor, "Movie."

2. Valkenburg and van der Ploeg, "Materialities between Security."

3. By *force* we mean literal force that is affectively inscribed on bodies, in the same way that Marco Abel describes the effect of violent films such as *Fargo* in his critically important book *Violent Affect*. Force is not reducible to bodily injury in the colloquial sense; it is an affective response to objects that themselves inflict forceful sensations on bodies. Such is the way securitized objects work: they forcefully (viz., affectively) impinge bodies, spaces, and discourses by creating the very feelings of insecurity and vulnerability that they are designed to prevent. This is a point we will return to in chapter 4. Abel, *Violent Affect*.

4. See Abel and Foster, *Architecture and Identity*.

5. Herbert Muschamp, "Don't Rebuild, Reimagine," *New York Times*, last modified September 8, 2001, paragraph 7, http://www.nytimes.com/2002/09/08 /magazine/don-t-rebuild-reimagine.html.

6. Fisher, "Architecture," 96.

7. Young, "Counter-Monument."

8. Hajer, "Rebuilding Ground Zero," 446.

9. Ada Louise Huxtable, "Another World Trade Center Horror," *Wall Street Journal*, last modified July 25, 2002, paragraph 1, http://www.wsj.com/articles /SB1027555114818134800.

10. See Hendry, "Decide, Announce, Defend."

11. Hendry, "Decide, Announce, Defend."

12. Lower Manhattan Development Corporation, "Lower Manhattan Development Corporation Announces Six Teams of Architects and Planners to Participate in Design Study of World Trade Center Site," *LMDC*, last modified September 26, 2002, http://www.renewnyc.com/displaynews.aspx ?newsid=655798f4-b8ee-4583-bf27-b3b9a9c29f1f.

13. Lower Manhattan Development Corporation and the Port Authority of New York and New Jersey, "The Public Dialogue: Innovative Design Study," *Renewnyc.com*, February 27, 2003, 4, www.renewnyc.com/content/pdfs /public_dialogue_innovative_design.pdf.

14. Martin Filler, "Into the Void," *New Republic*, September 30, 2001, https:// newrepublic.com/article/66008/the-void.

15. Tom McGeveran, "Pataki Grabs Center Stage as Zero Nero," *Observer*, last modified April 28, 2013, paragraph 8, http://observer.com/2003/04/pataki -grabs-center-stage-as-zero-nero/.

16. McGeveran, "Pataki Grabs Center."

17. Lower Manhattan Development Corporation and The Port Authority of NY and NJ, "Public Dialogue," 10.

18. "Listening to the City: Report of Proceedings," *A Project of the Civic Alliance to Rebuild Downtown New York to Rebuild Downtown New York*, February 7, 2002, 5, http://www.weblab.org/ltc/LTC_Report.pdf.

19. Steven Edwards, "9/11 Memorial Delay Angers Survivors," *Pressreader*, July 2, 2008, paragraph 6, https://www.pressreader.com/canada/times-colonist /20080702/282157877010208.

20. Rowan Moore, "9/11 Ground Zero: Why Has Its Rebirth Turned Sour?" *Guardian*, paragraph 4, last modified July 30, 2011, https://www.theguardian .com/world/2011/jul/31/new-york-towers-memorial-architecture.

21. Filler, "Into the Void," paragraph 48.

22. Edward Wyatt, "Ground Zero: The Site," *New York Times*, last modified September 13, 2003, http://www.nytimes.com/2003/09/13/nyregion/ground -zero-the-site-ground-zero-plan-seems-to-circle-back.html.

23. See Goldberger, "Designing Downtown."

24. Joel Roberts, "World Trade Center Finalists Named," *CBS News*, last modified February 4, 2003, http://www.cbsnews.com/news/world-trade-center-finalists-named/.

25. Greenspan, *Battle for Ground Zero*, 145.

26. Greenspan, *Battle for Ground Zero*, 87.

27. Nobel, *Sixteen Acres*, 175

28. Nobel, *Sixteen Acres*.

29. Goldberger, "Designing Downtown."

30. Tom McGeveran, "The Man Who Is Almost There," *New York Observer*, paragraph 32, January 20, 2003, http://observer.com/2003/01/the-man-who-is-almost-there/.

31. "World Trade Center Master Plan, 2003," *Studio Libeskind*, paragraph 2, accessed July 5, 2017, http://libeskind.com/work/ground-zero-master-plan/.

32. In Greenspan, *Battle for Ground Zero*, 94.

33. Irina Vinnitskaya, "Ground Zero Master Plan/Studio Daniel Libeskind," *Arch Daily*, last modified September 23, 2012, paragraph 1, http://www.archdaily .com/272280/ground-zero-master-plan-studio-daniel-libeskind.

34. Vinnitskaya, "Ground Zero Master Plan," paragraph 7.

35. Vinnitskaya, "Ground Zero Master Plan," paragraph 2.

36. Dunlap and Collins, "New Design for Freedom Tower Calls for 200-Foot Pedestal," *New York Times*, last modified June 29, 2005, paragraph 2, http://www .nytimes.com/2005/06/29/nyregion/new-design-for-freedom-tower-calls-for -200foot-pedestal.html.

37. Karrie Jacobs, "How Security Concerns and Developers Undermine the Design of 1 World Trade Center," *Fast Company*, last modified September 11, 2014, paragraph 2, https://www.fastcompany.com/3035461/how-cops-and -developers-compromised-the-design-of-1-world-trade-center.

38. Nicolai Ouroussoff, "Critic's Notebook; For Freedom Tower and Ground Zero, Disarray Reigns, and Opportunity Awaits," *New York Times*, last modified May 2, 2005, paragraph 3, http://query.nytimes.com/gst/fullpage.html?res= 9E03E6DF1F31F931A35756C0A9639C8B63.

39. Jacobs, "How Security Concerns," paragraph 27.

40. Daniel Benjamin, "The 1,776-Foot-Tall Target," *New York Times*, last modified March 23, 2004, http://www.nytimes.com/2004/03/23/opinion/the-1776 -foot-tall-target.html?_r=0.

41. Benjamin, "1,776-Foot-Tall," paragraph 2.
42. Ron Rosenbaum, "Ground Zero Hype: Is Giant Skyscraper a Freedom Folly?" *Observer*, last modified June 27, 2005, paragraph 11, http://observer.com /2005/06/ground-zero-hype-is-giant-skyscraper-a-freedom-folly/.
43. Deborah Sontag, "The Hole in the City's Heart," *New York Times*, last modified September 11, 2006, http://www.nytimes.com/2006/09/11/world /americas/11iht-web.0911groundzero.2762587.html?pagewanted=all.
44. Sontag, "Hole," paragraph 114.
45. Sontag, "Hole," paragraph 115.
46. Julia Lester, "Post-9/11 WTC Security: Never Forget, Never Again," *CNBC*, paragraph 29, last modified September 2, 2016, http://www.cnbc.com/2016 /09/02/post-911-wtc-security-never-forget-never-again.
47. Sontag, "Hole," 117.
48. Sontag, "Hole," paragraph 120.
49. Sontag, "Hole," 123.
50. Sontag, "Hole."
51. Sontag, "Hole," paragraph 2.
52. Patrick D. Healy and William K. Rashbaum, "Security Issues Force a Review at Ground Zero," *New York Times*, last modified May 1, 2005, paragraph 16, http://www.nytimes.com/2005/05/01/nyregion/security-concerns-force-a -review-of-plans-for-ground-zero.html.
53. Edwards, "Still a Zero-Sum," paragraph 17.
54. Jill Gardiner, "Freedom Tower Security Issues Worry Police," *New York Sun*, last modified November 19, 2004, paragraph 8, http://www.lexisnexis.com /hottopics/lnacademic/?.
55. Gardiner, "Freedom Tower Security," paragraph 9.
56. Gardiner, "Freedom Tower Security," paragraph 10.
57. Rosenbaum, "Ground Zero Hype," paragraph 8.
58. Healy and Rashbaum, "Security Concerns," paragraph 25.
59. Frankie Edozien and Michael White, "Still Just a Big 'Zero'—Gov: Tower Redesign Will Stick to WTC-Site Plan," *New York Post*, last modified May 7, 2005, paragraph 29, http://nypost.com/2005/05/07/still-just-a-big-zero -gov-tower-redesign-will-stick-to-wtc-site-plan/.
60. Adam Brodsky, "Our Only Real Security," *New York Post*, last modified May 15, 2005, paragraphs 6, 10, 22, http://www.lexisnexis.com/hottopics/lnacademic/?.
61. David Saltonstall, "New Design to Delay Freedom Tower Plan," *Daily News*, last modified May 5, 2005, paragraph 19, http://www.nydailynews.com /archives/news/new-design-delay-freedom-tower-plan-article-1.634193.

62. Healy and Rashbaum, "Security Concerns," paragraph 21.

63. Healy and Rashbaum, "Security Concerns," paragraph 22.

64. Glenn Collins and David W. Dunlap, "Many Demands on New Tower at Ground Zero; Seeking Better Security at a Symbol of Resolve," *New York Times*, last modified June 7, 2005, paragraph 38, http://www.nytimes.com /2005/06/07/nyregion/many-demands-on-new-tower-at-ground-zero -seeking-better-security-a.html.

65. David W. Dunlap and Glenn Collins, "Redesign Puts Freedom Tower on a Fortified Base," *New York Times*, last modified June 30, 2005, paragraph 12, http://www.nytimes.com/2005/06/30/nyregion/front%20page/redesign -puts-freedom-tower-on-a-fortified-base.html.

66. Sontag, "Hole," paragraph 142.

67. Sontag, "Hole," 145.

68. David Saltonstall, "Freedom Tower Plan Sent Back, 1 Yr. Delay," *Daily News*, last modified May 5, 2005, paragraph 1, http://www.nydailynews.com /archives/news/freedom-tower-plan-back-1-yr-delay-article-1.581278.

69. David Usborne, "New York Divided Over Memorial: Absolutely Zero," *Independent*, paragraph 13, last modified June 2, 2005, Lexis Nexis.

70. Tom Topousis, "New Tower Plan in June: Pataki, FBI Legend Kallstrom on Board," *New York Post*, last modified May 13, 2005, paragraphs 5–6, http://nypost.com/2005/05/13/new-tower-plan-in-june-pataki-fbi-legend -kallstrom-on-board/.

71. Dunlap and Collins, "Redesign Puts Freedom Tower," paragraph 1.

72. Alan Boyle, "How Ground Zero's Supertower Rose above New York's 9/11 Nightmare," *NBC News*, last modified September 10, 2013, paragraph 14, http://www.nbcnews.com/technology/how-ground-zeros-supertower-rose -above-new-yorks-9-11-8C11111444. Italics added for emphasis.

73. Boyle, "How Ground Zero's," paragraph 5.

74. Boyle, "How Ground Zero's," paragraph 19.

75. Matthew Schuerman, "In City Security Squabbles, a Banker Restores Order," *New York Observer*, last modified August 29, 2005, paragraph 12, http:// observer.com/2005/08/in-city-security-squabbles-a-banker-restores -order/.

76. Alexandra Marks, "Signs of Life from Hole in the Heart," *Courier Mail*, last modified September 10, 2005, http://www.lexisnexis.com/hottopics /lnacademic/?.

77. Schuerman, "In City Security Squabbles."

78. Schuerman, "In City Security Squabbles," paragraph 134.

79. Healy and Rashbaum, "Security Concerns," paragraph 33.

80. Sontag, "Hole," paragraph 141.

81. Agamben, *Homo Sacer.*

82. Schuerman, "Security Squabbles," paragraph 16.

83. Schuerman, "Security Squabbles."

84. Schuerman, "Security Squabbles."

85. Valkenburg and van der Ploeg, "Materialities," 2. For another example of a Latourian way of thinking about the citizen-police relationship in securitized situations, see Valkenburg, "Security Technologies."

86. Healy and Rashbaum, "Security Concerns," paragraph 32.

87. Healy and Rashbaum, "Security Concerns," paragraph 11.

88. Dunlap and Collins, "Redesign Puts Freedom Tower," paragraph 37.

89. Collins and Dunlap, "Many Demands," paragraph 14.

90. Rosenbaum, "Ground Zero Hype," paragraph 25.

91. Rosenbaum, "Ground Zero Hype," paragraph 27.

92. Rosenbaum, "Ground Zero Hype," paragraph 11.

93. Steven Edwards, "Still a Zero-Sum Game: WTC Four Years Later," *National Post*, last modified November 5, 2005," paragraph 29, Lexus Uni.

94. Tom Topousis, "2 Years of WTC Plans Lie in Ruins as Pataki Orders a New Tower," *New York Post*, last modified May 5, 2002, paragraph 19, http://nypost.com/2005/05/05/2-years-of-wtc-plans-lie-in-ruins-as-pataki-orders-a-new-tower/.

95. Molly Cotter, "What Ever Happened to Daniel Libeskind's Original WTC Freedom Tower Design?," *Inhabitat New York City*, last modified September 7, 2011, paragraph, 3, http://inhabitat.com/nyc/the-tower-that-could-have-been-daniel-libeskinds-award-winning-wtc-design/.

96. Sagalyn, *Power at Ground Zero*, 271.

97. Greenspan, *Battle for Ground Zero*, 95.

98. Elizabeth Greenspan, "Daniel Libeskind's World," paragraph, 9.

99. Elizabeth Greenspan, "Daniel Libeskind's World," paragraph 16.

100. David W. Dunlap, "Libeskind Sues Silverstein for Design Fee," *New York Times*, last modified July 14, 2004, http://www.nytimes.com/2004/07/14/nyregion/libeskind-sues-silverstein-for-design-fee.html.

101. David Saltonstall, "New Design to Delay Freedom Tower Plan," *Daily News*, last modified May 5, 2005, paragraph 4, http://www.nydailynews.com/archives/news/new-design-delay-freedom-tower-plan-article-1.634193.

102. Janz, "Terror."

103. Dunlap and Collins, "Redesign Puts Freedom Tower," paragraph 8.

104. Dunlap and Collins, "Redesign Puts Freedom Tower."

105. Steve Rose, "The Indestructibles," *Guardian*, last modified September 11, 2006, paragraph 10, https://www.theguardian.com/artanddesign/2006/sep/11/architecture.art.

106. Rose, "Indestructibles," paragraph 12.

107. David Dunlap, "Venting Ideas, Then Hiding Them, Turns Out to Be a Tall Order," *New York Times*, last modified September 15, 2005, paragraph 7, http://www.nytimes.com/2005/09/15/nyregion/venting-ideas-then-hiding-them-turns-out-to-be-a-tall-order.html.

108. Dunlap, "Venting Ideas," paragraph 11.

109. Dunlap, "Venting Ideas."

110. Dunlap, "Venting Ideas," paragraph 18.

111. Joe Hagan, "The Breaking of Michael Arad," *New York Magazine*, May 14, 2006, 6, http://nymag.com/arts/architecture/features/17015/.

112. Maggie Haberman, "WTC Columns in Memorial," *New York Daily News*, last modified December 17, 2004, paragraph 1, https://www.nydailynews.com/archives/news/wtc-columns-memorial-article-1.650253.

113. Haberman, "WTC Columns."

114. David W. Dunlap, "Order of Victims' Names on Memorial Turns Out to Be Not Quite Settled," *New York Times*, March 30, 2006, http://www.nytimes.com/2006/03/30/nyregion/order-of-victims-names-on-memorial-turns-out-to-be-not-quite.html.

115. Dunlap, "Order of Victims' Names," paragraph 14.

116. Dunlap, "Order of Victims' Names," paragraph 15.

117. Dunlap and Collins, "Redesign Puts Freedom Tower," paragraph 35.

118. Haberman, "WTC Columns," paragraph 1.

119. Haberman, "WTC Columns."

120. Grusin, *Premediation*.

3. POLICING MEMORY

1. Deborah Sontag, "The Hole in the City's Heart," *New York Times*, last modified September 11, 2006, http://www.nytimes.com/2006/09/11/world/americas/11iht-web.0911groundzero.2762587.html?pagewanted=all.

2. Waldman, *Submission*.

3. William Skidelski, "*The Submission* by Amy Waldman—A Review," *Guardian*, last modified September 10, 2011, https://www.theguardian.com/books/2011/sep/11/the-submission-amy-waldman-review.

4. See Mamdani, *Good Muslim, Bad Muslim*.

5. For more on the ideological meaning of this "felt necessities of the time" phrase see Anthony Lewis, "Abroad at Home: 'The Felt Necessities,'" *New York Times*, last modified January 26, 1986, https://www.nytimes.com/1986/01/23/opinion/abroad-at-home-the-felt-necessities.html.

6. Julie Mason and Josh Gerstein, "Osama Bin Laden Buried at Sea," *Politico*, last modified May 1, 2011, paragraph 7, http://www.politico.com/story/2011/05/osama-bin-laden-buried-at-sea-054050.

7. Mason and Gerstein, "Osama Bin Laden," paragraphs 18–19.

8. See, for example, Debra Burlingame, "Obama and the 9/11 Families: The President Isn't Sincere about 'Swift and Certain' Justice for Terrorists," *9/11 Families for a Safe and Strong America*, last modified May 8, 2009, https://911familiesforamerica.org/obama-and-the-911-families-the-president-isnt-sincere-about-swift-and-certain-justice-for-terrorists/.

9. Debra Burlingame, quoted in Joe Palca, "Former Guantanamo Detainee Bombed Iraqi Base," *NPR*, last modified February 23, 2009, paragraph 35, http://www.npr.org/templates/transcript/transcript.php?storyId=101055378.

10. Middleton et al., *Participatory Critical Rhetoric*, 118.

11. Jan Aronson, "After 15 Years, The Political Power of the 9/11 Victims Endures," *Washington Post*, last modified September 11, 2016, https://www.washingtonpost.com/news/monkey-cage/wp/2016/09/11/the-political-power-of-the-dead-in-the-long-wake-of-911/?utm_term=.9f2e9bdc114c.

12. Aronson, "After 15 Years," paragraphs 8–9.

13. Aronson, "After 15 Years," paragraph 9.

14. Joanna Slater, "In New York, Making Space to Remember 9/11," *Globe and Mail*, last modified March 31, 2014, paragraph 3, http://www.theglobeandmail.com/news/world/in-new-york-making-space-to-remember-911/article17751858/?page=all.

15. Wilson, "Rethinking 1807," 168.

16. Anemona Hartocollis, "Developer Sues to Win $12.3 Billion in 9/11 Attack," *New York Times*, last modified March 27, 2008, http://www.nytimes.com/2008/03/27/nyregion/27rebuild.html.

17. Nora, "Between Memory and History," 7.

18. Rick Hampson, "Americans Rush to Build Memorials to 9/11," *USA Today*, last modified May 22, 2003, http://usatoday30.usatoday.com/news/nation/2003-05-21-memorial-cover_x.htm.

19. See Doss, *Memorial Mania*.

20. Donofrio, "Ground Zero," 156.

21. Donofrio, "Ground Zero," 157.

22. Donofrio, "Ground Zero," 157.

23. Denis Hamill, "The National September 11 Memorial & Museum Should Be Free to All," *New York Daily News*, last modified May 17, 2014, http://www .nydailynews.com/new-york/hamill-9-11-museum-free-article-1.1796718; Josh Nathan-Kazis, "From Gettysburg to Ground Zero, 'Sacred Space' Debated," *Jewish Daily*, last modified August 18, 2010, http://forward.com /articles/130181/from-gettysburg-to-ground-zero-sacred-space/; Will Pavia and Steven Edwards, "Paying Tribute to 'Terrible Loss,'" *Ottawa Citizen*, last modified May 6, 2011, http://www2.canada.com/ottawacitizen/news/story .html?id=8e9ca26b-2996-411a-8fb2-b073715a8953.

24. On the problematic nature of some "competitive" memories, see Rothberg, *Multidirectional Memory*.

25. Joshi Pradnya, "Families Protest WTC Museum," *New York Newsday*, last modified June 20, 2005, paragraph 5, http://www.nynewsday.com /news/local/manhattan/wtc/nyc-wtc0621,0,4229004.story?coll=nyc -multimedia-wtc.

26. Janz, "Terror," 195.

27. Donofrio, "Ground Zero"; Kolker, "Grief Police."

28. Debra Burlingame, "The Great Ground Zero Heist," *Wall Street Journal*, last modified June 7, 2005, paragraph 4, http://www.wsj.com/news/articles /SB111810145819652326.

29. Nancy Dillon, "WTC Museum Panned: Focus on Attack, Kin Urge," *New York Daily News*, last modified June 21, 2005, paragraph 8, http://www .nydailynews.com/archives/news/wtc-museum-panned-focus-attack-kin -urge-article-1.572628.

30. Hoskins, "Politics of Memory."

31. Glenn Collins, "Protestors Step Up Calls for 9/11 Memorial above Ground," *New York Times*, last modified February 28, 2006, paragraph 4, http://www.nytimes .com/2006/02/28/nyregion/28protest.html?pagewanted=print&_r=0.

32. David W. Dunlap, "9/11 Memorial Faces Setback over Names," *New York Times*, June 27, 2006, B1.

33. Redfield, "Virtual Trauma."

34. Kolker, "Grief Police," paragraph 1.

35. Donofrio, "Ground Zero," 164.

36. Benitez, "Why Victims' Families Are Furious about 9/11 Memorial Museum," *ABC News*, last modified May 19, 2014, paragraph 2, http://abcnews.go.com /US/victims-families-furious-911-memorial-museum/story?id=23774869.

37. Benitez, "Why Victims' Families," paragraphs 3–6; See *WTC Neighborhood Alliance by Mary Perillo v. Kelly*, 2014 NY Slip Op 30327 (U).

38. Edgar Sandoval and Corky Siemaszo, "Relatives of Missing World Trade Center Victims Want Remains Moved from 9/11 Museum," *New York Daily News*, last modified May 27, 2014, http://www.nydailynews.com/new-york/wtc-victims-relatives-remains-removed-article-1.1807117.

39. Stephen Farrell, "In 'Ceremonial Transfer,' Remains of 9/11 Victims Are Moved to Memorial," *New York Times*, last modified May 10, 2014, paragraph 8, http://www.nytimes.com/2014/05/11/nyregion/remains-of-9-11-victims-are-transferred-to-trade-center-site.html.

40. David W. Dunlap, "A 9/11 Shrine Where Families Mourned for Years, Now Open to Others," *New York Times*, last modified September 10, 2014, http://www.nytimes.com/2014/09/11/nyregion/family-room-for-relatives-of-9-11-victims-is-recreated-in-albany.html?_r=0. For more on the visual materials that can be found in the Family Room, as well as a virtual tour that can be taken of this site of memory, see Tara Snow Hanson, "The Family Room at One Liberty Plaza," *Exhibitions.nysm*, accessed January 31, 2018, http://exhibitions.nysm.nysed.gov/familyroom/.

41. Jackson, "Unknown Knowns."

42. Donofrio, "Ground Zero," 157.

43. Foucault, "'Of Other Spaces.'"

44. Foucault, "'Of Other Spaces.'"

45. Holland Cotter, "The 9/11 Story Told at Bedrock, Powerful as a Punch to the Gut: Sept. 11 Memorial Museum at Ground Zero Prepares for Opening," *New York Times*, last modified May 14, 2014, paragraph 2, http://www.nytimes.com/2014/05/14/arts/design/sept-11-memorial-museum-at-ground-zero-prepares-for-opening.html.

46. Cotter, "9/11 Story," paragraphs 1–4.

47. Dunlap, "9/11 Shrine," paragraphs 1, 2.

48. Dunlap, "A 9/11 Shrine," paragraphs 2, 3.

49. Stern quoted in Dunlap, "9/11 Shrine," paragraph 4.

50. Hanson, "Family Room," paragraph 3.

51. Hanson, "Family Room," paragraphs 4, 5.

52. See Rebecca Fishbein, "A Look inside the Powerful 9/11 Family Room," *Gothamist*, last modified September 11, 2014, http://gothamist.com/2014/09/11/911_family_room_inside.php.

53. Sturken, "Aesthetics of Absence," 321.

54. 9/11 Memorial and Museum staff, "White Rose Signifies Remembrance of 9/11 Victims' Birthdays," *The Memo Blog*, last modified September 23, 2016, https://www.911memorial.org/blog/white-rose-signifies-remembrance-911 -victims-birthdays.

55. Butler, *Precarious Life*. See McIvor, "Bringing Ourselves to Grief."

56. Pettitt, "On Stuff."

57. Brown, *Sense of Things*.

58. Farrell, "'Ceremonial Transfer,'" paragraph 8.

59. Alan Feuer, "As 9/11 Museum Opens, These New Yorkers Will Stay Away," *New York Times*, last modified May 16, 2014, paragraph 2, http://www .nytimes.com/2014/05/17/nyregion/9-11-museum-not-a-must-see-site-for -all-new-yorkers.html.

60. Feuer, "As 9/11 Museum," paragraph 13.

4. MELANCHOLIC COMMEMORATION

1. "Solemn Crowd Gathers in a Healing City," *Daily News of Los Angeles*, last modified September 12, 2011, paragraphs 11–13, Lexis Nexis.

2. Alison Gendar and Douglas Feiden, "Security Plan for WTC Means Army of Cops, Barriers and Traffic Hell," *New York Daily News*, last modified April 6, 2008, paragraph 7, http://www.nydailynews.com/news/security-plan-wtc -means-army-cops-barriers-traffic-hell-article-1.278339.

3. David W. Dunlap, "With Security, Trade Center Faces New Isolation," *New York Times*, last modified May 16, 2013, paragraph 18, https://cityroom.blogs .nytimes.com/2013/05/16/world-trade-center-may-be-isolated-again-this -time-by-security-measures/?_r=0.

4. Julia Lester, "Post-9/11 WTC Security: Never Forget, Never Again," *CNBC*, last modified September 2, 2016, paragraph 27, http://www.cnbc.com/2016 /09/02/post-911-wtc-security-never-forget-never-again.html.

5. "Mayor Bloomberg Looks Back at New York City on September 12, 2001, and Out-lines Progress on Economic Recovery, Major Growth in Population and Historic Decreases in Crime," *US Official News*, last modified September 12, 2013, paragraph 4, http://www1.nyc.gov/office-of-the-mayor/news/298-13/mayor-bloomberg -looks-back-new-york-city-september-12-2001-outlines-progress-on#/0.

6. "Mayor Bloomberg Looks Back," paragraph 76.

7. Cerny, "From Warriors to Police?"

8. Janz, "Terror," 192.

9. Erik Ortiz, "NYC Keeps Security Tight following 9/11 Memorial," *amN-ewYork*, last modified September 11, 2011, Lexis Nexis.

10. We are course not the only nation worried about policing tourist attractions. See, for example, Alanna Petroff, "London Tourist Attractions Closed after U.K. Warns Another Attack Likely," *CNN.Money*, last modified May 24, 2017, http://money.cnn.com/2017/05/24/news/london-travel-tourism-terrorism -manchester/index.html.

11. Ortiz, "NYC Keeps Security Tight," paragraph 10.

12. Ortiz, "NYC Keeps Security Tight," paragraph 1.

13. Josh Margolin and Rebecca Rosenberg, "Open Door to Terror 'Bomb Plot' Raises White House Border Fear," *New York Post*, last modified September 11, 2011, Lexis Nexis.

14. Margolin and Rosenberg, "Open Door," paragraph 13.

15. Ortiz, "NYC Keeps Security Tight," paragraph 3.

16. Ortiz, "NYC Keeps Security Tight," paragraph 7.

17. Margolin and Rosenberg, "Open Door," paragraph 14.

18. Larry Celona and Bruce Golding, "WTC Neighbors Rip Fortress Mentality," *New York Post*, last modified November 13, 2013, paragraph 7, http://nypost .com/2013/11/13/wtc-neighbors-rip-fortress-mentality/.

19. Schuck, "Citizen Terrorist."

20. Ortiz, "NYC Keeps Security Tight," paragraph 9.

21. Coscarelli, "World Trade Center Neighbors," paragraph 3.

22. John Ost, "Towering Insecurity at Top NY Terror Target," *New York Post*, April 9, 2014, Lexis Nexis.

23. "World Trade Center Security at Center of New Yorkers' Lawsuit," *CBS News*, last modified January 9, 2014, paragraph 6, http://www.cbsnews.com/news /world-trade-center-security-at-center-of-new-yorkers-lawsuit/.

24. Kate Briquelet, "Cops Nix WTC Trash Cans," *New York Post*, last modified August 12, 2012, paragraph 4, http://nypost.com/2012/08/12/cops-nix-wtc -trash-cans/.

25. Briquelet, "Cops Nix WTC Trash," paragraph 6.

26. Briquelet, "Cops Nix WTC Trash," paragraph 1.

27. Briquelet, "Cops Nix WTC Trash," paragraph 14.

28. Woolgar and Neyland, *Mundane Governance*, 2.

29. Michael A. Bloomberg, "Mayor Bloomberg Looks Back at New York City at September 12, 2001, and Outlines Progress on Economic Recovery, Major Growth in Population and Historic Decreases in Crime" (speech, New York City, September 12, 2013), *NYC*, paragraph 22, http://www1.nyc.gov/office -of-the-mayor/news/298-13/mayor-bloomberg-looks-back-new-york-city -september-12–2001-outlines-progress-on#/0.

30. Ron Rosenbaum, "Who Needs Tower? NY Politicians Do—But It's Folly," *New York Observer*, last modified May 16, 2005, http://observer.com/2005 /05/who-needs-tower-ny-politicians-dobut-its-a-folly/.

31. *New York Times* Editorial Staff, "Ground Zero, Safe and Vibrant," *New York Times*, last modified August 12, 2008, paragraph 2, http://www.nytimes.com /2008/08/13/opinion/13wed4.html.

32. David W. Dunlap, "Residents Suing to Stop 'Fortresslike Plan for World Trade Center," *New York Times*, last modified November 13, 2013, paragraph 4. https://www.nytimes.com/2013/11/14/nyregion/residents-suing-to-stop -fortresslike-security-plan-for-world-trade-center.html.

33. Türetken, "Breathing Space."

34. National Preservation Institute staff, "The NEPA Review Process," National Preservation Institute, last accessed January 31, 2018, paragraph 14, https:// www.npi.org/NEPA/process.

35. Dunlap, "Residents Suing," paragraph 5.

36. Dunlap, "Residents Suing," paragraph 19.

37. *Neighborhood Alliance v. Kelly*, 6–8.

38. *Neighborhood Alliance v. Kelly*, 8–9.

39. *Neighborhood Alliance v. Kelly*, 19.

40. *Neighborhood Alliance v. Kelly*, 19.

41. *Neighborhood Alliance v. Kelly*, 19.

42. Hana R. Alberts, "Lawsuits," *Curbed New York*, last modified January 7, 2014, paragraph 1, https://ny.curbed.com/2014/1/7/10157152/lawsuits.

43. *Neighborhood Alliance v. Kelly*, 10.

44. *Neighborhood Alliance v. Kelly*, 10.

45. *Neighborhood Alliance v. Kelly*, 10.

46. *Neighborhood Alliance v. Kelly*, 10.

47. *Neighborhood Alliance v. Kelly*, 13.

48. *Neighborhood Alliance v. Kelly*, 13.

49. *Neighborhood Alliance v. Kelly*, 14.

50. *Neighborhood Alliance v. Kelly*, 21.

51. *Neighborhood Alliance v. Kelly*, 21.

52. *Neighborhood Alliance v. Kelly*, 22.

53. Josh Rogers, "In a Shift, W.T.C Residents Like What They Hear on Security," *Downtown Express*, last modified April 24, 2014, paragraph 4, http://www .downtownexpress.com/2014/04/24/in-a-shift-w-t-c-residents-like-what -they-hear-on-security/.

54. Rogers, "In a Shift," paragraph 3.

55. Verena Dopnik, "NY Residents Sue over World Trade Center Security," *San Diego Union Tribune*, last modified January 9, 2014, paragraph 11, http://www.sandiegouniontribune.com/sdut-ny-residents-sue-over-world-trade-center-security-2014jan08-story.html.

56. Ivan Pereira, "NYPD Remains on High Alert, Mayor Tells New Yorkers to Remain Calm," *Newsday*, last modified April 16, 2013, paragraph 9, http://www.newsday.com/news/new-york/nypd-remains-on-high-alert-mayor-tells-new-yorkers-to-remain-calm-1.5085487?view=print.

57. Vera Chinese and Barry Paddock, "In Races, Fear Finishes Last," *Daily News*, last modified April 22, 2013, line 6, http://www.lexisnexis.com.echo.louisville.edu/hottopics/lnacademic/?.

58. Chinese and Paddock, "Fear Finishes Last," lines 31–32.

59. Chinese and Paddock, "Fear Finishes Last," line 34.

60. Chinese and Paddock, "Fear Finishes Last," line 45.

61. Chinese and Paddock, "Fear Finishes Last," lines 26 and 27.

62. Forest and Johnson, "Security and Atonement," 405.

63. Forest and Johnson, "Security and Atonement," 406.

64. Light, "Visualizing Homeland," 3.

65. Light, "Visualizing Homeland," 8.

66. Light, "Visualizing Homeland," 6.

67. Michael Goodwin, "To NYPD Critics: Never Forget!," *New York Post*, last modified March 11, 2012, paragraph 15, http://nypost.com/2012/03/11/to-nypd-critics-never-forget/.

68. 9/11 Memorial, "9/11 Memorial Design Competition," 9/11 Memorial (2013), paragraphs 1, 9, last accessed January 31, 2018, http://www.911memorial.org/design-competition.

69. 9/11 Memorial, "9/11 Memorial Design," paragraph 1.

70. G. Roger Denson, "Michael Arad's 9/11 Memorial 'Reflecting Absence': More Than a Metaphor or a Monument," *Huffington Post*, last modified September 9, 2011, paragraphs 4, https://www.huffingtonpost.com/g-roger-denson/michael-arads-911-memoria_b_955454.html.

71. Denson, "Michael Arad's 9/11," paragraph 9.

72. Stephen Foley, "'We Were Able to Put a Hand on Him, Feel Part of Him. We're at Peace Now,'" *Independent*, last modified September 12, 2011, paragraph 5, http://www.independent.co.uk/news/world/americas/we-were-able-to-put-a-hand-on-him-feel-part-of-him-were-at-peace-now-2353169.html.

73. Anemona Hartocollis, "Connecting with Lost Loved Ones, if Only by the Tips of Fingers," *New York Times*, last modified September 11, 2011, paragraph 12,

http://www.nytimes.com/2011/09/12/nyregion/families-touch-the-names
-of-911-victims.html.

74. Colum McCann, "The Nation," *New York Times*, last modified December
    25, 2011, paragraph 1, http://query.nytimes.com/gst/fullpage.html?res=
    9403E5DC153DF936A15751C1A9679D8B63.

75. Phillip Kennicott, "Two Stark Voids. But in a City of Life," *Washington Post*,
    August 28, 2011, E7.

76. Al Baker, "At 9/11 Memorial, Police Raise Fears of Suicide," *New York Times*,
    last modified February 15, 2012, paragraph 5, http://www.nytimes.com/2012
    /02/16/nyregion/at-9-11-memorial-police-raise-suicide-fears.html.

77. Edward Helmore, "The Battle to Build the New World Trade Center,"
    Telegraph.co.uk, last modified March 23, 2013, paragraph 10, http://www
    .telegraph.co.uk/news/worldnews/northamerica/usa/9942760/The-battle
    -to-build-the-new-World-Trade-Center.html.

78. G. Roger Denson, "Michael Arad's 9/11 Memorial 'Reflecting Absence': More
    than a Metaphor or a Monument," *Huffington Post*, last modified December
    56, 2017, paragraph 18, https://www.huffingtonpost.com/g-roger-denson
    /michael-arads-911-memoria_b_955454.html.

79. Hilker, "Comfort of Melancholy," 31.

80. Lotringer and Virilio, *Accident of Art*.

81. Michael Kimmelman, "Space for the Living at a Memorial," *New York Times*,
    last modified May 28, 2014, https://www.nytimes.com/2014/05/29/arts
    /design/finding-space-for-the-living-at-a-memorial.html.

82. Biesecker, "No Time for Mourning," 157.

83. Sci, "(Re)thinking the Memorial."

84. Stow, "From Upper Canal," 689.

85. Martin Filler, "A Masterpiece at Ground Zero," *New York Review of Books*,
    last modified October 27, 2011, paragraphs 1–2, http://www.nybooks.com
    /articles/archives/2011/oct/27/masterpiece-ground-zero/?pagination=false.

5. HOLOCAUST MEMORIES

1. James E. Young, "James Young: The Stages of Memory and the Monument;
   From Berlin to New York," *YouTube*, video file, accessed July 17, 2015,
   https://www.youtube.com/watch?v=1wWK36TVPP8.

2. Examples of Young's renowned work include Young, *Texture of Memory*, and
   Young, *At Memory's Edge*.

3. Young, *Stages of Memory*, 2.

4. Young, *Stages of Memory*, 2.

5. Young, *Stages of Memory*, 2.

6. Young, *Stages of Memory*, 2.

7. Young, *Stages of Memory*, 2.

8. Young, "James Young: The Stages of Memory," video file.

9. Barack Obama, "President Obama Speaks at 9/11 Museum Dedication: 'A Sacred Place of Healing and Hope,'" *The White House Blog*, last modified May 15, 2014, paragraph 4, http://www.whitehouse.gov/blog/2014/05/15 /president-obama-speaks-911-museum-dedication-sacred-place-healing -and-hope.

10. Holland Cotter, "The 9/11 Story Told at Bedrock, Powerful as a Punch to the Gut: Sept. 11 Memorial Museum at Ground Zero Prepares for Opening," *New York Times*, last modified May 14, 2014, paragraph 3, http://www.nytimes .com/2014/05/14/arts/design/sept-11-memorial-museum-at-ground-zero -prepares-for-opening.html.

11. Donofrio, "Ground Zero."

12. Cotter, "9/11 Story."

13. Ehrenhaus, "Why We Fought."

14. Greenwald, "'Passions on All Sides,'" 117.

15. Greenwald, "'Passions on All Sides,'" 117.

16. Greenwald, "'Passions on All Sides,'" 118.

17. National September 11 Memorial and Museum staff, "2015 Annual Report," National September 11 Memorial and Museum, *9/11memorial.org*, http://2015 .911memorial.org/ (accessed January 11, 2017).

18. National September 11 Memorial and Museum Staff, "9/11 Memorial Museum Welcomes More Than 10 Million Visitors," 911 *Memorial.org.*, July 28, 2017, https://www.911memorial.org/blog/911-memorial-museum-welcomes-more -10-million-visitors.

19. See Ivie and Giner, "American Exceptionalism."

20. Bowman and Pezzullo, "What's So 'Dark,'" 187.

21. Rothberg, *Multidirectional Memory*, 3.

22. For another example of a scholar using dingpolitik approaches to explain some of this competitiveness in other genocidal contexts see Rindzeviciute, "Hegemony or Legitimacy."

23. See Greenwald, "Passions on All Sides."

24. Greenwald, "Passions on All Sides," 118.

25. Lew, "Debating Tourism," 1.

26. Foucault, "Other Spaces."

27. Bellah, "Civil Religion."

28. Foucault, "Society Must Be Defended"; Foucault, *Security, Territory, Population*.
29. Agamben, *Homo Sacer*.
30. See Murray, "Thanatopolitics"; Kuljić, "Thanatopolitics and Thanatosociology."
31. Lennon and Foley, *Dark Tourism*.
32. Bigley et al., "War-Related Tourism."
33. Algeo, "Underground Tourists/Tourists."
34. Stone and Sharpley, "Consuming Dark Tourism."
35. See Žižek, *Desert of the Real!*
36. Isin, "Neurotic Citizen," 232.
37. Crandall and Armitage, "Envisioning the Homefront," 30.
38. De Goede, "Beyond Risk," 161; Isin, "Neurotic Citizen," 232.
39. Alicia Colon, "Make WTC More Than 9/11 Memorial," *New York Sun*, last modified June 17, 2005, http://www.nysun.com/new-york/make-wtc-more -than-9-11-memorial/15620/; Donofrio, "Ground Zero."
40. Debra Burlingame, "The Great Ground Zero Heist," *Wall Street Journal*, last modified June 7, 2005, http://online.wsj.com/news/articles /SB111810145819652326.
41. Calev Ben-David, "The Man at Ground Zero," *Jerusalem Post*, September 26, 2003, paragraph 10, Lexis Nexis.
42. Ben-David, "Man at Ground," paragraph 14.
43. Barbara Sofer, "Elul at Ground Zero," *Jerusalem Post*, August 16, 2013, para- graphs 11, 15.
44. Forest and Johnson, "Security and Atonement."
45. Forest and Johnson, "Security and Atonement," 409.
46. *CBSNews* staff, "Some Question 9/11 Memorial's $60M Annual Cost," *CBSNews*, last modified September 10, 2012, accessed July 17, 2015, http:// www.cbsnews.com/news/some-question-9-11-memorials-60m-annual-cost/.
47. Forest and Johnson, "Security and Atonement," 408.
48. Mark Vanhoenacker, "Do You Have a Photo ID, Young Man?," *Slate*, last modified September 10, 2012, paragraph 4, http://www.slate.com/articles /life/culturebox/2012/09/sept_11_memorial_does_the_world_trade_center _site_really_need_so_much_security_.html.
49. Vanhoenacker, "Do You Have," paragraph 6.
50. Mueller, *Overblown*, 1.
51. Sedgwick, review of *Overblown*, 439.
52. Schneier, *Beyond Fear*, 38.
53. Mann, "Smoke Screening," paragraph 21.

54. Janz, "Terror," 191.

55. Huyssen, "Review Essay"; Beck, "Cosmopolitan Society."

56. Sterritt, "Representing Atrocity," 142.

57. Cohen, "Tears of a Nation," paragraph 6.

58. Sterritt, "Representing Atrocity," 142.

59. Ehrenhaus, "Why We Fought," 332.

60. Mamdani, *Good Muslim, Bad Muslim*, 11.

61. Carr, "Staying for Time." See Lotringer and Virilio, *Accident of Art*.

62. Levy and Sznaider, *Globalen Zeitalter*. See also Huyssen, "Review Essay"; Huyssen, *Present Pasts*, 154.

63. See Steinweiss, "Auschwitz Analogy."

64. Krauthammer, "Greater the Evil," paragraphs 2, 4.

65. Holland, "From September 11th," 289.

66. Holland, "From September 11th," 287.

67. Diken and Lausten, "7-11, 9/11," 89.

68. Gregory J. Wallance, "The American Public Will Tolerate Intrusive Surveillance, but Only If They Are Convinced the Threat Justifies It," *Jerusalem Post*, last modified September 13, 2013, paragraph 15, http://www.jpost.com /Opinion/Op-Ed-Contributors/The-American-public-will-tolerate-intrusive -surveillance-but-only-if-they-are-convinced-the-threat-justifies-it-326295.

69. Grant, "Ground Zero as Holy," 54.

70. MacDonald, "Bush's American," 1107, 1109.

71. Jonathan Stempel, "Saudi Arabia Must Face U.S. Lawsuits over Sept. 11 Attacks," Reuters," paragraph 2, https://www.reuters.com/article/us-usa -saudi-sept11/saudi-arabia-must-face-u-s-lawsuits-over-sept-11-attacks -idUSKBN1H43Al.

72. Lapeter, "Now We Know Evil Has Power," *St. Petersburg Times*, February 22, 2002, paragraph 9.

73. Carr, "Staying for Time"; Jenkins, "Ethical Responsibility"; Sterritt, "Representing Atrocity."

74. Sterritt, "Representing Atrocity." See Virilio, *War and Cinema*; Virilio, *9/11*.

75. Sterritt, "Representing Atrocity," 143.

76. 9/11 Museum staff, "About the Museum," 9/11 Memorial and Museum, paragraph 1, https://www.911memorial.org/about-museum.

77. Vivian, *Public Forgetting*, 206.

78. Vivian, *Public Forgetting*, 206–7.

79. Holland Cotter, "The 9/11 Story Told at Bedrock, Powerful as a Punch to the Gut: Sept. 11 Memorial Museum at Ground Zero Prepares for Opening," *New*

York Times, last modified May 14, 2014, paragraph 2, http://www.nytimes
.com/2014/05/14/arts/design/sept-11-memorial-museum-at-ground-zero
-prepares-for-opening.html.

80. Cotter, "9/11 Story," paragraph 21.
81. See Brown, *Sense of Things*; Pettitt, "On Stuff."
82. See Hasian, "Remembering and Forgetting."
83. Cotter, "9/11 Story," paragraph 6.
84. Cotter, "9/11 Story," paragraph 7.
85. Cotter, "9/11 Story," paragraph 5.
86. Cotter, "9/11 Story," paragraph 8.
87. Cotter, "9/11 Story," paragraph 10.
88. Cotter, "9/11 Story," paragraph 15.
89. Stephen Farrell and Peter Baker, "At 9/11 Museum Dedication, Remembrance and Resilience," *New York Times*, last modified May 15, 2014, http://www.nytimes.com/2014/05/16/nyregion/at-9-11-museum-dedication-remembrance-and-resilience.html.
90. Cotter, "9/11 Story."
91. Steve Kandell, "The Worst Day of My Life Is Now New York's Hottest Tourist Attraction," *BuzzFeedNews*, last modified May 19, 2014, paragraph 14, http://www.buzzfeed.com/stevekandell/the-worst-day-of-my-life-is-now-new-yorks-hottest-tourist-at#.lgv8v3k7gw.
92. Farrell and Baker, "At 9/11 Museum Dedication," paragraph 8.
93. Charles Wolf, "Let the 9/11 Museum Remains Rest in Peace: A Small Band of Dissenters Reopens Old Wounds," *New York Daily News*, last modified May 29, 2014, http://www.nydailynews.com/opinion/9-11-museum-remains-rest-peace-article-1.1809125.
94. Adam Gopnik, "Stones and Bones: Visiting the 9/11 Memorial and Museum," *New Yorker*, last modified July 7, 2014, paragraph 30, http://www.newyorker.com/magazine/2014/07/07/stones-and-bones.
95. Gopnik, "Stones and Bones," paragraph 8.
96. See Lennon and Foley, *Dark Tourism*.
97. Alan Feuer, "As 9/11 Museum Opens, These New Yorkers Will Stay Away," *New York Times*, last modified May 16, 2014, paragraph 20, http://www.nytimes.com/2014/05/17/nyregion/9-11-museum-not-a-must-see-site-for-all-new-yorkers.html.
98. Feuer, "As 9/11 Museum Opens," paragraph 13.
99. Feuer, "As 9/11 Museum Opens," paragraph 3, http://www.nytimes.com/2014/05/17/nyregion/9-11-museum-not-a-must-see-site-for-all-new-yorkers.html.

100. De Goede, "Beyond Risk."
101. Lennon and Foley, *Dark Tourism.*
102. Foucault, "Other Spaces."
103. Rindzeviciute, "Hegemony or Legitimacy?," 153.
104. Rindzeviciute, "Hegemony or Legitimacy?," 176–77.

CONCLUSION

1. See Matthew Rothschild, "Comment: Plan for Quagmire," *Progressive*, last modified December 26, 2005, http://progressive.org/dispatches/comment -plan-quagmire/.
2. See, for example, Norman Solomon, "The Quagmire of the U.S. Media," *Al Jazeera*, last modified March 16, 2004, http://www.aljazeera.com/archive /2004/03/2008410113325867819.html.
3. Mark Danner, "Rumsfeld's War and Its Consequences Now," *New York Review of Books*, last modified December 19, 2013, http://www.nybooks.com /articles/2013/12/19/rumsfelds-war-and-its-consequences-now/.
4. See Young, "Counter-Monument."
5. For a more detailed discussion of the various ways that publics not only accept but also demand the discursive and material formation of an American national security state, see Hasian et al., *Rhetorical Invention.*
6. *USA Today* staff, "Bush Makes Surprise Visit to 9/11 Memorial," *USA Today*, last modified December 11, 2014, http://www.aljazeera.com/archive/2004 /03/2008410113325867819.html; Bonnie Azab Powell, "Investigative Journalist Seymour Hersh Spills the Secrets of the Iraq Quagmire and the War on Terror," *UC Berkeley News*, last modified October 11, 2004, https://www .berkeley.edu/news/media/releases/2004/10/11_hersh.shtml.
7. For diverse discussions of this site's link to commemorate the lives of those killed by terrorists, see Young, "Memorial's Arc."
8. Cheryl K. Chumley, "George W. Bush Makes Surprise Visit to 9/11 Memorial Museum," *Washington Times*, last modified December 15, 2014, http://www .washingtontimes.com/news/2014/dec/15/george-w-bush-makes-surprise -visit-to-911-memorial/.
9. Chumley, "George W. Bush Makes," paragraph 5.
10. *Fox News* team, "'Breaking the Silence' Moment Captured on Video, Aired by *Fox News*," *RobertJONeill*, last modified November 11, 2014, http://www.robertjoneill.com/2014-11-11_Rob-ONeill-FOXnews-Breaking -the-Silence.html.
11. *Fox News* Team, "'Breaking the Silence,'" paragraph 3.

12. FBI New York Office Press Office, "Remembering 9/11," FBI, last modified September 11, 2014, https://www.fbi.gov/contact-us/field-offices/newyork/news/press-releases/remembering-9-11.

13. *CBS News* staff, "Remembering 9/11: 'We Must Never Forget That Day,'" *CBS News*, last modified September 11, 2015, paragraph 3, http://www.cbsnews.com/news/september-11-terror-attacks-14th-anniversary/.

14. *CBS News* Staff, "Remembering 9/11," paragraphs 2–3.

15. *CBS News* staff, "Remembering 9/11," paragraphs 4–5.

16. Ivie and Giner, *Hunt the Devil*. This is not to say that all veterans consistently support all facets of perpetual wars. For examples of dissenters, see Ivie and Giner, "Waging Peace."

17. Pope Francis, quoted in "Full Text: Pope Francis' Speech at the 9/11 Memorial and Museum," *Catholic News Agency*, last modified September 25, 2015, http://www.catholicnewsagency.com/news/full-text-pope-francis-speech-at-the-911-memorial-and-museum-39576/.

18. Pope Francis, "Pope Francis' Speech," paragraph 2.

19. Pope Francis, "Pope Francis' Speech," paragraph 7.

20. Maggie Haberman, "Donald Trump, in First Visit to 9/11 Memorial, Praises 'New York Values' in Jab at Ted Cruz," *New York Times*, last modified April 9, 2016, paragraph 9, https://www.nytimes.com/politics/first-draft/2016/04/09/donald-trump-in-first-visit-to-911-memorial-praises-new-york-values-in-jab-at-ted-cruz/.

21. 9/11 Memorial and Museum staff, "FBI Agent Who Supervised 9/11 Investigation Speaks at Museum," *9/11 Memorial.org*, last modified December 2, 2016, https://www.911memorial.org/blog/fbi-agent-who-supervised-911-investigation-speaks-museum.

22. John Brennan, "Remarks as Prepared for Delivery by Central Intelligence Agency Director John O. Brennan at the 9/11 Memorial Museum in New York City," *CIA.gov*, last modified September 26, 2016, paragraph 1, https://www.cia.gov/news-information/speeches-testimony/2016-speeches-testimony/director-brennan-speaks-at-the-9-11-memorial-museum-in-new-york-city.html.

23. Brennan, "Remarks as Prepared," paragraph 2.

24. For more on Operation Jawbreaker see Gary Berntsen and Ralph Pezzullo, *Jawbreaker: The Attack on Bin Laden and Al-Qaeda; A Personal Account of the CIA's Key Field Commander* (New York: Crown Publishers, 2005). Many years later journalists and members of the public were still being presented with fragmentary information about these secret Afghanistan missions. See Thomas Gibbons-Neff, "After 13 Years, CIA Honors Green Beret Killed on

Secret Afghanistan Mission," *Washington Post*, last modified April 17, 2016, https://www.washingtonpost.com/news/checkpoint/wp/2016/04/17/after -13-years-cia-honors-green-beret-killed-on-secret-afghanistan-mission/?utm _term=.ee7d4801d3e4.

25. Brennan, "Remarks as Prepared," paragraph 5.
26. Brennan, "Remarks as Prepared," paragraph 9.
27. Brennan, "Remarks as Prepared," paragraph 12.
28. Brennan, "Remarks as Prepared," paragraph 13.
29. Brennan, "Remarks as Prepared," paragraph 17.
30. Brennan, "Remarks as Prepared," paragraph 19.
31. Brennan, "Remarks as Prepared," paragraph 24.
32. Brennan, "Remarks as Prepared," paragraphs 27–29.
33. Brennan, "Remarks as Prepared," paragraph 31.
34. Brennan, "Remarks as Prepared," paragraphs 47–50.
35. Brennan, "Remarks as Prepared," paragraph 38.
36. Brennan, "Remarks as Prepared," paragraphs 41–44.
37. Arthur Dominic Villasanta, "Bin Laden's Body Pulverized by Over 100 Rounds Fired by SEAL TEAM Six Operation. *China Topix*, last modified April 11, 2017. http://www.chinatopix.com/articles/113372/20170411/bin -laden-body-pulverized-over-100-rounds-fired-seal.htm.
38. *Fox News Insider* staff, "SEAL Who Killed Bin Laden Meets 9/11 Families at Memorial Museum," filmed 2015, *Fox News Insider*, last modified April 30, 2015. http://insider.foxnews.com/2015/04/30/seal-who-killed-bin-laden -meets-911-families-memorial-museum.
39. Jordan Friedman, "Navy SEAL Rob O'Neill Recounts bin Laden's Death," 9/11 Memorial and Museum, last modified May 1, 2015, paragraph 4, https://www .911memorial.org/blog/navy-seal-rob-oneill-recounts-bin-ladens-death.
40. Friedman, "Navy SEAL," paragraph 4.
41. Robert J. O'Neill, "The Meaning behind the Mission," *robertjoneill.com*, paragraph 8, last modified September 11, 2015, http://www.robertjoneill.com /2015-09-11_Fox-and-Friends.html.
42. Friedman, "Navy SEAL Rob O'Neill," paragraph 5.
43. Friedman, "Navy SEAL," paragraph 6.
44. *Fox News Insider* staff, "SEAL Who Killed Bin Laden," video.
45. *Fox News Insider* staff, "SEAL Who Killed Bin Laden."
46. *Fox News Insider* staff, "SEAL Who Killed Bin Laden."
47. "I Fired Twice and bin Laden Crumpled," *Sunday Times* (London), last modified February 8, 2015, Lexis Nexis.

48. Toby Harnden, "Rob O'Neill: The Man Who Shot Osama bin Laden," *Australian*, last modified February 11, 2015, paragraph 27, http://www.theaustralian .com.au/news/world/the-times/rob-oneill-the-man-who-shot-osama-bin -laden/news-story/50fe923d82d76f02cfac27de9a7ea4ab.

49. Friedman, "Navy SEAL Rob O'Neill."

50. "I Fired Twice and bin Laden Crumpled," paragraph 36.

51. Hasian, *Drone Warfare*.

52. For essays on the symbolic meaning of the movie *Saving Private Ryan*, see Hasian, "Nostalgic Longings"; Owen, "Memory, War"; Ehrenhaus, "Why We Fought."

53. Hasian and McFarlane, *Cultural Rhetorics*.

54. Stahl, *Militainment, Inc.*, 6.

55. Stahl, *Militainment, Inc.*, 6.

56. See Vivian, *Commonplace Witnessing*; Vivian, "Witnessing Time."

57. Weizman, *Least of All*.

58. Friedman, "Navy SEAL Rob O'Neill."

59. Friedman, "Navy SEAL Rob O'Neill."

60. Burlingame quoted in Friedman, "Navy SEAL Rob O'Neill."

61. Butler, *Precarious Life*, xv.

62. Butler, *Precarious Life*, xv.

63. Conquergood, "Lethal Theatre," 367.

64. Villasanta, "Bin Laden's Body," paragraph 5.

65. Harold and DeLuca, "Behold the Corpse."

66. See Owen and Maurer, *No Easy Day*. Also see Hasian and McFarlane, *Cultural Rhetorics*, for more detail about this particular book and how it is deeply inscribed with cultural and rhetorical notions of American exceptionalism.

67. Jim Sciutto, Ryan Browne, Deirdre Walsh, "Congress Releases Secret '28 Pages' on Alleged Saudi 9/11 Ties," *CNN*, lasted modified July 15, 2016, paragraph 3, http://www.cnn.com/2016/07/15/politics/congress-releases -28-pages-saudis-9–11/index.html.

68. Sciutto et al., "Congress Releases Secret," paragraph 4.

69. Sciutto et al., "Congress Releases Secret," paragraph 4.

70. See Hasian, *Drone Warfare*.

71. Buncombe, "How Trump's ME Trip Could Make Saudi Compensate Families of 9/11 Victims," *Tehran Times*, last modified June 12, 2017, http://www .tehrantimes.com/news/414159/How-Trump-s-ME-trip-could-make-Saudi -compensate-families-of-9-11.

72. Buncombe, "How Trump's ME Trip," paragraph 13.

73. Brandon Jones, "Congress Unites to Override Obama's Veto of 9/11 Victim Bill, JASTA, Allowing Families to Sue Saudis," *Global Dispatch*, last modified September 28, 2016, paragraph 16, http://www.theglobaldispatch.com /congress-unites-to-override-obamas-veto-of-911-victim-bill-jasta-allowing -families-to-sue-saudis-69366/.

74. Jones, "Congress Unites," paragraph 6.

75. Ruth Sherlock, "Barack Obama Suffers Blow as Congress Overrides Veto of 9/11 Bill Allowing Families to Sue Saudi Arabia," *Telegraph*, last modified September 28, 2016, paragraph 3, http://www.telegraph.co.uk/news/2016 /09/28/barack-obama-suffers-blow-as-congress-overrides-veto-of-911-bill/.

76. Sherlock, "Barack Obama Suffers," paragraph 9.

77. Sherlock, "Barack Obama Suffers," paragraph 16.

78. Seung Min Kim, Congress Hands Obama First Veto Override," *Politico*, last modified September 28, 2016, http://www.politico.com/story/2016/09 /senate-jasta-228841.

79. Karoun Demirjian and Juliet Eilperin, "Congress Overrides Obama's Veto of 9/11 Bill," *Washington Post*, last modified, September 28, 2016, paragraphs 6, 8, https://www.washingtonpost.com/news/powerpost/wp/2016/09/27/senate -poised-to-vote-to-override-obamas-veto-of-911-bill/?utm_term=.c658f1ec4e5a.

80. Kim, "Congress Hands Obama First," paragraph 4.

81. Vera Bergengruen, "Why Families of the 9/11 Victims Feel Betrayed by Obama," *McClatchy DC*, last modified September 20, 2016, paragraph 5, http://www.mcclatchydc.com/news/politics-government/congress /article103033037.html.

82. Bergengruen, "Why Families," paragraph 8.

83. Bergengruen, "Why Families," paragraph 15.

84. Bergengruen, "Why Families," paragraph 14.

85. Bergengruen, "Why Families," paragraph 18.

86. Bergengruen, "Why Families," paragraph 20.

87. Max Greenwood and Akbar Shahid Ahmed, "Barack Obama Makes Last-Minute Push to Block Saudi 9/11 Bill, *Huffington Post*, last modified September 28, 2016, paragraph 4, http://www.huffingtonpost.com/entry /barack-obama-jasta-letter_us_57ebd8d3e4b082aad9b81a75.

88. Patton, "Saudis Paid Veterans," paragraph 9.

89. Buncombe, "Trump's ME Trip," paragraph 10.

90. Patton, "Saudis Paid Veterans," paragraph 10.

91. *Zee News* staff, "Pakistan Banks Sent Funds to UAE to Finance 9/11, 26/11 Terror Attacks," *Zeenews*, last modified June 27, 2017, http://zeenews.india

.com/asia/pakistan-banks-sent-funds-to-uae-to-finance-9/11-26/11-terror-attacks
-2019256.html.

92. *Zee News* staff, "Pakistan Banks Sent Funds," paragraph 6.

93. *Zee News* staff, "Pakistan Banks Sent Funds," paragraph 10.

94. Edward Malnick and Luke Heighton, "UAE Warned US It Could End Intelligence Cooperation over 9/11 Victims' Claims," *Telegraph*, last modified June 21, 2017, paragraph 24, http://www.telegraph.co.uk/news/2017/06/21/uae-warned-us-could-end-intelligence-cooperation-911-victims/.

95. Buncombe, "How Trump's ME Trip," paragraph 10.

96. See *New York Times* staff, "How the US Became More Involved in the War in Yemen," *New York Times*, last modified October 15, 2016, https://www.nytimes.com/interactive/2016/10/14/world/middleeast/yemen-saudi-arabia-us-airstrikes.html.

97. Buncombe, "How Trump's ME Trip," paragraph 6.

98. See Paliewicz and McHendry, "When Good Arguments."

99. Foucault, *Security, Territory, Population*, 20.

Abel, Chris, and Norman Foster. *Architecture and Identity: Responses to Cultural and Technological Change*. New York: Routledge, 2000.

Abel, Marco. *Violent Affect: Literature, Cinema, and Critique after Representation*. Lincoln: University of Nebraska Press, 2007.

Africa News. "Uganda; Good Muslim or Bad." The Monitor. *Africa News*. August 7, 2004.

Agamben, Giorgio. *Homo Sacer: Sovereign Power and Bare Life*. Translated by Daniel Heller-Roazen. Palo Alto CA: Stanford University Press, 1998.

———. *What Is an Apparatus?* Translated by David Kishik and Stefan Pedatella. Palo Alto CA: Stanford University Press, 2009.

Algeo, Katie. "Underground Tourists/Tourists Underground: African American Tourism to Mammoth Cave." *Tourism Geographies* 15, no. 3 (2013): 380–404. Accessed February 8, 2018. http://www.tandfonline.com/doi/abs/10.1080/14616688.2012.675514.

Ali Nasir, Muhammad. "Biopolitics, Thanatopolitics and the Right to Life." *Theory, Culture & Society* 34, no. 1 (2017): 75–95. Accessed February 8, 2018. http://journals.sagepub.com/doi/abs/10.1177/0263276416657881.

Baer, Elizabeth. "Fallout of Various Kinds." In *Trauma at Home: After 9/11*, edited by Judith Greenberg, 158–67. Lincoln: University of Nebraska Press, 2002.

Beck, Ulrich. "The Cosmopolitan Society and Its Enemies." *Theory, Culture & Society* 19, no. 1–2 (2002): 17–44. Accessed February 8, 2018. http://journals.sagepub.com/doi/abs/10.1177/026327640201900101.

Bellah, Robert. "Civil Religion in America." *Daedalus* 96, no. 1 (1967): 1–21. Accessed February 8, 2018. http://www.jstor.org/stable/20027022?seq=1#page_scan_tab_contents.

Bennett, Jane. *Vibrant Matter: A Political Ecology of Things*. Durham NC: Duke University Press, 2010.

Berntsen, Gary, and Ralph Pezzullo. *Jawbreaker: The Attack on Bin Laden and Al-Qaeda; A Personal Account by the CIA's Key Field Commander*. New York: Crown Publishers, 2005.

Biesecker, Barbara. "No Time for Mourning: The Rhetorical Production of the Melancholic Citizen-Subject." *Philosophy & Rhetoric* 40, no. 1 (2007): 147–69. Accessed February 8, 2018. http://www.jstor.org/stable/25655263?seq=1#page_scan_tab_contents.

Bigley, James, Choong-Ki Lee, Jinhyng Chon, and Yooshik Yoon. "Motivations for War-Related Tourism: A Case of DMZ Visitors in Korea." *Tourism Geographies* 12, no. 3 (2010): 371–94. Accessed February 8, 2018. http://www.tandfonline.com/doi/abs/10.1080/14616688.2010.494687.

Blair, Carole. "Reflections on Criticism and Bodies: Parables from Public Places." *Western Journal of Communication* 65, no. 3 (2001): 271–94. Accessed February 8, 2018. https://search.proquest.com/openview/a37112b1642007287d82b17fe289bdb8/1?pq-origsite=gscholar&cbl=47214.

Blair, Carole, Marsha Jeppeson, and Enrico Pucci Jr. "Public Memorializing in Postmodernity: The Vietnam Veterans Memorial as Prototype." *Quarterly Journal of Speech* 77, no. 3 (1991): 263–88. Accessed February 8, 2018. http://www.tandfonline.com/doi/abs/10.1080/00335639109383960.

Blair, Carole, and Neil Michel. "Reproducing Civil Rights Tactics: The Rhetorical Performances of the Civil Rights Memorial." *Rhetoric Society Quarterly* 30, no. 2 (2000): 31–55. Accessed February 8, 2018. http://www.tandfonline.com/doi/abs/10.1080/02773940009391174.

Borradori, Giovanna. *Philosophy in a Time of Terror: Dialogues with Jürgen Habermas and Jacques Derrida*. Chicago: University of Chicago Press, 2013.

Bowman, Michael, and Phaedra Pezzullo. "What's So 'Dark' about 'Dark Tourism'? Death, Tours, and Performance." *Tourist Studies* 9, no. 3 (2009): 187–202. Accessed February 8, 2018. http://journals.sagepub.com/doi/abs/10.1177/1468797610382699.

Brager, Jenna. "The Selfie and the Other: Consuming Viral Tragedy and Social Media (After) Lives." *International Journal of Communication* 9 (2015): 1660–71. Accessed February 8, 2018. http://ijoc.org/index.php/ijoc/article/view/3137.

Brill, Steven. "Are We Any Safer?" *Atlantic*, September 2016. https://www.theatlantic.com/magazine/archive/2016/09/are-we-any-safer/492761/.

Brown, Bill. *A Sense of Things: The Object Matter of American Literature*. Chicago: University of Chicago Press, 2004.

Butler, Judith. *Precarious Life: The Powers of Mourning and Violence*. London, UK: Verso, 2006.

Carr, Steven. "Staying for Time: The Holocaust and Atrocity Footage in American Public Memory." In *Violating Time: History, Memory and Nostalgia in Cinema*, edited by Christina Lee, 57–69. New York: Continuum, 2008.

Cerny, Philip. "From Warriors to Police? The Civilianisation of Security in a Globalising World." *International Politics* 52, no. 4 (2015): 389–407. Accessed February 8, 2018. https://link.springer.com/article/10.1057/ip.2015.7.

Chouliaraki, Lilie, and Angelos Kissas. "The Communication of Horrorism: A Typology of ISIS Online Death Videos." *Critical Studies in Media Communication* 35, no. 1 (2018): 24–39, Accessed February 8, 2018. http://nca.tandfonline.com/doi/abs/10.1080/15295036.2017.1393096.

Conquergood, Dwight. "Lethal Theatre: Performance, Punishment, and the Death Penalty." *Theatre Journal* 54, no. 3 (2002): 339–67. Accessed February 8, 2018. https://muse.jhu.edu/article/35005/summary.

Coscarelli, Joe. "World Trade Center Neighbors Suing over Super-Safe, 'Fortresslike' Security." *New York Magazine*, November 14, 2013. http://nymag.com/daily/intelligencer/2013/11/world-trade-center-neighbors-sue-over-security.html.

Crandall, Jordan, and John Armitage. "Envisioning the Homefront: Militarization, Tracking and Security Culture." *Journal of Visual Culture* 4, no. 1 (2005): 17–37. Accessed February 8, 2018. http://journals.sagepub.com/doi/abs/10.1177/1470412905050636.

De Goede, Marieke. "Beyond Risk: Premediation and the Post 9/11 Security Imagination." *Security Dialogue* 39, no. 203 (2008): 155–76. Accessed February 8, 2018. http://journals.sagepub.com/doi/abs/10.1177/0967010608088773.

Dehncke-Fisher, Heidi, dir. *Dust to Dust: The Health Effects of 9/11*. 2006; Productions and Tinderbox Media Group. DVD.

Deleuze, Gilles, and Claire Parnet, *Dialogues*. Translated by Hugh Tomlinson and Barbara Habberjam. New York: Columbia University Press, 1987.

Dickinson, Greg. "Joe's Rhetoric: Finding Authenticity at Starbucks." *Rhetoric Society Quarterly* 32, no. 4 (2002): 5–27. Accessed February 8, 2018. http://www.tandfonline.com/doi/abs/10.1080/02773940209391238.

Dickinson, Greg, Brian L. Ott, and Eric Aoki. "Memory and Myth at the Buffalo Bill Museum." *Western Journal of Communication* 69, no. 2 (2005): 85–108. Accessed February 8, 2018. http://www.tandfonline.com/doi/abs/10.1080/10570310500076684.

Diken, Bülent, and Carston Bagge Lausten. "7-11, 9/11, and Postpolitics." *Alternatives: Global, Local, Political* 29, no. 1 (2004): 89–113. Accessed February 8, 2018. https://www.jstor.org/stable/40645106?seq=1#page_scan_tab_contents.

Donofrio, Theresa. "Ground Zero and Place-Making Authority: The Conservative Metaphors in 9/11 Families' 'Take Back the Memorial' Rhetoric." *Western Journal of Communication* 74, no. 2 (2010): 150–69. Accessed February 8, 2018. http://www.tandfonline.com/doi/abs/10.1080 /10570311003614492.

Doss, Erika. *The Emotional Life of Contemporary Public Memorials: Towards a Theory of Temporary Memorials*. Amsterdam, Netherlands: University of Amsterdam Press, 2008.

———. *Memorial Mania: Public Feeling in America*. Chicago: University of Chicago Press, 2010.

Douglas, Mary. *Purity and Danger*. New York: Routledge, 1966.

Duvall, John N., and Robert P. Marzec. *Narrating 9/11: Fantasies of State, Security, and Terrorism*. Baltimore: Johns Hopkins University Press, 2015.

Edkins, Jenny. *The Absence of Meaning: Trauma and the Events of 11 September 2001*. Providence RI: Watson Institute for International Studies, Brown University, 2004. Web publication.

———. "Forget Trauma? Responses to September 11." *International Relations* 16, no. 2 (2002): 243–56. Accessed February 8, 2018. http://journals.sagepub .com/doi/abs/10.1177/0047117802016002005.

Ehrenhaus, Peter. "Why We Fought: Holocaust Memory in Spielberg's *Saving Private Ryan*." *Critical Studies in Media Communication* 18, no. 3 (2001): 321–37. Accessed February 8, 2018. http://www.tandfonline.com/doi/abs/10 .1080/07393180128089.

Fisher, Thomas. "Architecture in the Crosshairs." *Architecture* 92, no. 6 (2003): 96.

Foote, Kenneth. *Shadowed Ground: America's Landscapes of Violence and Tragedy*. Austin: University of Texas Press, 2003.

Forest, Benjamin, and Juliet Johnson. "Security and Atonement: Controlling Access to the World Trade Center Memorial." *Cultural Geographies* 20, no. 3 (2012): 405–11. Accessed February 8, 2018. http://journals.sagepub.com/doi /abs/10.1177/1474474012455000.

Foucault, Michel. "Other Spaces." In *Foucault: Aesthetics, Method, and Epistemology*, edited by James D. Faubian and Paul Rabinow, pp. 175–85. 1967. Repr., New York: New Press, 1998.

———. *Security, Territory, Population: Lectures at the Collège De France, 1977–78*, edited by Michel Sennellart. Translated by Graham Burchell. London: Palgrave Macmillan, 2007.

———. "Society Must Be Defended: Lectures at the College de France, 1975–1976." In *The Essential Foucault: Selections from Essential Works of Foucault*,

1954–1984, edited by Paul Rabinow and Nikolas Rose, 294–99. New York: New Press, 2003.

Goldberger, Paul. "Designing Downtown." *New Yorker,* January 6, 2003, http:// www.newyorker.com/magazine/2003/01/06/designing-downtown.

——— . "Up From Zero." *New Yorker,* July 29, 2002. http://www.newyorker.com /magazine/2002/07/29/up-from-zero.

Gopnik, Adam. "Stones and Bones: Visiting the 9/11 Memorial and Museum." *New Yorker.* Last Modified July 7, 2014. http://www.newyorker.com /magazine/2014/07/07/stones-and-bones.

Gordon, Avery. *Ghostly Matters: Haunting and the Sociological Imagination.* Minneapolis: University of Minnesota Press, 2008.

Grant, A. J. "Ground Zero as Holy Ground and Prelude to Holy War." *Journal of American Culture* 28, no. 1 (2005): 49–60. Accessed February 8, 2018. http:// onlinelibrary.wiley.com/doi/10.1111/j.1542-734X.2005.00153.x/abstract.

Greenspan, Elizabeth. "Daniel Libeskind's World Trade Center Change of Heart." *New Yorker,* August 28, 2013. http://www.newyorker.com/business /currency/daniel-libeskinds-world-trade-center-change-of-heart.

——— . *Battle for Ground Zero: Inside the Political Struggle to Rebuild the World Trade Center.* New York: St. Martin's Press, 2013.

Greenwald, Alice. " 'Passions on All Sides': Lessons for Planning the September 11 Memorial Museum." *Curator* 53, no. 1 (2010): 117–25. Accessed February 8, 2018. https://www.911memorial.org/blog/passion-behind-building-911 -memorial-museum.

Grusin, Richard. *Premediation: Affect and Mediality after 9/11.* London: Palgrave, 2010.

Gunn, Joshua. "Mourning Speech: Haunting and the Spectral Voices of Nine-Eleven." *Text and Performance Quarterly* 24, no. 2 (2004): 91–114. Accessed February 8, 2018. http://www.tandfonline.com/doi/abs/10.1080 /1046293042000288344.

Hagan, Joe. "The Breaking of Michael Arad." *New York Magazine,* May 14, 2006. http://nymag.com/arts/architecture/features/17015/.

Hajer, Marteen. "Rebuilding Ground Zero. The Politics of Performance." *Planning Theory & Practice* 6, no. 4 (2005): 445–64. Accessed February 8, 2018. http://www.tandfonline.com/doi/abs/10.1080/14649350500349623.

Harold, Christine, and Kevin Michael DeLuca, "Behold the Corpse: Violent Images and the Case of Emmett Till." *Rhetoric and Public Affairs* 8, no. 2 (2005): 263– 86. Accessed February 8, 2018. https://muse.jhu.edu/article/189491.

Hasian, Marouf, Jr. *Drone Warfare and Lawfare in a Post-Heroic Age.* Tuscaloosa: University of Alabama Press, 2016.

———. "Nostalgic Longings, Memories of the 'Good War,' and Cinematic Representations in Saving Private Ryan." *Critical Studies in Media Communication* 18, no. 3 (2001): 338–58. Accessed February 8, 2018. http://www.tandfonline.com/doi/abs/10.1080/07393180128083.

———. "Remembering and Forgetting the 'Final Solution': A Rhetorical Pilgrimage through the US Holocaust Memorial Museum." *Critical Studies in Media Communication* 21, no. 1 (2004): 64–92. Accessed February 8, 2018. http://www.tandfonline.com/doi/abs/10.1080/0739318042000184352.

Hasian, Marouf, Jr., and Megan McFarlane. *Cultural Rhetorics of American Exceptionalism and the bin Laden Raid*. New York: Peter Lang, 2013).

Hasian, Marouf, Jr., Sean Lawson, and Megan D. McFarlane. *The Rhetorical Invention of America's National Security State*. Lanham MD: Lexington Books, 2015.

Haskins, Ekaterina V., and Justin DeRose. "Memory, Visibility, and Public Space: Reflections on Commemoration(s) of 9/11." *Space and Culture* 6, no. 4 (2003): 377–93. Accessed February 8, 2018. http://journals.sagepub.com/doi/abs/10.1177/1206331203258373.

Hauser, Gerard. *Vernacular Voices: The Rhetoric of Publics and Public Spheres*. Columbia SC: South Carolina University Press, 1999.

Heath-Kelly, Charlotte. *Death and Security: Memory and Mortality at the Bombsite*. Manchester, UK: Manchester University Press, 2017.

Hendry, Judith. "Decide, Announce, Defend: Turning the NEPA Process into an Advocacy Tool Rather Than a Decision-Making Tool." In *Communication and Public Participation in Environmental Decision Making*, edited by Stephen Depoe, John Delicath, and Marie-France Aepil Elsenbeer, 99–112. Albany: SUNY Press, 2004.

Hilker, Anne. "Comfort of Melancholy: Understanding the Experience of Absence at American Memorials." *Journal of American Culture* 37, no. 1 (2014): 29–36. Accessed February 8, 2018. http://onlinelibrary.wiley.com/doi/10.1111/jacc.12104/pdf.

Holland, Jack. "From September 11th, 2001, to 9-11: From Void to Crisis." *International Political Sociology* 3, no. 3 (2009): 275–92. Accessed February 8, 2018. http://onlinelibrary.wiley.com/doi/10.1111/j.1749-5687.2009.00076.x/abstract.

Hoskins, Gregory. "The Politics of Memory and the World Trade Center Memorial Site." *Social Philosophy* 38, no. 2 (2007): 242–54. Accessed February 8, 2018. http://onlinelibrary.wiley.com/doi/10.1111/j.1467-9833.2007.00377.x/abstract.

Huyssen, Andreas. *Present Pasts: Urban Palimpsests and the Politics of Memory*. Redwood City: Stanford University Press, 2003.

———. "Review Essay." *German Literature Review* 78, no. 1 (2003): 86–91.

Isin, Engim. "The Neurotic Citizen," *Citizenship Studies* 8, no. 3 (2004): 217–35. Accessed February 8, 2018. http://www.tandfonline.com/doi/abs/10.1080 /1362102042000256970.

Ivie, Robert, and Oscar Giner. "American Exceptionalism in a Democratic Idiom: Transacting the Mythos of Change in the 2008 Presidential Campaign." *Communication Studies* 60 (2009): 359–75. Accessed February 8, 2018. http:// www.tandfonline.com/doi/abs/10.1080/10510970903109961.

———. *Hunt the Devil: A Demonology of U.S. War Culture.* Tuscaloosa: University of Alabama Press, 2015.

———. "Waging Peace: Transformations of the Warrior Myth by U.S. Military Veterans." *Journal of Multicultural Discourse* 11, no. 2 (2016): 199–213. Accessed February 8, 2018. http://www.tandfonline.com/doi/abs/10.1080 /17447143.2016.1182174?journalCode=rmmd20.

Jackson, Richard. "Unknown Knowns: The Subjugated Knowledge of Terrorism Studies." *Critical Studies on Terrorism* 5, no. 1 (April 2012): 11–29.

Janz, Bruce. "The Terror of the Place: Anxieties of Place and the Cultural Narrative of Terrorism." *Ethics Place and Environment* 11, no. 2 (2008): 191–203. Accessed February 8, 2018. http://www.tandfonline.com/doi/abs/10.1080 /13668790802252389.

Jenkins, Keith. "Ethical Responsibility and the Historian: On the Possible End of a History 'of a Certain Kind.'" *History and Theory* 43, no. 4 (2004): 43–60. Accessed February 8, 2018. https://www.jstor.org/stable/3590635?seq=1#page_scan_tab_contents.

Johnson, Paul Christopher. "Savage Civil Religion." *Numen* 52, no. 3 (2005): 289–324. Accessed February 8, 2018. http://booksandjournals.brillonline.com /content/journals/10.1163/156852705774342842/.

Kelly, Casey Ryan. "It Follows: Precarity, Thanatopolitics, and the Ambient Horror Film." *Critical Studies in Media Communication* 34, no. 3 (2017): 234–49. Accessed February 8, 2018. http://www.tandfonline.com/doi/abs/10.1080 /15295036.2016.1268699?journalCode=rcsm20.

Kennicott, Phillip. "Two Stark Voids. But in a City of Life." *Washington Post,* August 28, 2011.

Kirshenblatt-Gimblett, Barbara. "Kodak Moments, Flashbulb Memories: Reflections on 9/11." *Drama Review* 47, no. 1 (2003): 11–48. Accessed February 8, 2018. https://www.mitpressjournals.org/doi/abs/10.1162 /105420403321249983.

Kolker, Robert. "Grief Police," *New York Magazine,* November 28, 2005. http:// nymag.com/nymetro/news/sept11/features/15140/

Krauthammer, Charles. "The Greater the Evil, the More It Disarms." *Time*, September 24, 2001, http://content.time.com/time/magazine/article/0,9171,1000889,00.html.

Kuljić, Todor. "Thanatopolitics and Thanatosociology—Draft on the Theoretical and Conceptual Framework—." *Sociological Discourse* 3, no. 5 (2013): 5–20.

Laclau, Ernesto, and Chantal Mouffe. *Hegemony and Socialist Strategy: Towards a Radical Democratic Politics*. New York: Verso, 2001.

Latour, Bruno. "From Realpolitik to Dingpolitik: Or How to Make Things Public." *Making Things Public: Atmospheres of Democracy*, edited by Bruno Latour and Peter Weibel, 14–43. Cambridge: MIT Press, 2005.

———. *An Inquiry Into Modes of Existence*. Translated by Catherine Porter. Cambridge: Harvard University Press, 2013.

———. *The Pasteurization of France*. Translated by Alan Sheridan and John Law. Cambridge MA: Harvard University Press, 1993.

———. "War and Peace in an Age of Ecological Conflicts." Lecture at Peter Wall Institute Vancouver, Canada, 2013. Accessed February 8, 2018. http://www.bruno-latour.fr/sites/default/files/130-VANCOUVER-RJE-14pdf.pdf.

———. *We Have Never Been Modern*. Translated by Catherine Porter. Cambridge MA: Harvard University Press, 1993.

———. "Where Are The Missing Masses?" In *The Sociology of a Few Mundane Artifacts, Shaping Technology/Building Society: Studies in Sociotechnical Change*, edited by Wiebe Bijker and John Law, 225–58. Cambridge MA: MIT Press, 1992.

Law, John. "Actor Network Theory and Material Semiotics." In *The New Blackwell Companion to Social Theory*, edited by Bryan S. Turner, 141–58. West Sussex, UK: 2009.

Lennon, John, and Malcolm Foley. *Dark Tourism: The Attraction of Death and Disaster*. New York: Continuum Press, 2000.

Levy, Daniel, and Natan Sznaider. *Erinnerung Im Globalen Zeitalter: Der Holocaust*. Berlin: Suhrkamp Verlag KG, 2007.

Lew, Alan. "Debating Tourism after 9/11." *Tourism Geographies* 5, no. 1 (2003): 1–2.

Light, Elinor. "Visualizing Homeland: Remembering 9/11 and the Production of the Surveilling Flâneur." *Cultural Studies* ↔ *Critical Methodologies* 16, no. 6 (2016): 536–47. Accessed February 8, 2018. http://journals.sagepub.com/doi/abs/10.1177/1532708616655823.

Lotringer, Sylvère, and Paul Virilio. *The Accident of Art*. Cambridge MA: Semiotext(e), 2005.

Low, Setha. *Behind the Gates: Life, Security, and the Pursuit of Happiness in Fortress America*. New York: Routledge, 2004.

———. "The Memorialization of September 11: Dominant and Local Discourses on the Rebuilding of the World Trade Center Site." *American Ethnologist* 31, no. 3 (2004): 326–39. Accessed February 8, 2018. http://www.jstor.org /stable/3805361.

Low, Setha, Dana Taplin, and Mike Lamb. "Battery Park City: An Ethnographic Field Study of the Community Impact of 9/11." *Urban Affairs Review* 40, no. 5 (2004): 655–82. Accessed February 8, 2018. http://journals.sagepub.com /doi/pdf/10.1177/1078087404272304.

MacDonald, David. "Bush's American and the New Exceptionalism: Anti-Americanism, the Holocaust and the Transatlantic Rift." *Third World Quarterly* 29, no. 6 (2008): 1101–18. Accessed February 8, 2018. http://www .tandfonline.com/doi/abs/10.1080/01436590802201063.

Mamdani, Mahmood. *Good Muslim, Bad Muslim: America, the Cold War, and the Roots of Terror.* New York: Three Leaves Press, 2005.

Mann, Charles. "Smoke Screening." *Vanity Fair*, December 20, 2011. http://www .vanityfair.com/culture/features/2011/12/tsa-insanity-201112.

McHendry, George F., Jr., Michael Middleton, Danielle Endres, Samantha Senda-Cook, and Megan O'Byrne. "Rhetorical Critic(ism)'s Body: Affect and Fieldwork on a Plane of Immanence." *Southern Communication Journal* 79, no. 4 (2014): 293–310. Accessed February 8, 2018. http://www.tandfonline .com/doi/abs/10.1080/1041794X.2014.906643.

McIvor, David. "Bringing Ourselves to Grief: Judith Butler and the Politics of Mourning." *Political Theory* 40, no. 4 (2012): 409–36. Accessed February 8, 2018. https://www.jstor.org/stable/41703076?seq=1#page_scan_tab_contents.

Middleton, Michael, Aaron Hess, Danielle Endres, and Samantha Senda-Cook. *Participatory Critical Rhetoric: Theoretical and Methodological Foundations for Studying Rhetoric in Situ.* Lanham MD: Lexington Books, 2015.

Mitchell, Gordon. *Strategic Deception: Rhetoric, Science, and Politics in Missile Defense Advocacy.* East Lansing: Michigan State University Press, 2000.

Mitchell, W. J. T. *What Do Pictures Want? The Lives and Loves of Images.* Chicago: University of Chicago Press, 2005.

Mueller, John. *Overblown: How Politicians and the Terrorism Industry Inflate National Security Treats, and Why We Believe Them.* New York: Free Press, 2009.

Muller, Benjamin. "Securing the Political Imagination: Popular Culture, the Security *Dispositif*, and the Biometric State." *Security Dialogue* 39, no. 2–3 (2008): 199–220.

Murray, Stuart. "Thanatopolitics: Reading in Agamben a Rejoinder to Biopolitical Life." *Communication and Critical/Cultural Studies* 5, no. 2 (2008): 203–7.

Accessed February 8, 2018. http://www.tandfonline.com/doi/abs/10.1080 /14791420802024350.

National Commission on Terrorist Attacks. *The 9/11 Commission Report: Final Report of the National Commission on Terrorist Attacks upon the United States.* Washington DC: Government Printing Office, 2011.

Naudet, Jules, Gedeon Naudet, and James Hanlon, dirs. *9/11.* Los Angeles: Paramount Pictures, 2002. 129 minutes.

Nobel, Phillip. *Sixteen Acres: Architecture and the Outrageous Struggle for the Future of Ground Zero.* New York: Metropolitan Books, 2005.

Nora, Pierre. "Between Memory and History: Les Lieux de Mémoire." *Representations* 26 (1989): 7–24. Accessed February 8, 2018. https://www.jstor.org /stable/2928520?seq=1#page_scan_tab_contents.

Nyers, Peter. "Moving Borders: The Politics of Dirt." *Radical Philosophy: Philosophical Journal of the Independent Left* 174 (2012): 1–6. Accessed February 8, 2018. https://www.radicalphilosophy.com/commentary/moving-borders.

Owen, Mark, and Kevin Maurer. *No Easy Day.* New York: New American Library, 2014.

Owen, Susan A. "Memory, War and American Identity: *Saving Private Ryan* as Cinematic Jeremiad." *Critical Studies in Media Communication* 19, no. 3 (2002): 249–82. Accessed February 8, 2018. http://www.tandfonline.com /doi/abs/10.1080/07393180216565?journalCode=rcsm20.

Paliewicz, Nicholas, and George F. McHendry Jr. "When Good Arguments Do Not Work: Post-Dialectics, Argument Assemblages, and the Networks of Climate Skepticism." *Argumentation and Advocacy* 53, no. 4 (2017): 287–309. Accessed February 8, 2018. http://www.tandfonline.com/doi/abs/10.1080 /00028533.2017.1375738.

Parr, Adrian. *Deleuze and Memorial Culture: Desire, Singular Memory, and the Politics of Trauma.* Edinburgh, UK: Edinburgh University Press, 2008.

Patton, Callum. "Saudis Paid Veterans to Oppose Bill," *Newsweek,* May 11, 2017. http://www.newsweek.com/saudi-arabia-paid-veterans-lobby-congress -against-911-lawsuit-law-607655.

Pettitt, Clare. "On Stuff." *19: Interdisciplinary Studies in the Long Nineteenth Century* 6 (2008): 1–12.

Phillips, Kendall. *Framing Public Memory.* Tuscaloosa: University of Alabama Press, 2004.

Portero, Ashley. "9/11—The Dust That Refuses to Settle." *International Business Times,* September 9, 2011. http://www.ibtimes.com/911-dust-refuses -settle-311340.

Redfield, Marc. "Virtual Trauma: The Idiom of 9/11." *diacritics* 37, no. 1 (2007): 55–80. Accessed February 8, 2018. https://muse.jhu.edu/article/247592/summary.

Rickert, Thomas. *Ambient Rhetoric: The Attunements of Rhetorical Being*. Pittsburgh PA: University of Pittsburgh Press.

Rindzeviciute, Egle. "Hegemony or Legitimacy? Assembling Soviet Deportations in Lithuanian Museums." In *Maps of Memory: Trauma, Identity, and Exile in Deportation Memoirs from the Baltic States*, edited by Violeta Davoliute and Tomas Balkelis, 153–77. Vilnius: Institute of Lithuanian Literature and Folklore, 2012.

Rothberg, Michael. *Multidirectional Memory: Remembering the Holocaust in the Age of Decolonization*. Palo Alto CA: Stanford University Press, 2009.

Sagalyn, Lynne. *Power at Ground Zero: Politics, Money, and the Remaking of Lower Manhattan*. Oxford: Oxford University Press, 2016.

Salter, Mark. "Risk and Imagination in the War on Terror." In *Risk and the War on Terror*, edited by Louise Amoore and Marieke De Goede, 233–46. London: Routledge, 2008.

Schneier, Bruce. *Beyond Fear: Thinking Sensibly about Security in an Uncertain World*. Göttingen: Copernicus Books, 2003.

Schmitt, Carl. *Political Theology: Four Chapters on the Concept of Sovereignty*. Edited and translated by George Schwab. Chicago: University of Chicago Press, 1985.

Schuck, Peter. "Citizen Terrorist." *Policy Review*, no. 164 (2010): 61–73. Accessed February 8, 2018. https://search.proquest.com/docview/857722579?pq-origsite=gscholar.

Sci, Susan "(Re)thinking the Memorial as a Place of Aesthetic Negotiation." *Culture, Theory and Critique* 50, no. 1 (2009): 41–57. Accessed February 8, 2018. http://www.tandfonline.com/doi/abs/10.1080/14735780802696351.

Sciulo, Nick. "The Ghost in the Global War on Terror: Critical Perspectives and Dangerous Implications for National Security and the Law." *Drexel Law Review* 3 (2010): 561.

Sedgwick, Mark. Review of *Overblown: How Politicians and the Terrorism Industry Inflate National Security Threats, and Why We Believe Them*, by John Mueller. *Terrorism and Political Violence* 19, no. 3 (2007): 438–40. Accessed February 8, 2018. http://www.tandfonline.com/doi/abs/10.1080/09546550701476125?journalCode=ftpv20.

Senie, Harriet F. "A Difference in Kind: Spontaneous Memorials after 9/11." *Sculpture*, July/August 2003. https://www.sculpture.org/documents/scmag03/jul_aug03/webspecial/senie.shtml.

Shields, Rachel, Jason Laurendeau, and Carly Adams. "The Logic of Memory: 'Paroxysms of Tears and Joy' for the London Olympics and the Bhopal Disaster." *Memory Studies* 10, no. 2 (2017): 193–209. Accessed February 8, 2018. http://journals.sagepub.com/doi/abs/10.1177/1750698016638407.

Simons, Massimiliano. "The Parliament of Things and the Anthropocene: How to Listen to 'Quasi-Objects." *Techné: Research in Philosophy and Technology* 21, no. 2–3 (2017): 1–25.

Sitaraman, Ganesh. "Counterinsurgency, the War on Terror, and the Laws of War." *Virginia Law Review* 95 (2009): 1745–839.

Stahl, Roger. *Militainment, Inc.: War, Media, and Popular Culture.* New York: Routledge, 2009.

Steinweiss, Alan. "The Auschwitz Analogy: Holocaust Memory and American Debates over Intervention in Bosnia and Kosovo in the 1990s." *Holocaust and Genocide Studies* 19, no. 2 (2005): 276–89. Accessed February 8, 2018. https://academic.oup.com/hgs/article/19/2/276/630458.

Sterritt, David. "Representing Atrocity." In *Hollywood's Chosen People: The Jewish Experience in American Cinema,* edited by Daniel Bernardi, Murray Pomerance, and Hava Tirosh-Samuelson, 141–58. Detroit: Wayne State University Press, 2013.

Stone, Philip, and Richard Sharpley. "Consuming Dark Tourism: A Thanatological Perspective." *Annals of Tourism Research* 35, no. 2 (2008): 574–95. Accessed February 8, 2018. https://www.sciencedirect.com/science/article/pii/S0160738308000261.

Stow, Simon. "From Upper Canal to Lower Manhattan: Memorialization and the Politics of Loss." *Perspectives on Politics* 10, no. 3 (2012): 687–700. Accessed February 8, 2018. https://www.cambridge.org/core/journals/perspectives-on-politics/article/from-upper-canal-to-lower-manhattan-memorialization-and-the-politics-of-loss/EC020A4BBEB79D1C4A5FD12B9A9675EA.

Sturken, Marita. "The Aesthetics of Absence: Rebuilding Ground Zero." *American Ethnologist* 31, no. 3 (2004): 311–25. Accessed February 8, 2018. http://onlinelibrary.wiley.com/doi/10.1525/ae.2004.31.3.311/abstract.

———. *Tourists of History: Memory, Kitsch, and Consumerism from Oklahoma City to Ground Zero.* Durham NC: Duke University Press, 2007.

Supreme Court of New York. New York County. 42 Misc. 3d 1223(A); 992 N.Y.S.2d 161; 2014 N.Y., February 4, 2014.

Tanenhaus, Jeffrey. "America's Phoenix." *Jerusalem Post.* September 8, 2006.

Taylor, Bryan. "'The Movie Has to Go Forward': Surveying the Media-Security Relationship." *Annals of the International Communication Association* 41

(2017): 46–69. Accessed February 8, 2018. http://www.tandfonline.com/doi
/abs/10.1080/23808985.2017.1288069?journalCode=rica20.

Taylor, Diana. *The Archive and the Repertoire: Performing Cultural Memory in the Americas*. Durham NC: Duke University Press, 2003.

Toom, Victor. "Whose Body Is It? Technological Materialization of Victims' Bodies and Remains after the World Trade Center Terrorist Attacks." *Science, Technology & Human Values* 41, no. 4 (2016): 686–708. Accessed February 8, 2018. http://journals.sagepub.com/doi/abs/10.1177/0162243915624145.

Trigg, Dylan. *Topophobia: A Phenomenology of Anxiety*. New York: Bloomsbury, 2016.

Türetken, Füsun. "Breathing Space: The Amalgamated Toxicity of Ground Zero." In *Forensis: The Architecture of Public Truth*, edited by Eyal Weizman, 261–62. Berlin: Sternberg Press, 2014.

Valkenburg, Govert. "Security Technologies Versus Citizen Roles?" *Science as Culture* 26, no. 3 (2017): 307–29. Accessed February 8, 2018. http://www .tandfonline.com/doi/pdf/10.1080/09505431.2016.1255723.

Valkenburg, Govert, and Irma van der Ploeg. "Materialities between Security and Privacy: A Constructivist Account of Airport Security Scanners." *Security Dialogue* 46, no. 4 (2015): 1–19. Accessed February 8, 2018. http://journals .sagepub.com/doi/abs/10.1177/0967010615577855.

van Toor, Bob, and Hanneke Ronnes. "Reflecting Absence, or How Ground Zero Was Purged of Its Material History (2001–2010)." *International Journal of Cultural Property* 22 (2015): 85–110. Accessed February 8, 2018. https://www .cambridge.org/core/journals/international-journal-of-cultural-property /article/reflecting-absence-or-how-ground-zero-was-purged-of-its-material -history-20012010/893975D14584D7BEBD6E1226DEDC3387.

Virilio, Paul. *9/11*. New York: Verso Press, 2002.

——— . *War and Cinema: The Logistics of Perception*. New York: Radical Thinkers, 1984.

Vivian, Bradford. *Commonplace Witnessing: Rhetorical Invention, Historical Remembrance, and Public Culture*. New York: Oxford Press, 2017. doi: 10.1080/02773945.2014.911558.

——— . *Public Forgetting: The Rhetoric and Politics of Beginning* Again. State College PA: Penn State University Press, 2010.

——— . "Witnessing Time: Rhetorical Form, Public Culture, and Popular Historical Education." *Rhetoric Society Quarterly* 44, no. 3 (2014): 204–19. Accessed February 8, 2018.

Waldman, Amy. *The Submission*. New York: Random House, 2011.

Walters, William. "Drone Strikes, Dingpolitik and Beyond: Furthering the Debate on Materiality and Security." *Security Dialogue* 45, no. 2 (2014): 101–18.

Accessed February 8, 2018. http://www.tandfonline.com/doi/abs/10.1080 /02773945.2014.911558.

Weizman, Eyal. *The Least of All Possible Evils: Humanitarian Violence from Arendt to Gaza*. New York: Verso Books, 2011.

Weizman, Eyal, Paulo Tavares, Susan Schuppli, and Situ Studio. "Forensic Architecture," *Architectural Design* 80, no. 5 (2010): 58–63. Accessed February 8, 2018. http://onlinelibrary.wiley.com/doi/10.1002/ad.1134/abstract.

Wenner, Lawrence. "The Unbearable Dirtiness of Being: On the Commodification of MediaSport and the Need for Ethical Criticism." *Journal of Sports Media* 4, no. 1, (2009): 85–94. Accessed February 8, 2018. https://muse.jhu.edu /article/259806.

Williams, Paul. *Memorial Museums: The Global Rush to Commemorate Atrocities*. New York: Bloomsbury, 2007.

Wilson, Ross. "Rethinking 1807: Museums, Knowledge and Expertise." *Museum and Society* 8, no. 3 (2010): 165–79. Accessed February 8, 2018. https:// journals.le.ac.uk/ojs1/index.php/mas/article/view/163/177.

Woolgar, Steve, and Daniel Neyland. *Mundane Governance: Ontology and Accountability*. Oxford, UK: Oxford University Press, 2013.

Yaeger, Patricia. "Rubble as Archive, or 9/11 as Dust, Debris and Bodily Vanishing." In *Trauma at Home: After 9/11*, edited by Judith Greenberg, 188. Lincoln: University of Nebraska Press, 2003.

Young, James. *At Memory's Edge: After-Images of the Holocaust in Contemporary Art and Architecture*. New Haven CT: Yale University Press, 2002.

——. "The Counter-Monument: Memory against Itself in Germany Today." *Critical Inquiry* 18, no. 2 (1992): 267–96. doi: 10.1086/448632. Accessed February 8, 2018. http://www.journals.uchicago.edu/doi/abs/10.1086/448632 ?journalCode=ci.

——. "James Young: The Stages of Memory and the Monument: From Berlin to New York." Video file, accessed July 17, 2015, https://www.youtube.com /watch?v=1wWK36TVPP8.

——. "The Memorial's Arc: Between *Denkmal* and New York City's 9/11 Memorial." *Memory Studies* 9, no. 3 (2016): 325–31. Accessed February 8, 2018. http://journals.sagepub.com/doi/abs/10.1177/1750698016645266.

——. *The Stages of Memory: Reflections on Memorial Art, Loss, and the Spaces Between*. Amherst MA: University of Massachusetts Press, 2016.

——. *The Texture of Memory: Holocaust Memorials and Meaning*. New Haven: Yale University Press, 1993.

Zelizer, Barbie. *About to Die: How News Images Move the Public.* New York: Oxford University Press, 2010.

———. "Reading the Past Against the Grain: The Shape of Memory Studies." *Critical Studies in Mass Communication* 12, no. 2 (1995): 214–39. Accessed January 11, 2019. https://nca.tandfonline.com/doi/abs/10.1080/15295039509366932?journalCode=rcsm19#.XDkVz_x7n5Y.

Žižek, Slavoj. *Welcome to the Desert of the Real! Five Essays on September 11 and Related Dates.* New York: Verso, 2002.

securitization: and ambiguities (2001–3), 37–39, 42–44, 46, 48–49, 52, 55–56, 58, 64–68; apparatus of, 9, 11, 68; concept of, 4–6, 8, 14, 23–25, 27; and counterterrorist futures, 197–98, 200–201, 204, 211, 214–15, 218, 222, 228, 230–34; of Ground Zero, 27, 41, 46, 64–67, 77, 79, 87–88, 105, 140; and Holocaust memories, 168, 172–75, 178–80, 182, 185; or (in)securitization, 14, 112, 143, 153, 198; of memorial space, 14, 23, 33, 37, 43–44, 49, 52, 75, 98, 127, 134, 147, 156; and moral authority (2004–14), 105, 112, 124, 133–34, 139–45, 147–49, 151, 153–54, 156, 160–62, 164–65; narratives of, 142; practices of, 8, 26, 35, 179, 215; and rebuilding (2002–5), 71–72, 74–77, 79–81, 84, 87–88, 91–92, 94, 96, 98, 101–2; and resecuritization, 6, 7–8, 25, 28, 31–32, 35–37, 39, 42, 43, 46, 68, 77, 80, 101, 109, 127; rhetorics of, 10, 24, 102, 124, 175, 179, 214, 231. *See also* Foucault, Michel; Ground Zero; National September 11 Memorial and Memorial Museum; O'Neill, Robert

security: apparatus of, 6, 14–15, 34, 37, 47, 58, 68, 75, 80, 107, 135, 137, 140, 147, 153, 155–57, 164, 177, 233; appearance of, 91; and (in)security, v, 1, 12, 24, 36, 56, 152, 155, 231, 234, 240; theater, 13, 180, 211, 217, 231. *See also* Ground Zero; National September 11 Memorial and Memorial Museum; New York Police Department; Port Authority of New York and New Jersey; securitization

Senda-Cook, Samantha, 30, 112

Silverstein, Larry, 85–87, 90–91, 93, 95–96, 116, 125

Skidmore, Owing, and Merrill, 81, 84

slurry wall, 191–92

soapbox arguments, 220, 222, 234

sovereignty: and authority, 28, 221; and immunity, 222–23, 226, 233; and order, 63; and security, 26; of state and nation, 55, 214, 230

space: ambiguities of, 37–39, 42–53, 55–61, 69; as cosmopolitan, 117; deterritorialization of, 19, 22, 45; as heterotopic, 47, 80–81, 132; at memorial, 8, 10, 13–14, 33, 37, 43, 49, 52, 61, 63, 75, 77, 107, 133, 135–36, 139–40, 147, 152, 156, 163; as negative, 78; weaponization of, 39, 77, 102. *See also* Ground Zero; rhetoric; securitization; topophobia

Stahl, Roger, 216

Sterritt, David, 186–87

Stow, Simon, 165

Sturken, Marita, 130, 198; and kitschification, 24

subjectivity, 8, 26, 132, 176, 188, 195, 232–33

surveillance, x, 13, 28, 33, 98, 138, 143–44, 155, 162, 180, 184; and flâneur, 155

Syria, 208, 210, 233

Take Back the Memorial (TBTM), 118–25, 128

Taliban, 111, 113, 139, 141, 162, 180, 197, 201, 207

tanks, 42, 56, 58, 63–64, 68, 73

Tenet, George, 206, 224

teratology, 21, 22; and demonology, 23; and demos, 21

CPSIA information can be obtained
at www.ICGtesting.com
Printed in the USA
LVHW111304031019
633090LV00003B/8/P